Bar *Service*

Levels 1 and 2

Roy Hayter

Hospitality Training Foundation

THOMSON
LEARNING

Australia • Canada • Mexico • Singapore • Spain • United Kingdom • United States

About this book

Bar Service Levels 1 & 2

Copyright © Hospitality Training
Foundation & Thomson Learning 2000

The Thomson Learning logo is a registered
trademark used herein under licence.

For more information, contact Thomson
Learning, Berkshire House, 168–173 High
Holborn, London, WC1V 7AA or visit us on
the World Wide Web at:
http://www.thomsonlearning.co.uk

*British Library Cataloguing-in-Publication
Data*
A catalogue record for this book is available
from the British Library

ISBN 1-86152-710-1

First edition 1996 by Macmillan Press Ltd
Reprinted 1997 & 1998
Reprinted 2000 by Thomson Learning

Printed by CTPS, Hong Kong

Your route to a qualification

To gain an NVQ/SVQ in Serving
Food and Drink (Bar) at Levels 1 or
2 you need seven units in total:

- the three core units which deal
  with customer care (Section 1),
  hygiene, safety and security
  (Section 2) and working
  relationships (Section 6)
- the two units on taking payment
  (Section 9) and providing a drink
  service (Section 10)

and for Level 1:

- the two units on preparing for
  drink service (Section 8), and
  cleaning and storing glassware
  (Section 8 also)

and for Level 2:

- the two units on receiving,
  storing and returning drinks
  (Section 7) and maintaining
  cellars, kegs and drinks dispense
  lines (Section 7 also).

At Level 2 three other units are
available, but not necessary for a
qualification: providing a table
drink service (Section 10), cocktails
(Section 10 also), and cask
conditioned beers (Section 7).

To help you find your way through
the book, the NVQ/SVQ unit and
element numbers are given above
the main headings used within each
section.

How to use this book

This book can be used in any way
which suits your needs:

- dip into it at the pages which
  catch your interest – perhaps
  because of an illustration, photograph or industry procedure
- to find information on a
  particular skill or technique,
  drink, or piece of equipment –
  use the index at the end of the
  book to find the page numbers
- concentrate on the topics you are
  preparing to be assessed in – the
  section titles closely match the
  titles of the NVQ/SVQ units.

This book and your assessment

The main text in each section helps
with the three aspects which relate
to your assessment:

- what you need to do – as defined
  in the NVQ/SVQ performance
  criteria for each element
- the situations, types of drink,
  equipment, etc. which apply – as
  set out in the NVQ/SVQ range
  list
- what you need to know – as
  given in the NVQ/SVQ underpinning knowledge statements.

Headings within sections use the
same or similar words to the
element titles, performance criteria
and range lists, or you will find
range words printed in *italics* in the
text.

Skills checks

To help you find out what stage you
are already at, to monitor progress
as you work towards a unit, and to
prepare for assessment, each
section includes a skills check.

The skills check summarises the
performance criteria for the two
(sometimes three or four) elements
of the unit, and the range list. Use
the tick box by each statement as
you wish.

Activity questions

These help you check what you have
learned and through the illustrations reinforce key points. Your
assessor will ask similar questions
to test your underpinning knowledge.

Industry examples

Throughout the book examples are
given of procedures, checklists and
test yourself questions from
different employers in the licensed
retailing, leisure, restaurants and
hotels sectors. These show how the
details of serving drink vary
according to customer needs and
workplace practices.

Acknowledgements

Industry liaison and research
Pam Frediani

Advice with text
Clive Finch, Visiting Professor,
Thames Valley University

Reviewers
June Barclay, The Scottish
Licensed Trade Association

Mike Connaboy, Alloa Pubs and
Restaurants

Mike Cowan, Whitbread Inns

Kate Cowie, Bass Taverns Ltd

Gaynor Curtis, Tom Cobleigh plc

Geoffrey Dixon, Allied Domecq
Retailing

Michael Finnis, Brewers and
Licensed Retailers Association

Malcolm Firth, Brunel College of
Arts and Technology

Chris Gillespie, Greenalls Inns

Val Glyn and Steve Gallagher,
Young & Co's Brewery plc

Jenny Grant, Bass Taverns Ltd

Marcus Harborne, Morland & Co
plc

Stephen Hawkins, Courage Ltd

Marshall Hodgkinson, Everards
Brewery Ltd

Kim Parish, Scottish & Newcastle
Retail

Fiona Price, J D Wetherspoon plc

Lorraine Ragosa and Roger
Loiselle, Corporate Catering
Company Ltd

Tim Sims, Haven Leisure Ltd

Graphics
Tom Lines

Cover photographs
Tom Stockill

Text photographs
Tom Stockill, Keith Turnbull

Photographic locations
The Bellhouse, Beaconsfield, De
Vere Hotels

Shenley Church Inn, Milton Keynes,
Toby Restaurants

Thames Valley University, Slough

Also: The Brewery Tap,
Wandsworth; Café Rouge, Putney;
Matt's Café, Chelsea Harbour; Pizza
Express, Clapham; The Whittington,
Pinner

Reproduction of material
John Artis Ltd

Gaskell & Chambers Ltd

Lockhart Catering Equipment

The Ravenhead Company Ltd and
Durobor SA

Staines Catering Equipment Ltd

*Contributing industry procedures
and other material*
Allied Domecq Retailing, Geoffrey
Dixon

Association for Payment Clearances

Australian Wine Bureau

Bass Taverns Ltd, Kate Cowie,
Jenny Grant, Allan Powers

The Committee of Scottish Clearing
Bankers and Clydesdale Bank plc

Coppid Beech Hotel, Michael Phipps

Corporate Catering Company Ltd,
Lorraine Ragosa

Courage Ltd, Derek Carr, Stephen
Hawkins

De Vere Hotels Ltd, Alan Makinson

Everards Brewery Ltd, Marshall
Hodgkinson

Finlandia Vodka, Jackie Cooper,
Annette Cremin

Gin and Vodka Association, Tricia
Crighton

Greenalls Inns

Haven Leisure Limited, Tim Sims

Morland & Co plc, Marcus Harborne

National Restaurant Association,
Washington DC

National Westminster Bank plc,
Streamline Section

Pizza Hut UK Ltd, Ingrid Newbould

The Portman Group, John McGovern

Rank Leisure, Mark Lindsell

Royal Naval Supply School

The Rum Information Bureau

The Scotch Whisky Association,
Caroline Thomson-Glover

Scottish & Newcastle Retail, Kim
Parish

TGI Friday's, David Graham, Jane
Moger

Toby Restaurants, David Hunt,
Graham Denning

Tom Cobleigh plc, Gaynor Curtis

J D Wetherspoon plc, Fiona Price

Whitbread Beer Co, Richard Prescott

Whitbread Inns, Mike Cowan,
Barbara Murray

*Also helped with information and
material*
Alambie Wine Cellars, Victoria
Morrell

Allied Distilleries

Britvic Soft Drinks Ltd, Shirley
Penn, Mary Sweeting

Californian Wines, Andrew
Montague

Cheltenham Wines, Glen Turvey

Cyprus Trade Commission

Food and Wine from France, Sophie
Vallejo

Percy Fox & Co, Ben Burbridge

Matthew Gloag & Son Ltd

William Grant & Sons, Alison
Phillips

Guinness Brewing GB, Alma
Edwards

John Harvey & Sons

Hotel and Catering International
Management Association, Rosemary
Morrison and Kalpana Amin

Ian McLeod & Co, Janice Macardle

Maison Marques et Domaine, Mark
Bingley

Moët and Chandon London Ltd,
Jenny Trevor

National Mineral Water Association,
Robert Heywood

New Zealand Wines

H Parrott & Co, Joanna Goodchild

Pavillon Publicity, Jo Simpson

Portuguese Trade Department

Pubmaster Ltd, Geoffrey Croxton

The Soft Drinks Association

Tanners Wines Ltd, John Melhuish

United Distillers plc, Lorna Finlay

Wines from Spain

Customer care
in bar service

Dealing with customers

Dealing with customers is a large part of barwork. It helps if you enjoy serving people, and talking to them. You may be naturally good at people skills, but you don't have to be to succeed. Everyone can become better at dealing with customers. You learn from:

- experience – by remembering each new situation, e.g. how you confused the customer who asked for 'whisky and pepper' by replying 'black or white?', but seeing your mistake when someone says 'pepper as in peppermint cordial!'

- observing – by noting how others at work deal with people and situations, successes as well as failures, e.g. when a customer is told 'sorry, we've no rolls', and not offered one of the delicious speciality sandwiches as an alternative

and from the basic principles and rules, presented here.

Understanding customers' needs and requirements

Most customers come to your place because they want a drink, food or both. These needs can be met by providing drinks and food of acceptable quality, but are drinks or food all they want?

Why do they choose your pub or bar? Are they regulars? Are they passing by? Are they locals meeting friends? Have they come because of the darts competition? Have they heard about the friendly service?

There are many more questions like this that you can ask and, as the diagram shows, a wide range of answers. Because it's a complex area, the answers won't always be the same – different customers have different priorities at different times.

The outcome of customers' visits to your workplace – how satisfied they are – depends on how well their needs and requirements are met. When you have an understanding of what these are, you are in a stronger position to give the quality of service that means:

- new customers come because they have been told how good it is

- new customers return

- regulars stay loyal

- all customers enjoy their visits, and spend more.

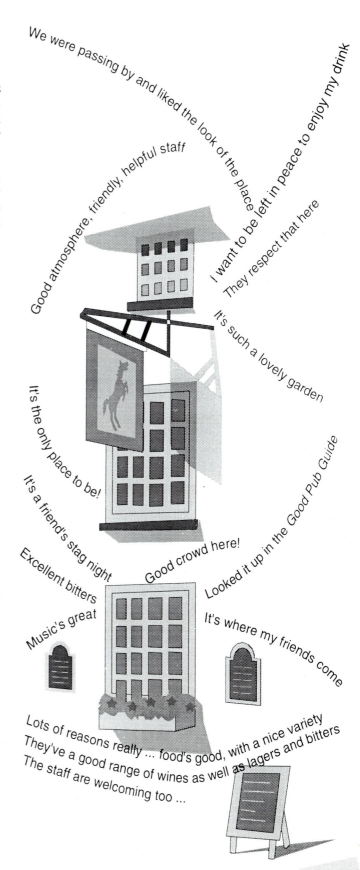

1 Customer care in bar service

Giving quality service

Customers are the judges of the quality of your service. But as it is not practical to ask customers – except as part of a special exercise, perhaps conducted by head office or consultants – many workplaces have their own measures, for example:

- every new customer should be acknowledged within 30 seconds of entering the bar area

- no customer should wait more than two minutes before being served

- ashtrays should be emptied and tables cleared at 20 minute intervals

- all customers leaving should be thanked, and given the appropriate greeting, e.g. 'good night'.

As these examples indicate, quality has a lot to do with providing a speedy, helpful, polite service. A more precise definition can only be made in the context of your workplace and your customers. For example, some:

- business people expect what they want to be available quickly

- people in their village local need less speed, but expect their regular drink to be known, and their usual seat to be available

- people in a fashionable, very crowded venue enjoy being in a throng of like-minded people, even when this makes it more difficult to get to and from the bar

- older customers prefer staff who are polite in a formal way, 'Yes, madam', 'Thank you, sir', and who keep their distance, not trying to engage in conversation

- younger people prefer informality and friendliness.

Answering customers' enquiries

It gives a good impression of your workplace if you can give helpful replies to questions about:

- the range of drinks and food available in your workplace – this is dealt with in Sections 4 and 5

- other facilities of your workplace – times when food is available, where children can be served, what day is karaoke night, where the toilets are, how much bed and breakfast costs, etc.

- other pubs, restaurants, hotels, etc. belonging to the company you work for

- the local area and what's going on – bus times, taxi services, opening times of the local leisure centre, places to stay in the area, where to visit, etc.

- services they would like – to book a table in the restaurant, enter the quiz competition, leave a message for another customer, etc.

and customers appreciate this service.

Providing information and help

No one can reasonably expect you to have the answer to every question, but not everyone is reasonable! Your aim must be to deal with every question helpfully.

There is no problem about providing information concerning your bar and about the local area. Even if you don't know all the details, you should be able to point the person towards accurate information. So you could direct them to the tourist information centre, or give the telephone number of the train enquiry service.

How much you can help

Some questions require decisions you shouldn't take.

For example, to reply that it's no problem to cash a cheque would go against the policy of most pubs and bars. Taking a booking for a table in the restaurant would be wrong if this is done by someone else who has the reservations book and up-to-date information about the availability of tables.

Scope of your authority

Questions like this go beyond the scope of your authority. Explain this to the customer and offer to get the publican, bar manager or someone with the authority to help.

Information that is not disclosable

There are some questions which require a careful answer, so as to avoid giving confidential information that the questioner is looking for:

- about the activities of customers – these are not your affair, and it would harm the reputation of your bar if it is seen as a source of gossip and personal information

- about security or business-related matters – people wanting to find out this sort of information might be planning a robbery, or to pass on useful facts to a business competitor.

It's easy to recognise direct questions, e.g. 'Has Roger left his wife?', or 'Where's the money kept?', and to give vague, unhelpful answers, 'No idea, I'm afraid'. Indirect questions are harder to spot, e.g. 'I hear you're rushed off your feet on Friday nights. You must get a hundred people or more in here. Is that a good guess, would you say?' Clever people collect little pieces of information, which when put together provide a valuable picture.

Customer comments

It is difficult when you work behind the scenes (in the cellar or kitchen) to get feedback from customers. What you may hear are the complaints, e.g. that the beer tastes flat.

You can avoid this if the people who receive customer comments share the good and the not-so-good news. In larger workplaces, or those which are part of a chain, there may be a system for recording and passing on customer comments. Otherwise, it's down to individual thoughtfulness. Remember to tell your colleagues and managers what customers have said.

Everyone likes compliments and positive feedback. The nice things customers say to you about the atmosphere, speed of service, quality of food, the guest beer, etc. will be appreciated by everyone who made these things possible:

- 'We've had a great time, thanks. The children especially have enjoyed themselves – fun menu, portions not too big, well cooked and nicely presented.'

You should also pass on comments which will be helpful to those in a decision-making role: cellar manager, head chef, publican, etc. Some indicate a change in the pattern of customer demand, for example:

- 'Oh, are those the only non-alcoholic drinks you have?'

- 'Menu's OK, but everything seems to be fried or have rather a lot of fat.'

Overheard customer remarks can draw attention to facilities or services which should be improved:

- 'The toilets are through that door and down the passage, but they're not well signed.'

- 'I always park on the street, the car park here is too dark.'

These comments show the customer is not satisfied.

When comments become complaints

Lack of satisfaction can easily turn into a complaint. Another customer, perhaps in a bad mood, or unhappy with other aspects of the service, could express the same views more forcibly, for example:

- 'We'll never come back here. It's a terrible place. My wife can't drink alcohol, and you offer nothing more interesting than a cordial or mineral water. The service is slow, no one smiles ...'

Try to notice – and report to your manager – other signs that may indicate dissatisfaction with the service or facilities. For example:

- customers who move to different seats – is it because they found the first place too draughty, or the room very smoky?

- a lot of food left on plates – is it because the portions were too large, or the food was not properly cooked, or it doesn't taste nice?

- customers leave abruptly, ignoring your good bye – is it because they were unhappy with the service, food, drinks, etc?

Incidents of this sort may mean they are customers who are very difficult to please, or have already eaten, or are of the unfriendly type. But it is still worth telling your manager, because he or she may see a pattern emerging.

Customer complaints

When you are face-to-face with a dissatisfied customer, try and put aside any feeling of anger, or hurt, or embarrassment. Deal with the situation calmly and professionally. Don't wait for the customer to actually use the word 'complain' or 'complaint' before acting. You can recognise dissatisfaction from the general behaviour of customers, words used, expressions on their faces, etc.

Dealt with well, unhappy customers can become your best customers. Instead of remembering the worst points, staying away and telling others of their bad experiences – the main dangers if the complaint is not properly acted upon – they return.

Many workplaces have their own procedure for handling complaints and rules limiting the action you can take, e.g. 'No free drinks to be offered except by the manager'.

Guidelines on dealing with complaints

1 Listen to the complaint until the customer has finished speaking. Do not interrupt, even when you know you will be asking someone else to handle the situation.

2 Apologise properly and sincerely, but do not admit that you or the pub/bar/company is at fault.

3 Do not make excuses or blame anyone else.

4 Never argue or disagree. You must react as if the customers are right, even when you believe otherwise, or think your manager will take a different view.

5 Keep calm and remain polite.

6 If appropriate, and it is the procedure in your workplace, consider offering a replacement (e.g. if the complaint was about flat lager), or an alternative drink/dish.

7 Where you do provide a replacement or alternative, do this as soon as possible, with another apology for the inconvenience. Check later that the new drink/dish is satisfactory. Complete the special order or form so that there are no problems with stock or cash control.

8 Never offer something you cannot provide – consider what would happen if the customer accepts your suggestion of another vegetarian special, but you find the kitchen have run out.

9 Thank the customer for bringing the matter to your attention – said with feeling, this will show the customer that you are genuine in your efforts to put things right.

Health and safety issues

Complaints to do with health and safety must be dealt with carefully for two reasons:

- your employer and every employee has a legal responsibility for the health and safety of customers and anyone else visiting the workplace (see Section 2)

- customers may seek compensation for injuries suffered.

The process of agreeing who is at fault must be left to your employers and the experts:

- never say or agree whose fault it was or whose responsibility it is

- if an accident has occurred, e.g. a cut lip from drinking out of a chipped glass, follow your workplace accident/emergency procedure

- if it is a complaint or information about a safety hazard, e.g. slippery steps at the main entrance, thank the person and inform your manager urgently.

Dealing with customer incidents

From time to time, things go wrong and customers are directly involved. Perhaps they have seen what has happened, or they caused the problem, or it involves their property. These are called 'customer incidents' and there are four main types:

- *spillages* – a drink or food is spilled by a customer, by you or by one of your colleagues, e.g. at the bar or food counter, at the customer's table, or when carrying food or drink on a tray through a customer area

- *breakages* – from a dropped glass, bottle, plate, cup, etc., or an accident near a window or in the toilets

- *lost property* – a customer claims to have left behind a bag, briefcase, coat, umbrella, etc.

- *equipment faults* – equipment provided for the customers' use or comfort does not work properly, e.g. a vending machine in the bar area or toilet takes the money but fails to deliver the paid-for items, or the central heating in a bedroom is not working.

Establishing priorities

You may find yourself in the centre of a drama, especially if people are upset. What do you do first? Wipe up the spill or breakage, call your manager, move the customers, or get another drink?

These decisions usually have to be made very quickly. Give priority to:

- safety – remove or clear away broken glass, china etc. which might cause a cut, wipe up liquid spills which might cause people to slip and fall, turn off and isolate equipment which might injure people (e.g. a faulty heater causing an electric shock)

- the comfort and convenience of your customers – tidy up the area affected by the breakage or spill, offer paper towelling so spills on customer clothes can be dried, move the customers to another table, get the details of lost property and ask the customer to be seated while you check (see page 31)

- getting things back to normal – bringing another drink or plate of food.

What you can do to help

No set rules cover all types of incident and the many circumstances which can happen.

Remain calm, polite and helpful. Although you may feel nervous, flustered or even angry, try to hide these feelings behind a calm exterior. This will help the other people involved to overcome their fear, anger or shock.

Getting help elsewhere

Often an extra pair of hands gets things back to normal more quickly. One person can concentrate on the clearing up, while the other helps the customers, or keeps the area clear.

When someone asks about lost property, but it has not been handed in, check if your colleagues noticed anything unusual at the time the loss was said to have occurred.

Some incidents are deliberately set up, e.g. to distract management and staff while money or stock is being stolen from the bar. To avoid this, someone should always keep an eye on what else is going on.

Limits of your authority

In many cases, others will have seen what has happened and come to your assistance. If not, you should let your manager know as soon as you have dealt with the immediate priorities.

It will usually be up to your manager to make the decisions about, for example:

- responsibility for the incident
- offering the customers free drinks or food, or making an allowance on their bill – because the incident was not their fault, or if it was, as a gesture of goodwill
- genuineness of the claim regarding property left behind, or money lost in the vending machine
- offering to pay for dry cleaning of a customer's clothes.

Other customer incidents

Of course, other things can go wrong which involve customers. For example:

- running out of a particular drink or dish on the menu
- the customer's reserved table is not free because the previous customers have taken much longer than usual over their meal
- the requested double bedroom was flooded in last night's storm (but a twin is available).

Wherever possible, inform customers before they order or check in. Always apologise and offer alternatives.

Occasionally you may not know of the problem until you have taken the order to the kitchen, dispense bar, etc. This can be much more irritating to customers. Return as quickly as possible with some alternatives to suggest, having made sure these are available and having checked details, e.g. no extra charge in spite of the price difference.

Reporting customer incidents

You may be asked to make a record of what happened:

- the date and time
- names of customers and members of staff/management involved
- description of the incident
- what action was taken, and by whom
- any follow-up action required, e.g. to arrange repair of faulty equipment.

Where workplaces have a system for recording incidents, this can help deal with claims for compensation and investigations into the cause of accidents or injury. Sometimes people exaggerate the circumstances to get increased compensation, or make claims for incidents which never occurred.

Local knowledge

Working in the bar or restaurant means that you are very likely to be asked questions on local knowledge. People may be new to the area and may wish to find out where they can go after leaving our restaurant.

An important part of your job is having an answer to everything and being a valuable source of information. But if you are asked something that you do not know, ask the guest to wait a moment and find somebody who does know the answer.

Listed on the right are the main items you have to find an answer for. Complete the table and keep it as a permanent reference.

CLOAKROOM/TOILETS ....

PUBLIC TELEPHONE ....

LOCAL TAXI TELEPHONE NUMBER ....

NEAREST TOBY HOTEL ....

LOCAL BANKS ....

LOCAL POST OFFICE ....

LOCAL GARAGE ....

LOCAL NEWSAGENT ....

NEAREST CINEMA ....

NEAREST THEATRE ....

NEAREST NIGHT CLUB ....

NEAREST SHOPPING CENTRE ....

NEAREST CHEMIST ....

NEAREST BUS STOP ....

1 Give examples of how you can help customers in your pub/bar be safer.

2 You are worried that a darts game is going to lead to an injury. What should you do?

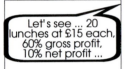

3 Give examples of questions from customers which you should not answer fully.

Let's see ... 20 lunches at £15 each, 60% gross profit, 10% net profit ...

No! The publican boasts 75% GP on food ...

4 And examples of questions which must be answered accurately.

The Manor Hotel
From £70 per night
No leathers

Oh yes! They welcome bikers at the Manor.

5 Give examples of customer comments you should pass on to a) the publican, b) the chef, c) the restaurant staff.

Great meal that!

It's got very smoky in that lounge bar.

You can't talk in there - the music's too loud!

6 Why must complaints be dealt with quickly?

7 What can go wrong if a spill or breakage is not cleared up quickly?

8 A customer tells you the hot-air hand dryer in the toilets is not working. What do you do?

Sorry out of order!

9 You're handed an umbrella by a customer who found it. What information can you get to help find the owner?

Who? What? Where? When?

10 A customer phones asking if an umbrella has been found. What information should you ask for?

Where? Who? What? When?

11 Describe what you would do if a group of customers have just knocked a full glass of wine over their table.

12 The pub is very crowded. Customers have stacked glasses everywhere, and some are broken. What problems could this lead to? What should be done to avoid them?

Illustration for question 1 with thanks to John Harvey & Sons

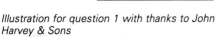

6

NVQ
SVQ

Skills check
Maintain customer care
Unit 1NG3
level 1

Use this to check your progress against the performance criteria.

Element 1

Deal with customers

Deal with customers in a polite and helpful manner ☐ PC1

▲ Customers: adults, children, those with mobility difficulties, those with communication difficulties

Act upon customers' needs and requirements without delay ☐ PC2

Answer customers' enquiries accurately, or refer to other help ☐ PC3

Give information in line with your authority ☐ PC4

Acknowledge customers' comments politely & pass on where appropriate ☐ PC5

Deal effectively with complaints ☐ PC6

Do your work in an organised, efficient and safe manner ☐ PC7

Element 2

Deal with customer incidents

Identify nature of incident quickly, and establish priorities ☐ PC1

▲ Incidents: spillage, breakage, lost property, equipment faults

Deal with customers politely and helpfully ☐ PC2

Assure customers that incident will receive immediate attention ☐ PC3

Resolve incidents within your authority calmly, as soon as possible ☐ PC4

Refer incidents outside your authority to appropriate person ☐ PC5

Report incidents according to procedures/the law ☐ PC6

Do your work in an organised, efficient and safe manner ☐ PC7

Presenting a positive image to customers

The atmosphere in your bar is one of the main reasons people visit. It's made up of many different things, but mostly by people – all the people who serve, and the other customers.

As a member of the bar team, what you contribute makes a real difference. Being well presented and cheerful ... these are some of the things that help everyone. Sometimes it is hard to have a positive influence, especially if you are tired, worried, or in a bad mood. Try not to let problems and negative feelings affect how you deal with customers or work colleagues.

Being courteous and helpful – always

If you were a robot, you might program yourself to give customers a smile, and use words like 'good evening', 'hullo', 'what can I get you to drink', 'certainly', 'please', 'thank you', etc.

One reason bars are not staffed by robots is that customers like someone with personality! The expressions and words you use should show:

- your personality – the positive aspects, that is, not any bad moods, depression, etc.

- the style of your workplace and the customers it attracts – formal, informal, business, tourists, local community, trendy, friendly, young, elderly, etc.

Handling stressful situations

Your people skills are really tested when the bar is packed and customers are waiting, some impatiently. In moments of stress, somehow you have to keep your cool. No one finds it easy.

Try to keep an even-handed approach. Remain polite. You only have a little time with each customer to make a good impression. But it only takes seconds to say 'What can I get you, sir?' when you come to take the order, and 'Thank you' when you are given the money.

Often people's bad temper can be overcome by an apology, 'I'm really sorry to keep you waiting'.

Try to ignore rudeness or bad temper which has nothing to do with the quality of service. Unlike you, customers are allowed to bring their problems with them! You should not take such behaviour personally, although it can be hurtful and unpleasant. Many people develop a sort of professional shield to protect themselves, keeping up the smiles, 'pleases' and 'thank you's', even though they are not returned.

The way you look

Your appearance should give the impression that you are:
FRIENDLY – CLEAN – SMART – ORDERLY – ORGANISED
If you are immaculate, your customers will be convinced that everything else is equally clean and fresh.

Your appearance is your responsibility and you are expected to take good care of it.

Check that your:

- uniform fits, is clean and well pressed
- name badge is on
- hair is clean and tidy
- personal freshness is OK – use a deodorant
- hands and fingernails are clean
- posture is upright and confident
- jewellery is not excessive

It's most important NOT to:

- play with your hair
- look at your watch
- yawn
- bite your nails
- fidget with jewellery
- pick your nose
- sneeze without a handkerchief

Remember:

- you are the centre of attention
- take pride in your appearance
- our customers expect it!
- you will feel better for it!

Keeping up standards

Take trouble over your appearance. Customers judge the standards of the bar by how you look and behave. For example, it gives a good impression of:

- hygiene standards – if they see clean hands and neatly trimmed figernails as you serve the drinks

- customer care – when you remain alert and attentive behind the bar, even though it is not busy at that moment.

Your clothes or uniform should be clean and look fresh. You should also be clean and fresh. Use a deodorant to help keep you sweat-free when it's hot or you're working hard.

Follow your workplace rules on the wearing of jewellery and make-up, and also hair styles. These reflect the atmosphere or style which is being offered, and the practicalities of hygiene and safety.

Customer care back-up

When customers ask if your pub caters for special parties, the cost of bed and breakfast, or which tourist attractions to visit, you can help by giving them leaflets or brochures which promote these facilities. If your workplace is one of a number owned and run by the brewery, or part of a hotel or leisure organisation, there will be a range of promotional material to tell potential customers what is offered.

Supplies

These are examples of customer care supplies. They are there to encourage sales, to provide information, and to support your role in providing quality customer service. You need to know where they are kept. It may also be part of your responsibility to maintain supplies and displays of brochures and similar items (see checklist).

The range might include;

- *literature* – brochures, price lists, posters, etc.
- *stationery* – till rolls, order pads, compliment slips, letterheads, bills and invoices, business cards, postcards, etc.
- *forms* – to take bookings and reservations, to record details of lost property, complaints, customer incidents, to enter quizzes or competitions, etc.
- *consumables* – give-away boxes of matches, drink mats, napkins with the name of the pub/brewery/ company, cocktail swizzles, engraved pens, etc.

CHECKlist
Displays of promotional material

- ✔ sufficient copies of each item
- ✔ different items in their proper place
- ✔ any inserts (e.g. price lists) present
- ✔ no damaged copies on display, e.g. torn or written on by customers
- ✔ overall arrangement is pleasing to look at

Back-up stocks

- ✔ tidy and well organised
- ✔ appropriate person advised when stocks are running low
- ✔ only most recent version of material is kept
- ✔ no material which has out-of-date information (e.g. last year's train timetable)

Equipment

Every time you take payment for a drink, you (or perhaps the cashier, in a bar restaurant) use the till to record the details (the procedures are described in Section 9). Most tills are *electronic*, some with pre-set keys so that you don't have to remember the price of individual drinks.

Some pubs have *mechanical* tills – the force you use to press each key works the price display, and perhaps prints the amount on the till roll.

Working to improve customer relations

You serve customers with the drinks and food they require. You also help create the atmosphere that they come to your bar to enjoy. One of the differences between your pub or bar and others in the area is the relationships you and your colleagues build up with the customers.

Building and maintaining constructive working relationships with customers

Even with those customers who only stay for a short time, the impression they take away is much more positive when you:

- are genuinely pleased to see them, and to serve them
- greet them as they arrive – if you're busy serving another customer, then a smile or a few words will reassure them that they have been noticed
- take an interest in what they order, making suggestions if appropriate, offering ice, lemon, a choice of glasses, etc.
- apologise when they have been kept waiting
- remember what they usually have to drink, but always give them the opportunity to confirm the order – or that they like to consider several different drinks before settling on the one they usually have!
- offer to move chairs or carry drinks when you can see customers are having difficulty (e.g. the elderly, those with mobility difficulties or other special needs, see pages 16 and 17)
- find out and use their names – colleagues will be able to tell you the names of most regulars, others you hear in conversations at the bar, or the names of people eating may be in the restaurant reservations book
- talk to them and listen to them – but don't interrupt or take over their conversations.

Balancing needs of customer and organisation

Some customers only ask for drinks they know you can provide, understand if the dish of the day has run out, etc. More familiar will be the occasion when you cannot provide exactly what customers ask for, or when you have to balance their needs with what it is practical to offer.

Being persistent

The first stage is to try. For example, if a customer asks for:

- a whisky in a larger glass from the one you normally use, don't say 'Sorry, it's a rule that we always serve whisky in these glasses'

- no pickle when ordering the ploughman's, don't say 'You can leave what you don't want, all the ploughman's come the same way'.

The first time you get an unusual request, your immediate reaction might be to think of the reasons why you can't do it. This is understandable. But stop for a moment before you say 'No'. Quickly review the alternatives, or if you need more time, say 'I'll see what we can do and get right back to you'.

Involving colleagues and other departments

Discussions with colleagues can be the way to get a wider perspective, review the options, and check the knock-on effects of each one. If the customer's needs will require cooperation from the kitchen, restaurant or cellar, then you need to agree with colleagues there what you can offer.

Consider the whisky request:

- wider perspective – whiskies are not usually served in large glasses because most people prefer whisky on its own or as a short drink, with a little water, lemonade, dry ginger, etc.

- the options – once you have identified that this customer wants a long drink, you should choose a suitable glass, e.g. one used for soft drinks

- knock-on effects – none in this example. There are no rules over the size of glass for whisky (in spite of what was said to the customer). The amount of whisky served is controlled by the spirit measure or optic, so you are not in danger of serving too much or too little (which would be illegal).

Now take the ploughman's example:

- wider perspective – if the customer dislikes pickle, seeing it on the plate will ruin the enjoyment of the bread and cheese. Most customers would consider a refusal to remove the pickle quite unreasonable

- the options – if ploughman's are prepared with the pickle in a small pot, you can remove this before you serve the customer. If ploughman's are made to order, you can ask for one without pickle. You might offer the customer chutney instead, or the kitchen might add extra salad garnish to compensate for the absence of pickle

- knock-on effects – if all cold dishes are prepared in advance (the ploughman's with a spoon of pickle on the dish), is there someone who can make up a special dish without pickle? If not, do you have the time to transfer one of the prepared ploughman's to a fresh plate, with a fresh garnish made up from the bowls of salad on the cold counter?

Organisational limitations

When you balance customers' needs with what it is practical to offer, you recognise organisational limitations. You take into account *time*, *resources* and *cost*.

In the example of the ploughman's:

- time and resources cannot be separated – if everyone in the kitchen is busy with hot dishes, and you have many other customers to serve, who can take one of the prepared ploughman's and put it on a fresh plate with a fresh garnish?

- cost – if ploughman's are made to order, then it will save money to omit the pickle. On the other hand, if the customer had asked for a double portion of pickle, or another, more expensive cheese, you might have to make an extra charge.

The prices charged at your workplace for drinks, food and the other facilities reflect the time, resources and cost which go into their preparation and service. The customer asking for a proper glass, not a plastic one, at a busy outdoor event, e.g. the bar at the local agricultural show, would be making an unreasonable request. But this would not be so in the VIP enclosure, where much higher prices are charged, and glasses can be more easily collected up.

Explaining to the customer

Telling customers that their request is unreasonable is best left to a manager. Usually you can avoid reaching this stage if you can:

- be flexible and creative – offer alternatives within the limits of your authority

- involve your colleagues – to get their ideas, to benefit from their experience, and when you need their cooperation

- present your proposals convincingly – ideally so that customers accept your ideas as better or equivalent to what they originally wanted. Or, if a compromise is necessary, they accept it because you have explained the circumstances.

Sometimes meeting a special request can create problems for the future. This might mean you have to say 'No, sorry' to the customer, or to make the conditions clear, for example:

- 'Usually the latest time for serving food is 9, but I've had a word with the chef. We could serve you at 9.30 in the restaurant. I hope this will suit you? Only, if we serve you in the bar, other customers might wonder why they are expected to eat before 9.'

Knowing what your workplace offers

It gets easier to respond helpfully to customers' special needs as you learn more about the range of drinks and food available.

Take an interest also in the other products and services offered by your workplace. Serving behind the bar puts you in line for all sorts of questions, especially when you have proved yourself helpful over the customers' drink and food order:

- 'We're having an office party soon. Do you know anywhere?'

- 'We're looking for a B&B for tonight.'

- 'It's our eldest child's birthday in a few weeks time. She's often mentioned what fun a barbecue would be, but without our own garden ...'

Promoting your workplace

Questions like these give you an opportunity to bring extra business to your workplace, or to other places belonging to the same group. So you could mention:

- the attractive room your pub has, ideal for private parties, anything from snacks to a sit-down dinner can be provided

- that many of the pubs in your group do bed and breakfast, and there is a freephone number to make reservations

- a barbecue is being built in the pub garden, which will be serving steaks, burgers, etc. at the weekends.

Also you can promote your workplace by being alert to what customers say in your hearing, e.g.:

- while you pour their drinks, the customers are discussing where to hold their office party

- as you say goodbye to a couple, the wife says 'Come along dear, we've still got to find somewhere to stay tonight'

- you are thanked for the nice meal you have served, and the eldest child says she's longing to try barbecued food.

Selling through bar service

To work behind a bar is not just a question of serving people, but also of *selling* products to customers:

WHITBREAD INNS

- have a thorough knowledge of products stocked – a background to new or unusual lines

- make the first approach to customers – don't wait to be asked for service.

The product

- the total pub is the product – entertainment, games, furnishing and service, etc.

- high standards are essential to attract new customers

- how can the product provide value for money and something different or better than our competitors?

Service

- the customers are being entertained – treat them with consideration – make them feel welcome

- if offered a drink or a tip, it is courtesy to appear surprised or pleased

- answer questions from customers fully but briefly

- some customers want to be left alone, others want to be entertained – be aware of customer moods

- guide customers in their choice if they appear doubtful

- if customers ask for a product that is not available, suggest an alternative

- keep your appearance neat, tidy and clean – tidy hair, hands and clean fingernails

- if there is a grievance behind the bar, raise the matter after the session, not in front of customers

- handle difficult customers discreetly, so that any trouble is not visible to other customers.

Service standards and codes of practice

In some pubs and bars – more so in the larger ones and those that are part of big companies – two types of formal document, statement or guidance are produced by top management:

- *service standards* – describe, in specific terms where possible, the level of service customers should expect. They give staff and management a common goal to work towards, and a means of measuring their achievement

- *codes of practice* – provide step-by-step instructions on how to handle certain situations, e.g. barring customers. Because everyone is following the same detailed guidance put together by experts, there is less risk of things going wrong.

If you have not already done so, find out what service standards and codes of practice apply to your work, and make sure you are working to them.

Giving accurate information to customers

When you are giving information, there is a danger of misleading the customers you are trying to help. This might happen because you have:

- remembered something wrongly – check the information first or warn customers that you cannot be sure

- made-up or guessed information – resist the pressure some customers try and put you under, in their anxiety for details

- left out a crucial fact – when you are describing other services available, or promoting a special event, be clear what the customers have to do, or where they can get more information.

Say you have had a discussion with a couple in the bar about food and places to eat. They are staying at a nearby caravan site. Taking the opportunity to promote your workplace, you tell them of the gourmet evenings in your restaurant every Friday. Next Friday the couple turn up to celebrate their wedding anniversary – but you hadn't said that early booking was essential, and the couple are turned away.

The 10 second and 2 minute rule

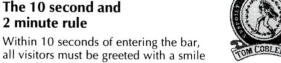

Within 10 seconds of entering the bar, all visitors must be greeted with a smile or 'Hullo, welcome to Tom Cobleigh'.

Within 2 minutes they must be served.

Learn the visitors' names. Develop a customer care style that encourages visitors to become Tom Cobleigh regulars.

Make conversation over the bar counter. Keep off religion and politics. Talk about what is in the newspaper that day, cricket, football, the national lottery, gardens, holidays, weather, hobbies, etc. Most importantly, tell the visitor about the company and how we value his or her visit.

Information that you should not disclose

In your enthusiasm to help customers, or promote your workplace, there is a danger of saying too much. This can happen quite easily, when the information you have given leads to an in-depth conversation.

Suppose you have been describing how the menu will be changed. As the conversation develops, you mention that the kitchen is being refitted, which is why the new menu is being brought in. The customer comments that standards for pub kitchens must be very high – you agree, and add that the work had cost over £25,000, which the landlord has had to borrow. When the customer comments that the landlord must be confident the new menu will be popular, you are once more indiscreet: 'No choice, it's the new hygiene regulations.'

When to seek assistance, when to use your own initiative

Another danger area, is when you have not been able to provide what a customer wants because it is against company policy or the law. If the customer tries to draw you into a discussion about the rights and wrongs of the policy, or different interpretations of the law, it is time to seek assistance.

Try and recognise when you are out of your depth in a situation, or have run out of suggestions and offers. Not calling on the help of a senior colleague or your manager can cause worse difficulties. The judgement is not always easy to make, but it is wise to be over-cautious.

Recording what you have done

In some workplaces, there are systems for recording customers' special or unusual needs. You will be asked to make a note of the time, place, people involved, etc., what was requested, what you proposed and the outcome. There may be a form for doing this.

Records help management monitor levels of customer service – usually a requirement of quality standard schemes like BS5750. They also help should the situation lead to a complaint, e.g. to head office.

Informal communication routes

It is always helpful to tell your manager if an incident has happened, especially if there is no formal system for recording the details. Then if the matter leads to a complaint, your manager is forewarned. And should the customer give a rather different description of events, your manager will be able to see both points of view, and support the action you took, knowing that you did the best you could.

Your manager is also in a position to make or propose changes which would avoid similar problems in the future, e.g. introducing a new range of drinks and food.

Legal aspects

There are four areas of possible conflict between the law and what customers ask for:

- *safe working practices* – you should not agree to or propose anything which would put at risk the safety of others in your workplace, e.g. blocking open fire doors to make the room cooler on a hot day

- *trade descriptions* – when you suggest drinks or dishes which are not exactly what the customer asked for, say what is different, e.g. that the vodka is brand X

- *weights and measures* – a customer asking for a partly-emptied glass of draught beer to be topped up, can only be served a measured quantity, i.e. half a pint (for reasons of hygiene, this should be served in a clean glass then poured into the customer's glass if requested)

- *licensing law* – a person you believe is under the legal age for buying alcohol should not be allowed to bully you into acceptance: ask for proof of age and, if this is not produced, get your manager.

Points of contact with customers in the bar

Providing creative solutions

1. Try and establish what the customer *really* wants. For example if someone asks 'Do you do food?', but seems put off by your answer 'Yes, we offer a 3-course meal in the restaurant for £8 per person'. Is this because:
   - £8 is more than the customer wants to pay?
   - a 3-course meal is not what the customer wants?
   In either case, you could suggest a choice from the bar snack menu, and offer some suggestions.

2. Identify the *key features* of what it is the customer wants. For example, if someone asks 'Do you do accommodation?', is it for a single, twin or double room, for how many people, in what price range?

3. Beware of *misunderstanding*. For example, some people booking accommodation assume all your rooms have private bathrooms.

4. Think around the request. For example, a customer may ask what the vegetarian special is. If there is none, or if the choice does not seem acceptable, suggest other dishes from the menu that do not contain meat or fish, or which could be prepared without these.

5. Learn from each situation you encounter. Once you have welcomed a mother who had booked a double room with you earlier, and you realise she is with her teenage son, you should remember that some people ask for a double when they mean a room with two beds (i.e. twin).

6. Think quickly. Show the mother and son to a twin room. Only if no twin is available will you have to explain why you misunderstood and suggest, if they are available, two single rooms.

7. Be tactful and sensitive. When you hand the menu to someone you think looks overweight, don't say as your opening remark: 'We have the very thing for you, a low-calorie summer salad'.

8. Be careful of bending the rules to please a particular customer. Don't let someone into the pub with a dog if dogs are not normally allowed (guide dogs are always an exception). It might be a small dog, and well behaved, but how do you explain to a customer with a bigger dog that it is not allowed?

9. Don't break the law or house rules to please a customer. If you have any doubt about whether someone is of the correct age, you must ask for proof.

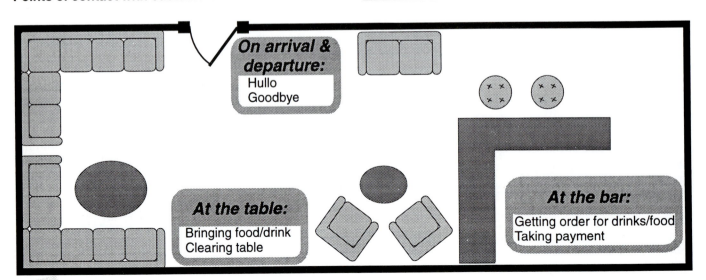

On arrival & departure:
Hullo
Goodbye

At the table:
Bringing food/drink
Clearing table

At the bar:
Getting order for drinks/food
Taking payment

Responding to customers' feelings

Barwork brings you into close contact with a very wide range of customers' feelings. These reflect the many reasons that people come to your place, and what happens while they are there – the effect of being with or among people, of the atmosphere, of alcohol, etc. Not everyone reacts in the same way, e.g. some get more cheerful, some have no obvious change of mood, a few get more depressed.

Barwork gives you the chance to respond to customers' feelings, helping them to enjoy their visit more. Customers who are cheerful, satisfied, content or good-humoured are likely to appreciate friendly, good-natured, good-humoured responses from you. There is usually no difficulty in responding to positive feelings like these.

Presenting more of a challenge are the feelings of the opposite sort. These include:

- *anger* – customers who are greatly annoyed or antagonistic. The customers may arrive angry (e.g. after an argument), become angry because of what another customer has said or done, and get angry with you or a colleague. This may be because of something you have said or done, or not said or done. Your action may just be the trigger for their anger

- *distress* – customers who are worried or upset. This may be because of a personal problem, worry, illness, side-effects of medicine, drugs, alcohol, etc.

- *vulnerability* – customers who are easily hurt or upset. This may be because they are worried, ill, etc. or because they are very shy, nervous, or feel ill at ease for some reason

- *frustration* – customers who feel dissatisfied. This may be because something has happened or not happened, or a more general feeling that things are against them.

By learning to judge or gauge anger, distress, vulnerability or frustration – 'negative feelings' – and respond in an appropriate way, you can reduce the risk of complaints, awkward situations and other difficulties.

Judging or gauging negative feelings

With someone you know well, you may be able to detect changes in their mood from small signs – not talking as much as usual, not listening to what you are saying, staring into the distance, etc. Perhaps you are naturally sensitive. Many people have to make an effort to pick up the signs. Indeed, you may know some people who never take notice until you have reached the stage of shouting, crying, etc. and then ask in a surprised tone of voice whether you have a problem!

Anger

Some customers when angry shout, swear, thump the bar counter or table, and gesture with their fists. Perhaps they cannot control their temper, or they want their anger to be obvious to the people around them.

Signs of more controlled forms of anger include: red face, unhappy expression, fidgeting, abrupt demands and sarcastic tone.

Distress

As with anger, the signs of distress vary from person to person. They may include: crying or sobbing, shaking of the body, higher pitch to the voice, fidgeting, wringing of the hands, covering the face with hands, wild expression in the eyes, and constantly going to the toilet.

Vulnerability

With customers you know, you may notice changes to their usual behaviour, worried expressions and nervousness. Other signs which help you judge the feelings of other customers include: keeping as far away as possible from everyone else, anxiety not to attract attention, or almost apologetic attitude when waiting to be served.

Frustration

This is quite difficult to pick up from people's behaviour. You might notice restlessness (e.g. moving from one seat to another), lack of enjoyment of drink or food (e.g. pushing it aside, leaving some), look of distraction (e.g. not involved in conversation), or difficulty to please (e.g. long discussion about order, rejecting most suggestions with a shake of the head).

Terms used to describe the outward signs

As these examples show, you can tell that all is not well by taking notice of – in other words, *observing* – customers' behaviour. The other two terms are:

- *body language* – the information you get on the customers' feelings from their gestures, facial expressions, how close or far away they are standing from other people, where they are looking, etc.

- *tone of voice* – the sound of the customer's voice, how loud or soft it is, the pitch (high, low, deep, shrill), the quality (warm, cold, hostile, aggressive), and the pace or speed of talking (fast, slow).

Using sensitive questioning to confirm outward signs

Sometimes you know from customers' behaviour that things are wrong, but you need to find out more about the cause (frustration, anger, etc.) to deal with the situation. Here carefully worded questions can play a useful role.

What you don't want is to make matters worse. What you do want is to help the person help himself or herself. Often just one or two very general questions give the opportunity to talk, and that is sufficient for the problem to blow over. The danger is to be seen to be prying, or trying to cause aggravation.

Consider, for example, a regular who has been drinking much more than usual. Jim has reached the stage when you should refuse him any more alcohol, but you would rather persuade him not to have another drink and to go home, than risk a row by refusing:

- a general comment might be sufficient to get him to talk, e.g. 'Jim, you seem rather low this evening ...'

- if you know from previous conversations that he has a problem, your question could be more specific, e.g. 'Have things at work been getting you down?'

- if you think it unwise to make any reference to his mood (because recognising that you and others have noticed it might depress him further), you can try the mutual sympathy line, e.g. 'I'm having a terrible time with my car at the moment, one expense after the other which I just can't afford'.

Responding to customers' feelings

Angry or distressed customers spoil the atmosphere in the bar, and create unpleasantness for everyone. Similar difficulties are caused by customers who feel frustrated or vulnerable, especially if this turns into anger or distress.

When you become aware of any negative feelings, or see the warning signs, your priorities are:

- keep calm

- remain polite

- act in as normal a manner as possible

- don't put yourself in danger.

Acknowledging customers' feelings

Usually it is sufficient to be with the customer, talking, listening to their problems or complaint, taking care not to make the situation worse. Through your action you show that you realise the customer is angry, distressed, etc. Putting it into words – e.g. 'I can tell you're frustrated' – is likely to aggravate the customer, especially if you are wrong about the nature of the problem.

Adapting your behaviour accordingly

You do this by not returning anger with anger, or getting distressed because a customer is distressed.

You may also have to control some of your natural characteristics. For example, being bubbly and humorous might cause a person feeling vulnerable to be even more worried and nervous.

Checking perception of customers' feelings

You have to be watchful that the anger or distress is not getting worse, or feelings of frustration or vulnerability are turning into anger or distress. When this happens, or at any time you feel the situation getting out of control, ask your manager to take over.

Hopefully, through your calm approach and awareness of difficulties, most situations will get easier. Normal relations can be restored, but avoid saying or doing things that might cause a relapse, such as a joke in poor taste.

WHITBREAD
INNS

Dissatisfied customers who don't complain

Not all customers complain. They may leave food untouched, or ask for the bill before they have finished their meal.

Try to establish if there is a problem. You may be able to remedy the situation and promote further sales.

Improving your skills at handling complaints

Handling complaints successfully can take practice and requires you to have confidence with your approach. You can help yourself by:

- finding out the house's policy on making refunds or changing items, and who can take these decisions
- asking colleagues to play the part of complaining customers, and give feedback on how you deal with them.

Complaints from customers with negative feelings

When customers complain to you about the service or some other subject to do with your workplace, they are quite likely to be frustrated. Some will be angry, some distressed, some feeling vulnerable.

Recognising these feelings helps you adapt the way you deal with the complaints (see page 4 for guidelines). For example:

- keeping a careful distance from someone who is very angry, and avoiding prolonged eye contact (this makes the person feel uncomfortable)

- persuading a very upset customer to move, so you can discuss matters calmly, away from others in the bar – 'Shall we sit over there, where you'll be more comfortable?'

- offering a distressed customer a cup of tea or coffee when you think this will calm the person down

- not leaving a distressed customer alone – if you have to go away, asking a colleague to remain with the customer.

Pizza Hut®

Complaint handling

1 Listen and respond with empathy.
2 Apologise sincerely.
3 Get all details of the complaint.
4 Respond by showing you understand.
5 Agree on specific action to be taken.
6 Thank the customer.

Angry customers

- remember it is not personal – try to avoid showing personal emotion
- empathise with problem by showing concern – think about your reaction if you were the customer
- listen to the complaint – if you can't agree and can't manage the problem, involve the support of the manager
- always follow up on what you have agreed.

Adopting methods of communication

Getting information across to customers, and understanding clearly what they are trying to communicate to you are not always straightforward. Think of the times when the bar is very noisy, or you've served the wrong drink because the customer's strong accent confused you.

Types of communication

In barwork, most of your communications with customers are spoken, talking to them *face-to-face*. Sometimes you deal with customers on the *telephone*, e.g. when they call to make a restaurant or room booking. And from time to time, you will use *written* communication, e.g. when taking down the details of a complaint or incident, or a message.

Using suitable language

Customers find it easy to understand what you are saying (or have written down) when you use everyday language. The bar is not the place to impress people with long or unusual words, or your command of English grammar. Nor is it the place to offend or shock (or try to impress) by using swear words or foul language.

With so few restrictions, you have plenty of scope for putting feeling and a sense of your personality into what you say. Customers prefer to be served by a person rather than a robot-like object who uses a few standard phrases said without thought or meaning.

Be sensitive to the customer's viewpoint and feelings:

- avoid words, remarks or jokes which might give offence because of their connection with religion, politics, race, skin colour, disabilities, sexual orientation, etc.

- try and match your language to the style of the people you are talking to – a chatty, casual response is unlikely to be appreciated by those who say to you 'Good afternoon, please may we have two glasses of your driest sherry?'

If in doubt, use the convential greetings – 'please', 'thank you', 'sir', 'madam', 'good afternoon', etc., and avoid any remarks or topics of conversation which might be controversial.

What information to communicate and when

You want customers to feel welcome and enjoy their visit. They appreciate a pleasant greeting when they arrive, come to the bar to order, the usual 'pleases' and 'thank you's' when they pay for their order, and farewells when they leave.

Customers also appreciate accurate, helpful information when they ask about the drinks and food available, or put more general questions to you (e.g. about taxi services).

The information is inappropriate if you:

- give too much so as to bore them – if the subject is a wide one (e.g. wines, and you have a lengthy wine list), ask some questions to establish their likely interest (e.g. red to go with their food order, Australian or French)

- give too little – saying that all spirits are half price, but not that 'happy hour' ends in 5 minutes' time

- time it poorly – after delivering food to customers sitting in the bar, saying that they could have eaten at a table in the restaurant if only they had mentioned it earlier

- give information they cannot use – describing the guest beer to a couple who have asked about non-alcoholic drinks

- are insensitive to their needs – customers will be irritated or embarrassed when you have heard them tell their children to have cokes because the other drinks are too expensive, and you answer their question on beers by starting with the top-price imported lagers

- pass on business or personal information which is not disclosable (i.e. confidential – discussed earlier in this section – see page 2).

Customers with special communication needs

All customers like special treatment, and it is one of the main reasons they enjoy their visits to your bar. But there are some customers who have special communication needs. Not noticing their needs, or treating them as strange, odd, weird, of subnormal intelligence or whatever, could turn the visit into a humiliating experience.

Acknowledging communication difficulties

If you do not have much experience of handling communication difficulties with customers, call on a more experienced colleague or your manager to help. Don't pretend to have experience and skills you don't have. This will only make things more difficult for the customer.

Speech impairment

When someone has difficulty talking or is unable to speak at all, you may have to take the lead in finding out what they would like. Show them the drinks list and menu, so they can point to their choice. Alternatively, talk them slowly through the range available and with each choice, wait for a sign, e.g. nod for yes, shake of the head for no. Before you get too far, check that you understand the sign as some people have difficulty controlling certain body movements.

Begin with the general, e.g. 'Would you like a drink?', then gradually home in on the choice, e.g.: 'Beer ... spirit ... soft drink ... still ... fizzy ... coke ... orange?'

When customers can speak a little, but it is very difficult to understand what they are saying, avoid correcting, interrupting or trying to finish what you think is being said. Wait before asking short questions that can be quickly answered (e.g. with a gesture) to clarify what is required.

Hearing impairment

The first step is to realise that the customer is having trouble hearing what you are saying. Those able to lip read might not give any clues until you say something with your face turned away.

Avoid remarks like 'Are you deaf?'– pointless because they won't hear the question.

1 Look directly at the person as you are talking. Seeing the expressions on your face and lip movement helps the person to follow what you are saying. Stand so the light is on your face (i.e. not in front of a window).

2 Keep your hands well away from your mouth. When this will help, use them to gesture and point.

3 Speak as clearly as you can, slowly, using short sentences and short words.

4 Raise the volume of your voice a little. Do not shout as this creates more noise and the words are no clearer.

5 Make use of printed drinks lists and menus. Point to items behind the bar that the customer might like. Use a notepad to write brief messages, e.g. 'ice?'

Sight impairment

Regulars who are partially sighted or blind will get to know their way around your pub so well that other customers and staff may be unaware of their situation. But the observant will notice, perhaps, a slowness of movement, use of a white stick, companionship of a guide dog (which should be allowed into the pub, no matter what the general rules are about animals), and wearing dark glasses.

Some of the ways you can help customers with sight impairment enjoy their visit to the pub are:

- assist them to a comfortable place to sit, explain the layout of the pub, where the toilets are, etc.

- describe the choice of food or drinks if they are not sure what to order

- gently touch them so they know you are there to help, and guide them to where you have put the chairs, their drink etc.

- serve their drink in an over-sized glass so they are less likely to spill it

- describe the arrangement of food on the plate, warn of any bones, and offer to help cut meat, etc.

- identify the value of each note when you return their change (many blind people fold each note in a certain way to help identify it).

If the customer is with a companion who is able to help in these and other ways, be careful not to ignore the blind person, e.g. by directing all your questions to the companion.

Some of the larger chains of pubs and restaurants have braille menus for the sight-impaired.

Physical disability

Customers who arrive in a wheelchair may need help to get to a place where they can be comfortable: by opening doors, moving chairs or tables aside, etc. If the customer is alone, offer to take the drink and food order to the table.

Wheelchair users may feel uncomfortable if they think other customers are being inconvenienced by their presence. Suggest somewhere to sit where there is more space available (but not a draughty corner or immediately outside the kitchen doors).

Be ready to help other customers with disabilities that affect their:

- walking – e.g. offering a steadying hand, taking the order to them

- control of their hands or head – e.g. offering to pour the drink into an over-sized glass, putting the food on an extra-large dish, cutting the food for them and providing a spoon.

Special mobility needs

If you know a visitor is due who has special mobility needs, you may be able to make special arrangements for when they arrive. Consider their needs from the moment of arrival, in particular:

- car parking
- access to the building
- ease of movement round the building
- access to facilities, such as toilets.

Language differences

Working in a pub or bar where many of the customers are from outside the area means that you will meet and have to try to understand a range of:

- *accents* – words said in a distinctive way, indicating the region, country or social class of the speaker, e.g. Cornish accent, Australian accent, 'English public school' accent

- *dialects* – form of the language (with different words, grammar and way of saying) spoken by a particular group of people, especially those living in one area, e.g. farm workers in Lincolnshire

- *other languages* – from any part of the world if you are near a top tourist attraction or major airport.

Some customers, especially those with regional accents, will expect you to know what they are saying – not out of any arrogance, but because they are used to being understood. One of your colleagues may be able to help interpret. Often you can persuade the customer (in a light-hearted way) to modify the accent.

Customers who don't speak English greatly appreciate the effort you make to learn and use the most important words and phrases of their language: 'hullo', 'good morning/afternoon', 'please', 'thank you', 'beer', 'wine', etc.

If all else fails, you can point to the drinks people seem to want, or show the bottles so they can read the label. Fingers come in useful for finding out how many drinks or servings of food they want.

Learning difficulties

Learning difficulties may explain why a customer asks you to read the menu, or write the cheque, or explain something again. Of course, these are matters you can easily help with. There is no reason to enquire what might be the problem.

Checking understanding of communication

Whoever the customers are, communication can easily go wrong and often does. This happens when people:

- hear what they want or expect to – e.g. that they can eat in the restaurant, but the 'different menu' you mentioned is taken to mean the same range of dishes and prices printed on restaurant menu cards, so they are upset to get to the restaurant and find more elaborate dishes and higher prices

- are distracted by their own thoughts or worries, or other activities in the bar, so they miss some of what you have said

- take a different meaning from what you meant – usually because you have been ambiguous or not sufficiently specific, e.g. 'Oh yes, smart casual wear is fine to get into the disco', when the customer considers designer jeans as smart casual, but the rules for the disco exclude anyone wearing jeans.

To reduce the risk of such misunderstandings, look the customer in the face as you are passing the information on. Watch out for blank expressions, the customer turning away while you are talking, looks being exchanged among the group and similar signs of inattention.

When you are dealing with important factual information, e.g. taking the customer's address to send details of Christmas lunches in the restaurant, or a B&B booking, repeat the information back to the customer.

Procedures for dealing with customer incidents

Remind yourself of what these are (see pages 4 and 5). Because of the nature of the customer's impairment or disability, things can go wrong no matter how carefully you try to help, for example:

- someone falls out of the wheelchair, or another customer trips over the chair

- there is an angry scene because no one seems to understand the customer's accent (or language)

- an adult with Down's syndrome becomes distressed.

Test yourself on customer service skills

BUSINESS BASICS

1 Why does Pizza Hut serve Pepsi drinks?

2 Who monitors the performance of the units and the quality of the product?

3 What must you do if a customer orders 'Coke'?

4 At which units can a customer order alcohol?

5 When can alcohol be sold?

SERVICE

6 How must a server be introduced?

7 What must all under 12's be given?

8 When should the bill be presented?

9 What should be offered with mineral water?

10 How many follow-ups should a customer receive?

11 Can change be given for sterling travellers' cheques?

12 Within what time should the bill be presented after a request?

13 What is meant by a service standard?

14 Why is it important to always repeat the order back to customers?

15 What parting remarks should we use when speaking on a telephone?

16 How many times is a phone allowed to ring before being answered?

17 How can we accommodate the special needs of families?

18 What are the three A's.

THE PRODUCT

19 List the forms of payment.

20 Do prices include VAT?

Questions which refer to Pizza Hut have been included in this selection because they show the sort of information employees of multi-unit companies need to know.

Answers

1 Because it is part-owned by Pepsi Cola.

2 Pepsi Cola International monitors the performance and product quality through the standards of operations.

3 Inform them politely that Pepsi is available. We cannot take an order for Coke and serve a different branded product. This is against the trade description laws.

4 Only at restaurant units which hold a licence.

5 During the licensing hours displayed in the relevant units.

6 By name.

7 Goody bags and kids' menus.

8 With the last item served.

9 Ice and lemon.

10 Two or more if appropriate.

11 Yes!

12 Within 3 minutes.

13 Questions 12 and 16 are examples.

14 To ensure both the customer and the server have the same products in mind.

15 Always be polite, confirm details such as times, products, name, etc. Give a cheerful general final remark.

16 As soon as possible, always before the fourth ring.

17 An environment where mothers can feed babies and always extra patience and a calming attitude. We can provide space for buggies, additional napkins, goody bags for children. Often we can provide baby changing facilities.

18 Attitude. Acknowledgement. Approach.

19 Cash. Cheques. Debit cards. Credit cards. VIP vouchers. LV vouchers.

20 Yes, VAT at current rates is included in the menu price.

1 Give the rules on behaviour and what you wear at work.

2 What stationery, promo material, etc. and equipment do you use to help serve customers?

3 'When you're really busy you don't have time for pleases and thank you's, etc.' Comment on this attitude.

4 How do you deal with customers who are rude to you?

5 'If a customer doesn't say "please", I won't.' Comment.

6 How do you identify the customers who a) want to be left on their own, b) like to have a conversation with the bar staff?

7 Give four examples of how you can promote the products/ services of your pub/bar and (if this applies) of the organisation it is part of.

8 'Regulars are the life-blood of many pubs – but it's hard laughing at the same jokes again and again.' Comment.

9 Give two examples of service standards in your pub/bar. What is the reason for having service standards and codes of practice?

10 Give examples of information about a) your workplace and b) customers, which must be treated as confidential.

11 To whom do you pass on customer comments about a) cleanliness of the toilets, b) range of lagers, c) speed of service in the restaurant?

12 Describe a situation when you used your initiative to meet a customer's needs, and another where you had to seek help.

13 Now describe a situation where the customer's needs could not be met. Why was this? What did you say to the customer?

14 Give an example of a customer request which cannot be met because of a) cost, b) time, c) resources?

15 Describe the steps for dealing with a complaint. For each step say what is important to remember and why.

16 How can you tell when a customer is feeling: a) angry, b) distressed, c) vulnerable, d) frustrated? What can you say and/or do to help the customer?

17 Describe how you can help a customer with a) hearing impairment, b) speech impairment, c) physical disability, d) learning difficulties, d) language differences.

Illustrations with thanks to Rank Leisure (questions 7 and 12)

NVQ SVQ

Skills check
Develop and maintain positive working relationships
with customers
Unit 2NG3

level
2

QUIZ – customer care

1. Why is a friendly greeting important?
2. How do you acknowledge a customer?
3. Why are regular customers important?
4. Why is it important to learn customers' names?
5. Why is eye contact important?
6. Why are first impressions important?
7. Why should all information given to customers be accurate?
8. Why should you not give information outside your authority?
9. How can you help customers with communication or mobility difficulties?
10. How do we encourage customers to stay in the pub?
11. What details should you give a customer who asks about function facilities?
12. How should you deal with customer complaints?
13. How do we leave the customer with a good impression?
14. How would you ask for help or advice from a) another member of staff, b) a manager, c) a customer?
15. How would you solve any difficulties you may have with another member of staff?

Use this to check your progress against the performance criteria.

Element 1

Present positive personal image to customer

Treat customers helpfully and courteously	☐ PC1
Meet workplace standards of personal appearance and behaviour	☐ PC2
Equipment/supplies for dealing with customers up-to-date, in good order	☐ PC3
⚠ Equipment and supplies: literature, stationery, forms, mechanical, electronic, consumables	
Seek opportunities for improving customer relations	☐ PC4

Element 2

Balance needs of customer and organisation

Make persistent attempts to meet customer needs	☐ PC1
Explain organisational limitations to customer	☐ PC2
⚠ Limitations: cost, time, resources	
Minimise conflict between customer needs and organisational limitations	☐ PC3
Recognise organisational limitations and seek assistance from managers	☐ PC4
Make record of outcome of proposals put to customers	☐ PC5

Element 3

Respond to feelings expressed by the customer

Accurately gauge customers' feelings	☐ PC1
⚠ Customers' feelings: anger, distress, vulnerability, frustration	
Acknowledge customers' feelings and adapt your behaviour	☐ PC2
Regularly check perception of customers' feelings	☐ PC3
Operate relevant procedures to respond to customer complaints	☐ PC4

Element 4

Adapt methods of communication to the customer

Select type of communication to inform customers	☐ PC1
⚠ Communication: face-to-face, telephone, written	
Use written and spoken language suited to the customer	☐ PC2
Use method of communication suited to customers with individual needs	☐ PC3
⚠ Individual needs: hearing impairment, speech impairment, physical disability, learning difficulties, language differences (includes dialects and accents)	
Regularly check customers' understanding of communication	☐ PC4
Openly acknowledge communication difficulties and seek help to overcome	☐ PC5

STARTER'S FIRST SESSION GUIDE

PUT YOURSELF IN THE CUSTOMER'S SHOES – THEIR CARE IS OUR NUMBER ONE PRIORITY

GUIDELINES FOR SUCCESS

- Customers deserve the service YOU would expect.
- Smile – it creates the right first impression.
- Always remember to welcome each customer and say good-bye.
- Be professional – look and feel the part.
- Try to relax – first night nerves are normal.
- Be friendly and confident.
- Open your eyes – never walk past what you could put right.

Welcome

Extracts from Service for Sales, *a training package which helps the staff of Scottish & Newcastle Retail gain their NVQ/SVQ*

SCOTTISH & NEWCASTLE RETAIL

QUIZ – your work unit

1. What type of unit do you work in?
2. Describe the main types of customer.
3. Name ten regulars and what they drink.
4. What does the unit offer that makes it attractive to customers?
5. What facilities are available, e.g. car parking?
6. What are the opening hours?

Hygiene, safety and security in the bar

Hygiene in the bar

Even if your bar or pub does not serve food, it must meet the legal requirements for food premises. This is because drinks are regarded as food. So is ice.

Like food, drinks become unsafe if they are contaminated. Ways this can happen include:

- someone sneezes over a tray of drinks

- hands are not washed properly after removing the empties

- in a busy service period, glasses are not properly washed

- glasses are refilled when customers order another drink – bacteria from customers' mouths and hands spread on to beer-dispense nozzles or spirit measures, and from there to other glasses and drinks.

How drinks and food can become contaminated

The examples above show how harmful bacteria can contaminate drinks and in a similar way, food. There are many varieties of bacteria, but they fall into two groups:

- those carried by people – all the examples above are of this type

- those mostly found on food.

Bacteria are also found in dust and dirt. They live on, and get spread by, pests – flies, ants, spiders, mice, rats, etc.

Bacteria are not the only cause of contamination. Drinks and food become unsafe to consume when:

- dirt, dust, pieces of broken glass or china or any other non-food object have got into them – known as *physical contamination*

- cleaning substances or agents get into them – known as *chemical contamination*.

Most people carry *Staphylococcus aureus* bacteria in their nose and mouth. Each time the nose or mouth is touched, or someone sneezes, bacteria are transferred to glasses, drinks, food, etc.

Salmonella is found in raw meats, chicken and turkey, *Clostridium perfringens* in the soil on unwashed vegetables and sometimes raw meat. The bacteria are killed by thorough cooking. The problems occur when bacteria are transferred from raw food to food which has already been cooked (e.g. by using the same knife to prepare both types). If that food is not kept sufficiently cold or sufficiently hot, the bacteria grow in numbers and can cause serious food poisoning.

Legal requirements relating to food safety

Under the Food Safety Act 1990, proprietors of food businesses (which include pubs and bars) commit an offence if they serve food (which includes drink) that is harmful to health. The scope of the Act is wide. It is an offence to make food harmful, offer for sale food that is contaminated, and describe food in a way that misleads the customer.

Regulations made under the Act deal with aspects of food safety. Of most significance to pubs and bars are the Food Safety (General Food Hygiene) Regulations 1995. These require:

- your employer to ensure that the preparation, storage and handling of food is carried out in a hygienic way. The regulations set general standards for the design and cleanliness of food premises and equipment, personal hygiene and training of food handlers

- you to report to your employer or manager any illness, wound, infection or other medical condition which might contaminate food – more details on page 23

- your employer to identify steps in the preparation, storage, handling and service of food that are critical to food safety, and ensure adequate safety procedures.

These safety procedures require you to follow cleaning schedules, workplace rules, and to check date marks on bottles and packets. You may also have to record temperatures of refrigerators and freezers, etc.

Personal health and hygiene

When you are tired or unwell, your concentration is below its best. You may find that you drop things – endangering yourself and the people around you. Your work seems more difficult. You find it less easy to relax. You are caught in a circle, which gets harder to break.

These problems are less likely if you follow a healthy lifestyle. Try to take regular exercise. Take enough sleep and relaxation, and keep a balance in what you eat and drink.

But it is another aspect of personal health that the following pages focus on: your responsibility to protect the safety of the drink and food you prepare and serve. This affects what you wear, your personal standards of hygiene, the wearing of jewellery, perfume and cosmetics, and what to do if you have a cut or graze, or feel ill.

What you wear at work

You spend long hours on your feet. Wear comfortable shoes that will not slip, and which protect your feet from dropped objects. Wash your feet every day, and keep your toe nails trimmed. Change socks daily.

If you change into a uniform at work, leave your outdoor clothing and footwear in the place provided for this purpose. Don't take it with you into the bar or cellar.

If you wear your own clothes at work, choose a combination that is comfortable, practical and safe. Avoid loose fitting clothes, accessories and jewellery which might get caught on things. What you wear should suit the style of your workplace, and give the right impression to customers.

How you look

Long flowing hair is not suitable behind the bar, in the cellar or kitchen. It might get trapped, e.g. in the door of the drinks cooling cabinet. Strands of hair are likely to fall into drinks and food. There is usually a rule that long hair must be tied back, and that anyone preparing food should keep their hair covered.

You will find that your hair (and this applies to beards and moustaches too) absorbs smoke and food smells. Daily washing will keep it clean and free from smells.

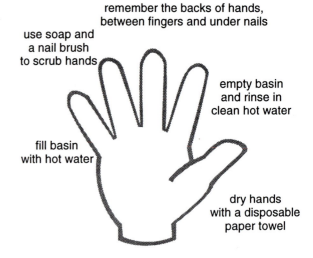

remember the backs of hands, between fingers and under nails

use soap and a nail brush to scrub hands

empty basin and rinse in clean hot water

fill basin with hot water

dry hands with a disposable paper towel

Personal hygiene

Keep yourself clean and fresh. The body excretes moisture constantly through sweat glands located all over it. You will perspire more when working under pressure in a hot environment. Sweat itself is virtually odourless and normally evaporates quickly. The smell comes from bacteria which live on the perspiration, especially in areas such as the underarms where it cannot evaporate freely. A daily bath or shower and a good deodorant are the best protection.

Pay special attention to your hands. You depend on them for most tasks. Your customers judge the hygiene standards of the pub from the state of your hands. Your fingernails should be clean and neatly trimmed. Nail varnish is best avoided, and must not be worn if you are preparing food.

Wash your hands thoroughly and often, and always before touching food. Use plenty of hot water and soap, rinse your hands, and then dry them well. Use the paper towels, roller towel or hot air drier provided – never a glass or drying-up cloth.

Do not wash glasses or drinks and food equipment in wash hand basins, and do not use food sinks for hand washing.

If you feel a sneeze coming, or you need to cough, turn away from any drinks or food. Hold a disposable paper tissue over your nose and mouth, and wash your hands afterwards. Control any impulse to lick your fingers, bite your nails, or touch your nose, mouth or hair.

Never smoke or spit in the bar, or any room where food is prepared, stored or served.

Reporting illness and infection

Report *any* illness or infection as soon as possible. Your manager will make the judgement of whether it is safe for you to serve behind the bar, or whether or not you can work with food. Don't break the law (see below) or put other people's health at risk, just because you don't want to admit to feeling ill.

Covering cuts, grazes and wounds

Cover cuts, grazes, open sores and wounds with a waterproof dressing. Dressings for kitchen staff (from the first aid box) are often coloured blue, so that if they do drop off they will be easily spotted.

If the wound or sore is infected, or you think it might be, report this to your manager.

Legal requirements

Under the Food Safety (General Food Hygiene) Regulations 1995 you must tell your manager if:

- you know or suspect you are suffering from, or may be a carrier, of any disease likely to be transmitted through food

- you have an infected wound, a skin infection, sores, diarrhoea or any similar medical condition such as stomach upset or vomiting.

Until you have been cleared of the condition, you will not be permitted to handle drinks or food, or work in any capacity where you might put at risk the safety of the food.

Your employer has a responsibility to ensure that every person working in the bar, restaurant and kitchen:

- maintains a high degree of personal cleanliness

- wears suitable, clean and, where appropriate, protective clothing.

The regulations also require the provision of adequate hand washing and toilet facilities, and somewhere to change into uniform and store personal and work clothing.

CHECK **list**
When to wash your hands

- ✔ when coming on duty
- ✔ after a break or visit to the toilet
- ✔ after clearing empties, or restocking
- ✔ after handling food
- ✔ after handling waste
- ✔ after handling cleaning materials
- ✔ after smoking

Element 2
Fire procedures

Pubs have a plentiful supply of the four things that can lead to really serious fires, those that cause thousands or millions of pounds of damage, destroy businesses, injure people and sometimes cost lives. The first three are the basic ingredients that any fire requires: oxygen (in other words, air), fuel (anything which will burn) and heat. The fourth is opportunity.

Discarded matches and cigarette ends not cleared away at the end of service are one of the most common sources of fires in pubs. Trapped in upholstered seats, or lying on a carpet, they have the opportunity to smoulder away unnoticed. Some time after everyone has gone, the fire starts in earnest. In the minutes it takes to trigger the fire detection system, and for someone to respond, the fire can cause considerable damage.

The other main causes of pub fires are cooking equipment, electrical faults (in wiring and equipment), arson (i.e. someone has started the fire deliberately to cause damage), poor storage of rubbish and room heating appliances (including open fires).

Raising the alarm

Some fires start when people are on the premises. Speed in raising the fire alarm is vital. The alarm will warn other people and give them time to get to safety. The alarm will bring help from those who have been trained to fight the fire and to rescue anyone who has been trapped by the smoke, heat or flames.

This means you need to know what to do now. Your employer has a legal duty to provide training, and there will be fire notices and other reminders in staff and customer areas of the pub telling you what to do. But you may be putting a lot of people at risk if you wait for a real emergency before you learn what has to be done.

Using fire fighting equipment

Never put yourself at risk in attempting to fight a fire. This is difficult to judge and you may be tempted to play the hero. The rule is, if in doubt, don't. Concentrate on raising the alarm and helping with the evacuation of the building.

In each of the customer areas of the bar, in the cellar, kitchen and other main behind-the-scenes rooms, there will be at least one fire extinguisher and possibly other appliances for fighting small fires. Familiarise yourself with their positions, how they should be used and what fires they are suitable for:

- public areas – usually water extinguishers, possibly a fire hose in larger pubs or automatic fire sprinklers

- rooms where there is electrical equipment – carbon dioxide or powder extinguishers, sometimes foam extinguishers (if the suitable type)

- kitchen – fire blanket, foam or powder extinguisher.

Remember, using the wrong extinguisher can make the fire worse. So can a few moments' delay, if you have to read the instructions and fumble around to get the fire extinguisher to work.

Water extinguishers

Coloured red, these are suitable for fires involving wood, paper and cloth:

- direct the jet at the base of the flames

- keep it moving across the area of the fire

- after the main fire is out, respray any remaining hot spot

- if the fire is spreading vertically, attack it at the lowest point, then follow upwards.

Do not use on live electrical equipment, burning fats or oils.

Carbon dioxide extinguishers

Coloured black, these are for fires involving flammable liquids or liquefiable solids, e.g. oil, fat, paint, petrol, paraffin or grease. They are safe on live electrical equipment. To use:

- direct the discharge horn at the base of the flames

- keep the jet moving across the area of the fire

- do not touch the discharge horn – this gets extremely cold.

The fumes can be harmful – ventilate the area as soon as the fire has been extinguished.

Carbon dioxide cuts off the oxygen supply to the fire, but whatever was on fire remains very hot. Watch that it does not re-ignite.

Extinguishers in use: carbon dioxide (above), *water* (top right), *foam* (lower right).

Foam extinguishers

Cream-coloured, these are used for fires involving paper, wood and cloth. AFFF (aqueous film-forming foam) extinguishers are suitable for fires involving flammable liquids. To use:

- stand well back and sweep jet from side to side

- for fires in a container, direct the jet at the inside edge.

Do not aim the foam directly into a burning liquid in case it splashes the fire further.

Some types of foam extinguisher are not suitable for live electrical equipment (check the instructions).

Powder extinguishers

Coloured blue, this type will put out fires involving flammable liquids or liquefiable solids, e.g. oil, fat or grease. It is safe for fires involving electrical equipment, but does not readily penetrate spaces inside equipment, so the fire may re-ignite. To use:

- direct the nozzle at the base of the flames

- with a rapid sweeping motion drive the flame towards the far edge of the fire until the flames are out

- repeat as necessary (some extinguishers can be shut off and used again if the fire re-starts).

For electrical equipment:

- disconnect the equipment from the mains

- direct the jet straight at the fire if possible, so that the powder can penetrate right inside the equipment.

Powder extinguishers have a limited cooling effect, so take care the fire does not re-ignite.

The powder makes a great mess. It can take several hours to clean up after even a small fire.

FIRE PREVENTION
is everybody's business

Fire exits and routes – are for your safety. Keep them free from obstruction at all times.

Extinguishers – are provided to tackle fires. Do you know where they are and how to operate them? Find out today – tomorrow may be too late. Never use them to prop open fire doors.

No smoking areas – are for your safety and comfort. Never try to beat the ban – that secret smoke could become embarrassingly public.

Security – protects against people who start fires for kicks.

Waste – is fuel for fire. Do not allow it to accumulate on the floor. Clear it away regularly.

Stock (of food, cleaning materials, etc.) – is always on the move. Keep it away from heaters and lights.

Storage areas – kept tidy help prevent fire and allow any outbreak to be tackled more easily.

Equipment servicing – and repair are jobs for the experts. Report suspected faults, damaged cables, etc. to your manager at once.

Shut-down check

Power	off at mains.
Appliances	switched off and unplugged.
Keep tidy	get waste outside to a safe place.
Lock up	you don't know who your next visitor might be.

Fire blanket

Used for small fires involving burning liquids and burning clothing. You will find one by the deep fat fryer.

Hold the blanket carefully so that it protects your body and hands from the fire, and place it over the flames. Take care not to waft the flames in your direction, or towards bystanders. You may need to put something across a large fryer, e.g. a metal tray, to stop the blanket falling into the oil.

For a fire involving clothing, wrap the blanket around the burning area, but not over the victim's nose and mouth. Roll the patient on the ground.

Fire hose

Used for fires involving wood, paper and cloth. To operate:

- release the locking mechanism on the reel

- open the valve (to allow water into the hose)

- unreel the length of hose required to reach the fire

- aim the jet of water at the base of the flames and move across the area of the fire.

Safety and emergency signs and notices

These are there for a purpose. Respect this. Don't make your own rules, or fall into the trap of thinking that nothing can go wrong because it hasn't so far in your experience.

Too many fires start because people have disobeyed a no smoking sign, or not followed instructions for using electrical equipment. Many fires cause great damage because people have ignored a notice saying FIRE DOOR KEEP SHUT. Too many people have been injured or lost their lives in fires because emergency exits have not been kept clear, or the doors have been locked in spite of the instructions.

A lot of effort goes into the appearance of safety signs, the symbols and the words they use. There are detailed regulations designed to ensure their uniformity throughout Europe, and specific requirements that your business has to meet when deciding on their use and location.

Evacuation procedures and the assembly point

You should be familiar with the fire notices around your bar. They tell you:

- what to do if the fire alarm sounds, how to leave the building and where to assemble

- how to raise the alarm if you discover a fire.

They also tell you what not to do:

- do not stop to collect personal belongings

- do not run

- do not open a door if you suspect there is a fire on the other side

- do not re-enter the building until advised to do so by the manager/officer in charge.

From time to time there will be a chance to practise an evacuation. If you find any problems during such a fire drill (e.g. a door which is hard to open, or uncertainty about your assembly point), tell your manager about them.

Be quite clear about any specific responsibilities you have been given, such as turning off the gas or electricity, or shutting windows.

Element 3
Maintaining a safe environment

Everyone at work, no matter how junior or senior their position, whether they are full-time, part-time or casual, has a duty to protect the health and safety of those around them. This is a legal and moral responsibility.

The ultimate sanctions of the law – many thousands of pounds in fines and legal costs, possibly a prison sentence – are usually reserved for top management. But your employer can dismiss you without notice for serious breaches of health and safety procedures.

While you would be concerned about being in trouble with the law or losing your job, the fact is that most workplace accidents are caused by inattention, carelessness, forgetfulness, or gradually falling into bad habits. None of these may be serious in themselves. Until, that is, an unlucky chain of events and one or more errors combine with fatal results.

When you and your colleagues are under many other pressures, it is not easy to maintain the highest safety standards. Whatever the effort involved, safety has to be a top priority.

Identifying hazards

Your work exposes you and others in your workplace (including customers) to a range of hazards.

Some hazards are unavoidable. Strong cleaning agents have the potential to cause harm, the accepted meaning of the word 'hazard'. Electrical equipment can go wrong, no matter how well maintained it has been.

Some hazards occur during the normal, day-to-day life of a busy pub or bar. Drinks or food get spilt. Glasses and bottles are knocked or fall over and break. Smokers drop smouldering cigarette ends or lighted matches. Customers put shopping bags in the way of other people.

Some hazards are avoidable:

- injury to your back from using the wrong method of lifting a crate of drinks or moving furniture
- cutting yourself when handling bottles and glasses
- burns or poisoning when using cleaning agents.

Lifting and carrying
- Straight back, knees bent.
- Keep the feet slightly apart to ensure balance.
- Lift with the whole length of the fingers, not just fingertips.
- Do not twist the body while lifting or carrying. Use your feet if you need to turn.
- Carry with arms close to your sides and fully extended.
- Make sure you can see over any loads being carried.
- Take care when carrying objects up and down stairs.

WHITBREAD INNS

Rectifying hazards

You can quickly deal with many of the everyday hazards. Close the fire door that was left propped open. Pick up things that have been dropped on to the floor. Move chairs back into place after customers have gone, so others can get by more easily.

Don't put safety at risk by doing nothing. You may be able to see your way down a corridor when the light bulb is not working, but someone less familiar with the route, or with poor eyesight, would be in danger.

Be prepared to put effort into keeping your workplace safe. For each hazard, consider how safety can get the priority it needs. For example, if you are rushing to serve some customers, and you spill a drink or food on the floor, do you:

- leave the spill while you get on with serving?
- ask a colleague to take over with the serving, while you attend to the spill?
- clear up the spill, explaining to the customers that you will be with them in a moment?

CHECK list
Preventing falls

✔ walk, don't run

✔ keep floor areas clean and dry. Spills or grease on the floor should be wiped up at once

✔ keep power cables to electrical equipment tidy, so they do not trail across floors or food preparation surfaces

✔ put up warning signs when cleaning floors or stairs

✔ wear sensible non-slip shoes, ideally with reinforced caps, which cover and protect your toes

Warning others and reporting hazards

Do not assume that because you can see a hazard, other people will too. Always:

- tell your manager when you find equipment not working properly

- label equipment which is out of order, so that no one else tries to use it

- unplug faulty electrical equipment or turn it off at the mains switch

- where practical, move faulty equipment to the maintenance area or to where it can be stored until repaired (this reduces the risk of someone using the equipment without realising it is faulty)

- report anything that is or might become a hazard, e.g. a broken leg on a chair or bar stool, a store shelf coming away from its fitting, or the smell of gas in the cellar

- position a hazard warning sign, rope off the entrance or put a safety barrier in place to prevent access to dangerous areas.

It is not enough to tell colleagues that equipment is not working, or not to go into a area which might be dangerous. Nor can you assume that customers won't enter closed parts of the bar or staff areas, nor that someone else will, who is unfamiliar with that part of the building. Safety notices must be put in place.

Safety with electricity

- Always switch off and disconnect from the mains before moving portable electrical equipment.
- Keep electrical supply cables and pumps away from wet floors (especially in cellars).
- Use only one appliance per plug. Do not use adaptors.
- Always switch off all equipment except coolers, when not required, especially during non-trading hours. TV sets and amplifiers should be disconnected at night by removing the plug from the socket.
- Switch off portable electric beer pumps in cellars before washing down floors.
- Always keep fuse-box covers closed.
- Always switch off the supply to any items of equipment which require renewal of the fuse, and replace with the correct rating of fuse. Repeated fuse-blowing must be notified, so that the installation is checked for defects.
- Do not allow electrical supply cables to remain in a position where they can be damaged by being walked over or knocked when moving goods about.

Calling an ambulance, the fire brigade or police

1 Use the nearest telephone.
2 Dial 999. No money is required.
3 Ask for the necessary service: ambulance, fire brigade or police.
4 When you get through, give the number of the telephone you are calling from so that the operator can call you back if necessary. Speak clearly.
5 Give the location of the accident.
6 State the nature of the accident or illness, the number of casualties, and as much detail of the injuries as you know.
7 Remain on the phone until the emergency service operator rings off – to be sure that you have given sufficient information.

While help is on its way, stay calm.

If the accident has been caused by an electric shock, break the contact by switching off the current at the plug or mains. Do not touch the casualty until the current has been switched off, or you will become a second victim.

Reassure any casualty kindly and confidently. Keep the casualty protected from the cold, but do not cover major burns.

Do not move the casualty unless absolutely necessary.

Learning safety

You will be trained or instructed on how to use and clean the various items of bar and cellar equipment you are expected to operate, and the safety precautions necessary. Don't be afraid to ask questions. Don't put yourself and others in danger and risk damaging equipment, by trying to use something you are not familiar with, or saying you have already had training when you haven't, or acting the expert when colleagues can't get equipment to work.

There is more information in later sections of this book on safety in the cellar (pages 75 and 78), when lifting or moving objects (page 76), and using cleaning agents (page 73).

Dealing with an accident

If you are a trained first-aider you will know what to do to help the injured person. Otherwise, immediately tell the publican, manager or other person who has been appointed to take charge if a serious injury or illness occurs. In larger pubs and in bars which are part of a hotel, leisure centre, nightclub, etc., there will be one or more first-aiders with this responsibility.

Check that you know who to contact and the location of the first-aid box. A notice or poster should be on display in your pub to remind everyone of this information.

In the first-aid box you will find a supply of dressings and bandages for minor injuries. There will also be a card with general first-aid guidance. Tell your manager if the first-aid box needs replenishing.

Reporting accidents

There should be an accident book (or an appropriate form) kept where you have ready access to it. By law you must tell your manager when you have had an accident. If you prefer, you can do this by writing about the accident in the accident book, or asking someone else to do this on your behalf. Details required include:

- date and time of incident
- your full name, address and occupation
- nature of the injury or illness
- place where the incident happened and description of the circumstances
- names of any witnesses, and their addresses if they are not usually based at your workplace
- details of the person making the report, and date the report was made.

The requirement to record accidents applies even to minor ones. For more serious incidents arising out of, or in connection with work, there is an additional procedure for reporting them to the enforcing authority (usually your local environmental health department). Normally it is the publican or manager in charge of the workplace who has to do this.

If you make a claim to the Department of Social Security for benefits in respect of personal injury, or work-related illness, your employer will have to provide detailed information on the accident. This includes where and what you were doing at the time, and whether you were authorised to be in that place and to do what you were doing.

More on the legal requirements

The main piece of legislation covering health and safety at work is the Health and Safety at Work Act 1974. Your employer must:

- provide safe equipment and safe ways of carrying out tasks
- ensure that the use, handling, storage and transport of articles and substances are safe and without health risks
- provide information, instruction, training and supervision to ensure health and safety
- maintain the workplace in a safe condition, and provide and maintain safe ways of getting into and out of the workplace
- provide a working environment which is safe, without risks to health and has adequate facilities and arrangements for the welfare of employees

- prepare, and as often as necessary, revise a written statement of general health and safety policy, which should also describe the organisations and arrangements for carrying out that policy, and bring the statement and any revisions to the notice of all employees.

Various regulations have been made under the Act on specific aspects of safety. These include first-aid and the reporting of accidents (described above), the control and use of hazardous substances (including cleaning agents and carbon dioxide cylinders – known as COSHH for short), gas and electrical equipment, noise and safety signs.

Regulations have also been made to bring the UK law into line with EC directives on equipment and workplace safety, the wearing of protective clothing, and manual handling.

Your legal responsibilities

You must follow the measures your employer has set up to reduce the risk of accident and injury. If the instructions are to use a trolley to move a heavy delivery, then you are at fault if you decide not to bother with the trolley. Similarly you must wear the gloves provided for cleaning and other tasks.

Under the Health and Safety at Work Act 1974 you must:

- not interfere or misuse anything provided in the interests of health, safety or welfare
- take reasonable care for the health and safety of yourself and of other persons who may be affected by what you do, or do not do, at work
- perform health and safety-related duties and comply with health and safety requirements imposed by your employer or any other person with health and safety responsibilities.

Under the Management of Health and Safety at Work Regulations 1992, you have a duty to:

- use correctly all work items provided by your employer, in accordance with the training and instructions you have received to enable you to use the items safely
- inform, without delay, your employer (or the person with responsibility for health and safety matters) of any work situation which might present a serious and immediate danger to health and safety
- notify your employer (or the person with responsibility for health and safety) of any short-comings in the health and safety arrangements at your workplace.

Getting information on current health and safety legislation

A copy of the Health and Safety Executive (HSE) poster *Health and safety law: what you should know* should be on display in your workplace. In the space provided on the poster you will find contact details of those who enforce the legislation in your area.

Alternatively (or in addition), you may have been given a copy of the leaflet published by the HSE (code number HSC5), and a separate note of the useful addresses.

Many employers in the licensed retailing sector have their own health and safety material. Others provide their employees with leaflets or books published for general industry use, and to meet special needs, e.g. of those whose first language is not English.

CHECK list
Protecting property

✔ keep keys on you, never left in locks, or lying around in supposedly safe places such as the top drawer of the storekeeper's desk

✔ be responsible for your own keys, never lend them to others

✔ leave your personal valuables at home. If you have to bring some to work, keep them safe in your locker while you are on duty

✔ keep personal lockers locked and the key with you

✔ put equipment and materials in the correct place after use. Storage areas must always be kept locked when unattended

✔ report anything belonging to you, colleagues, customers or your employer that appears to be missing. This means taking the trouble to notice what is going on around you

✔ respect workplace rules regarding, for example, taking personal handbags, shopping bags or baskets into work areas. Since these are a favourite way of removing stolen property from the premises, you will put yourself under suspicion

Maintaining a secure environment

Too often, pubs and bars are targets for the dishonest, for troublemakers, for the opportunist thief, and for terrorists.

Large sums of cash are on the premises – and even if this is not so, perhaps because the takings have just been banked, the expectation is that pubs and bars are cash-rich businesses. The stocks of drinks and cigarettes are very attractive to thieves because of their high value, ease of re-sale and the difficulty of tracing them back to the premises where they were stolen from.

In bars which are part of night clubs or entertainment venues, there may be people trying to get in without paying the entrance fee, or avoiding rules about membership or dress.

Pubs and bars sometimes have to ban certain customers because they are troublemakers, or dealers in drugs, or prostitutes.

Identifying and reporting security risks

Your workplace will have physical security systems appropriate to its needs – from a safe to keep cash, etc., to patrol dogs and remote control cameras. There will also be rules and procedures to reduce the risk of security problems – clearing cash tills regularly, using different routes to the bank, checking toilets and other places where people might hide before locking up time, and never leaving the bar unattended.

The effectiveness of these arrangements depends on you:

• what you notice going on around the pub or bar

• being alert to anything which is out-of-place, or unusual

• promptly reporting the unusual or out-of-place

• recognising the warning signs of violent behaviour, drug use, prostitutes, etc.

• remembering the faces of customers who have caused trouble, or who should not be served.

Preventing unauthorised access

There are parts of the premises where customers should not go, entrances (and exits) they should not use, and perhaps areas where you are not allowed, or only allowed at certain times or for particular reasons. This is to protect security and sometimes for safety reasons.

Entrances and exits

Ideally, no one should be able to enter or leave the building without being seen by a publican, manager or member of staff. This means that customers should have to pass through one of the bar areas and not, for example, be able to go direct to the carpark from the toilets. Otherwise there is a risk that people can leave with stolen property, unobserved, or by-pass the point where they should pay the disco entrance fee, show their membership card, or produce proof of their age.

Fire exits should never be locked or closed off in such a way that they cannot be used in an emergency.

If you do find a door open which should be locked, or see other signs that suggest people have been gaining unauthorised access, tell your manager at once.

Access to the cellar is restricted to as few people as possible. This is for reasons of safety and security.

Cellars and storerooms

When you have reason to enter the cellar, a storeroom or other area which is kept locked, it is normally your responsibility to see that it is locked again after you have finished. If you have to leave the room temporarily, relock it.

Do not let anyone else in while you are there, unless you are sure of the person's identity and reason for entering the room. Keep the key with you, not left in the door or some other place where it might be removed without your noticing.

Key control

Good key control is essential. You may be asked to sign keys in and out. Unless this is the usual practice, don't pass keys on to a colleague. If they go missing, it could be rather awkward proving that you were not responsible.

Missing keys are a very worrying matter. Have they been taken deliberately, by someone planning a break-in? If the keys turn up later, has someone had copies made? If someone found the keys by chance, might they be used dishonestly?

Usually the only solution is to change the locks. This will be expensive, especially as it has to be done quickly to limit the time when the old keys could be used.

Cash boxes

There may be a cash box in your workplace for small-value purchases in local shops, or emergency supplies. If you have use of this, you will be expected to produce receipts or some other record to account for what has been spent. Make quite sure you return the cash box to its proper place, and that it is locked.

Safes

Usually only the publican or manager will have access to the safe. It will be in a part of the premises where customers and staff do not normally go. Great care will be taken to prevent anyone else from knowing the combination which opens the safe (or getting hold of the key).

If you do see anyone behaving suspiciously near the safe, tell the publican at once.

Suspicious items

If you work in a bar or pub where politicians, royalty, celebrities and leading business people are customers, or your pub is in a target area for terrorists, you will be used to strict security procedures.

These will probably include regular searches of the entire building and restrictions on when deliveries come from suppliers. You will be expected to report anything that looks suspicious, and trained to recognise anything that is out of the ordinary. You may be asked to help search your area of the workplace if a bomb threat has been received.

In these and similar situations, there are two general rules that you should follow:

- if you see a suspicious-looking item, do not touch it yourself or let colleagues or customers put themselves in possible danger

- get help, from management and security officers. Tell them calmly and accurately where the item is and why you think it is suspicious. They will get in touch with the emergency services.

Reporting lost property

When a customer's or colleague's property, such as a coat, bag or umbrella, is left behind, it should be handed in immediately to a manager. Attach a note to the lost property with details of the place, time and date it was found. This will help identify the true owner.

When a claim is made for lost property, ask for a description of the item and where and when it might have been lost. If there is any doubt that the claim is genuine, or the lost property is a valuable item, ask a manager to deal with the matter.

Dealing with suspicious individuals

The identity of contractors, sales representatives, tradespeople, local authority officials, meter readers and so on should be checked before they are allowed into the premises. In large places, there will probably be a security officer who does this. All visitors and staff will be issued with an identity badge. In this case you should report anyone you see in the building who is not wearing a badge. Where appropriate, ask politely if you can help the person.

In a small pub, you will be very aware of the comings and goings, and perhaps have less reason to be suspicious. But there are people who take advantage of this, pretending to be an engineer calling to collect the jukebox for repair, or a supplier to take back a case of spirits delivered to the wrong address. They are relying on you not checking their story.

Dealing with violent customers

You will not be expected to handle this situation. The publican or your manager will be on hand to deal with the problem and call the police.

You can do much to help prevent violence from occurring:

- *spot the warning signs* – observing, watching and listening for rowdy behaviour, arguments, aggressive gestures, etc. (see checklist)
- *prevent frustration from building up* – serve customers in their turn, avoid treating some customers differently from others, don't argue with customers, apply rules fairly, apologise if you have made a mistake or keep customers waiting
- *tell your manager before the situation become serious* – do this quietly and calmly. Don't threaten the customers that you will get the manager. If you need to explain your absence, or feel they will be calmer once they know the publican is to be fetched, say what you are doing in your normal tone of voice. Speak firmly, slowly and deliberately.

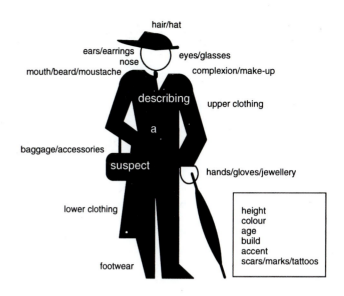

Dealing with bomb threats

There is no definitive description of what a bomb looks like. They vary in size, shape, colour and design as well as make-up. They can be disguised in many ways – in briefcases, handbags, carrier bags, holdalls, radio cassettes and even 'cigarette' packets, etc.

Receiving a bomb threat

Most threats are made by telephone because the caller:

- knows or believes an explosive device has been placed and wants to minimise injury
- wants to disrupt normal activities by creating anxiety and panic: this caller may simply be a disgruntled employee or customer.

If you take a telephone call which turns out to be a bomb threat, try to find out from the caller, and make note of:

- where the bomb is located
- what it looks like
- when it will go off
- what will make it go off
- why the bomb was planted.

Also note any details about the caller: accent, male/female, background noises, etc.

After taking the call, immediately tell a manager.

With thanks to Greenalls Inns/The Boddington Group plc

CHECK list
Warning signs of violence

- ✔ changes in the atmosphere or mood
- ✔ glasses deliberately broken or drinks spilled
- ✔ sudden silences
- ✔ higher-pitched voices
- ✔ aggressive gestures and language
- ✔ rowdy or silly behaviour
- ✔ heads turned in the same direction, watching
- ✔ people moving quickly away from an area
- ✔ a circle of people forming
- ✔ one group paying a lot of attention to another group

Dealing with drug abuse

High standards of cleanliness and service, vigilant staff and high profile management are the best defences against drug abuse.

Become familiar with the signs (see checklist). Tell the publican or your manager immediately you see or hear anything suspicious. Do this out of hearing of any customers, quietly and calmly.

Legal requirements

You have a duty to protect the property of your employer and of others in your workplace (e.g. bar or restaurant customers). You also have a duty to protect the safety and welfare of customers, staff and visitors by preventing unauthorised access to the premises.

The law is also there to support your action. For example, someone destroying or damaging property which is not their own, stealing or attempting to steal, is committing a criminal offence.

Drugs and their slang names

Ecstasy – 'E'
Amphetamines – speed, sulph, uppers, whiz
LSD – acid, tabs
Cocaine – coke, snow, Charlie, 'C'
Crack – stone, base, rock, wash
Cannabis – dope, hash, pot, weed, ganga, tac, bush, tarry, skunk, draw, grass, marijuana
Heroin – 'H', smack, horse, scag, gear, junk

CHECK list
Clues to drug abuse

✔ torn-up beer mats/cigarette packets/bits of cardboard left by customers, pieces of burnt tinfoil

✔ foam stuffing taken from seats and left around

✔ roaches (home-made filter tips from cannabis cigarettes)

✔ small packets made of folded paper, card or foil

✔ drinking straws, sweet wrappings, spoons left in toilets, traces of powder on seats or other surfaces in toilets (or obviously wiped-clean surfaces)

✔ syringes – danger of infection

✔ banknotes that have been tightly rolled

✔ traces of blood or powder on banknotes

Physical signs

✔ very dilated pupils

✔ excessive sniffing, dripping nose, watering or red eyes

✔ sudden severe cold symptoms following trip to toilet/garden/car park

✔ white mark/traces of powder around nostrils

Behavioural signs

✔ excessive giggling/laughing/ talking

✔ vacant staring, sleepy euphoria, dopey

✔ non-stop movement, jiggling about, dancing

✔ gagging or retching actions

✔ excessive consumption of soft drinks

✔ sudden, inexplicable tearfulness or fright

✔ any marked alteration in behaviour following trip to toilet/garden/car park

Signs of dealing

✔ a person holding court, with succession of 'visitors' who only remain a short time – if the business is being done in the toilet or garden, you may notice a lot of coming and going

✔ exchanges of small packages or cash, often done in a secretive manner, but may be quite open

✔ furtive, conspiratorial behaviour – huddling in corners and whispering

✔ conversation includes frequent references to drugs

with thanks to the Brewers and Licensed Retailers Association

Maintain a safe and secure working environment

1 Give three reasons why high standards of personal hygiene are required in pubs and bars.

2 What should you wear, and how should you look at work?

3 What should you wear (and not wear) if asked to prepare food?

4 If you are feeling unwell, who must you tell, when and why?

5 What must you do if you have a cut, graze or wound? Why?

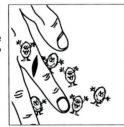

6 Give the main rules for working hygienically behind the bar.

7 What are the most likely causes of fire in your work area? How can you help reduce the risk?

8 Say what you should do if there is a fire. What must you do if you discover the fire?

9 When and how do you use each type of fire extinguisher: a) water, b) powder, c) foam, d) carbon dioxide, e) fire blanket, f) fire hose?

10 Give some ways you can help make your pub/bar safe for everyone.

11 What accidents or injury could occur in your work area? How can the risk be minimised?

12 What do you do about reporting hazards? How can they be made safe in the meantime?

13 Where is the first-aid equipment? Who is responsible for taking charge in the event of an accident?

14 State your legal responsibilities for health and safety in the workplace.

15 What would make you treat an item or package as suspicious? What do you do in this situation?

16 Give the main security risks in your pub/bar, and what you can do to prevent them.

17 What do you do when a) you find something a customer has left, b) lost property is handed to you by a customer, c) a customer claims lost property?

18 Describe the security and safety checks made after the pub/bar has closed.

Illustrations with thanks to De Vere Hotels (questions 2 and 12), Rank Leisure (questions 4 and 8)

Get to know how to use fire fighting equipment before there is an emergency.

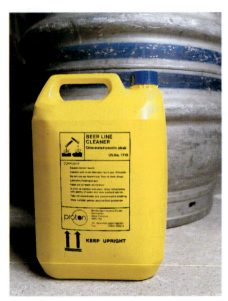

Always follow instructions on the use of hazardous substances.

NVQ
SVQ

Skills check
Maintain a safe and secure
working environment
Unit NG1

levels
1+2

Use this to check your progress against the performance criteria.

Element 1

Maintain personal health and hygiene

Wear clean, smart and appropriate work clothing ☐ PC1

Keep your hair neat and tidy ☐ PC2

Comply with workplace rules on jewellery, perfume, cosmetics ☐ PC3

Have cuts, grazes and wounds treated by the appropriate person ☐ PC4

Correctly report illness and infections ☐ PC5

Follow good hygiene practices ☐ PC6

Carry out your work in an organised, efficient and safe manner ☐ PC7

Element 2

Carry out procedures in the event of a fire

In the event of a fire, immediately raise the alarm ☐ PC1

Use fire fighting equipment correctly ☐ PC2

⚠ Fire hose, fire blanket, foam extinguisher, powder extinguisher, water extinguisher, carbon dioxide extinguisher

Conform to instructions on safety and emergency signs and notices ☐ PC3

Follow evacuation procedures in a calm and orderly manner ☐ PC4

Reach assembly point ☐ PC5

Carry out your work in an organised, efficient and safe manner ☐ PC6

Element 3

Maintain a safe environment for customers, staff and visitors

Identify and where possible rectify hazards and potential hazards ☐ PC1

Follow procedures for making people aware of hazards ☐ PC2

Follow procedures for giving warning of hazards ☐ PC3

Correctly report accidents, damage and hazards you cannot rectify ☐ PC4

Carry out your work in an organised, efficient and safe manner ☐ PC5

Element 4

Maintain a secure environment for customers, staff and visitors

Identify and report potential security risks ☐ PC1

⚠ Risks: prohibited areas, suspicious items, unauthorised open entrances/exits, missing keys

Secure customer and staff areas against unauthorised access ☐ PC2

⚠ Public facilities, public areas, work areas, staff facilities

Secure storage and security facilities against unauthorised access ☐ PC3

⚠ Storerooms, safes, cash boxes

Follow procedures for reporting lost property ☐ PC4

Challenge (politely) or report suspicious individuals ☐ PC5

Carry out your work in an organised, efficient and safe manner ☐ PC6

Before you lift something, examine the object. Plan the task and the route. If the load is too heavy for you, get assistance.

Controls over the sale of alcohol

The sale of alcoholic drinks is tightly controlled by law. To sell alcohol, your pub or bar must have a licence. This is issued to the person or people who manage the bar – it is specific to the premises and to the publican (and the wife, husband or partner).

Before a new owner or manager can take over existing premises, the licensing committee (licensing board in Scotland) has to be satisfied that the applicant(s) has the experience, knowledge and background necessary to run the pub satisfactorily.

For a new pub, bar, hotel or restaurant, the suitability of the premises (fire precautions, provision of toilets, etc.) will also be considered, and the likely effect on the local community of the sale of alcohol from the proposed outlet. People living in the area, other licensed premises, other businesses, the police and fire authorities will be told of the application. If there are objections, the licence may be refused.

Licences have to be renewed, usually every three years. Adverse reports on how the business has been conducted, in particular from the police, can lead to a refusal to renew. This means that the pub can no longer sell alcohol.

Decisions on what times the bar is open, who can be served alcohol and in what circumstances, together with the measures of alcoholic drink sold, must all take account of the law.

Responsibilities of the licensee and your role

When a licence is issued or renewed, a judgement is made about the licensee's conduct of the business. Can this person be trusted to sell alcohol according to the licensing laws? Will this person train and supervise staff so that they work within the licensing laws?

Your role is a key one. You don't need to know the licensing laws in detail. But you do need to appreciate that the rules you are expected to follow about the service of alcohol are made because of the law. If you do not learn these rules, ignore or disobey them, your job is at risk. The licence is also at risk, as well as the livelihood of the publican, your managers and colleagues.

Types of licence

The type of licence held determines who is served alcohol, whether this is all types of alcoholic drink or certain types only, and when and where customers can drink the alcohol. Scotland has a different system from England and Wales.

On-licence

In England and Wales, pubs, many bars and the larger hotels have an *on-licence*. This allows the sale of intoxicating liquor to customers who drink it on the premises, or take it elsewhere (e.g. buying bottles of lager to drink back home). When there are reasons for doing so (e.g. an important local market), the licence will allow alcohol to be sold at earlier or later times than the standard ones (see below). This may be for particular days (e.g. when the market is every Tuesday) or throughout the week.

Some bars have a limited licence. They can only sell wine (e.g. some wine bars), or wine, beer and cider. Bars licensed to sell beer and cider, or cider only, are more unusual.

Public house licence and hotel licence

In Scotland, these are the equivalent of the on-licence. They allow sale of liquor for drinking on and off the premises. The hotel licence is available to hotels with four or more letting rooms in towns and cities, and two or more in country areas.

Restaurant licence

Where the main business is serving food, a restaurant licence is required to sell alcohol. It can only be served as an ancillary to a table meal (i.e. with the meal, before the meal or directly after). Restaurants that only serve takeaway food cannot have this sort of licence.

In Scotland, a restaurant licence only allows drinks to be served at the table. Restaurants which serve drinks in a bar area before customers go to the table (or after their meal) must have a public house licence.

Residential licence

Guesthouses and smaller hotels in England and Wales can get a residential licence to sell alcohol to guests in the bar, the restaurant, etc. Usually one room, such as a lounge, must be available for the use of guests, where alcohol is not served – the 'dry room'.

Breakfast and at least one main meal must be provided. A place offering B&B only cannot sell alcohol.

Non-residents can drink alcohol in a hotel or guesthouse with this sort of licence only if their drinks are bought by a resident or if they are the guest of the proprietor or manager.

Restaurant and residential licence

Hotels without a full on-licence and guesthouses require a restaurant and residential licence to be able to sell alcohol with meals to non-residents.

Restricted hotel licence

This is the Scottish equivalent of the restaurant and residential licence. There must be no bar counter.

Off-licence

Customers wanting alcohol to drink at home or someplace other than licensed premises, can buy canned or bottled drinks from a pub, or go to a supermarket or shop which has an off-licence. This licenses the shop proprietor or manager to sell alcohol for drinking off the premises. Off-sales purchased from a pub must be taken off the premises within the drinking up time (see below).

Clubs

Night clubs and places which offer entertainment as well as alcoholic drinks are *licensed clubs*, i.e. operating to make a profit for the owners. They require a licence in the same way that a pub does, but the licence will specify opening times, such as 9 p.m. to 2 a.m., Tuesdays to Sundays. There may also be conditions, e.g. that the club is for members only.

Clubs owned by and operated for the benefit of their members are *registered clubs*. They are not regarded as licensed premises but they do have to be registered with the magistrate's court. The rules they follow, including opening hours and what members pay for drinks (anything over the actual cost of the drink is regarded as a contribution to the upkeep of the club), are those agreed by the members.

Refreshment licence

Cafés and similar places in Scotland which serve refreshment including food and non-alcoholic drinks require a refreshment licence to sell alcohol. There must be no bar counter and no off-sales. Young people under the age of 14 are not allowed on the premises after 8 p.m. At other times they must be accompanied by an adult.

When alcohol can be sold

The times which apply to most pubs and bars, *permitted hours,* are 11 a.m. to 11 p.m. on weekdays and 12 noon to 10.30 p.m. on Sundays. Good Friday hours are the same as a Sunday. Christmas Day has the shortest hours (see page 40). In Scotland, Sunday hours are 12.30 p.m. to 2.30 p.m. and 6.30 p.m. to 11 p.m.

Opening hours can be extended for special occasions, e.g. for a wedding reception. Regular extensions can be obtained, e.g. when there are meals and live entertainment, or when a music and dancing or an entertainment licence is held. Scottish pubs can open on Sunday afternoons with a regular extension, and later than 11 p.m. for the rest of the week.

Permitted hours can be modified to allow on-licensed premises to open earlier, but not before 10 a.m. The licensing committee can require the pub or particular bars in it to close for all or part of the afternoon. This may be for particular days of the week, or times of the year.

Pubs and bars do not have to be open throughout the permitted hours. Many of those in smaller places have kept the practice, once a requirement, of closing after the lunch session and not opening until 6 or 7 p.m. At weekends they may be open all day, whereas some pubs in the mainly-business areas of large towns and cities do not open at all on Saturdays and Sundays.

Licensed hotels and guesthouses can sell alcohol to residents at any time. For practical reasons, hotel bars usually keep to similar opening times as those of pubs. After hours, drinks can be obtained from room service or the porter, or a minibar in the guest's bedroom. In small places, the proprietor or manager may be willing to keep the bar open as late as guests require.

Drinking-up time

At the end of permitted hours, customers have a short time (20 minutes in England and Wales, 15 minutes in Scotland) to finish their drinks. When the drink is supplied with a meal, 30 minutes' drinking-up time is allowed.

Who can and cannot be sold alcohol

It is against the law to sell alcohol to anyone under the age of 18. However, in restaurants and areas of the pub set aside for eating food, 16 and 17 year olds can be sold beer, cider or perry provided they also have a meal.

The law on under-age drinking is strictly enforced. Many publicans insist that young people who they do not know produce proof of their age. National and local schemes have been set up so that proof-of-age identity cards are readily available to those who qualify (example on page 38).

The law also makes it illegal to serve a customer who is drunk. Sometimes it is not easy to recognise when a customer is drunk. And refusing to serve such a customer can lead to an unpleasant scene. Warn your manager when you think a customer is drunk, or is getting towards that state. The licensee has the right to refuse to serve anyone, so it is more difficult for the customer to argue. Customers who create problems can be banned.

Recognising the stages of intoxication

GREEN LEVEL – no noticeable behaviour change, customer:
- is talkative
- seems relaxed, comfortable, happy

YELLOW LEVEL – relaxed inhibitions and impaired judgement, customer:
- becomes louder or more talkative
- becomes quieter
- behaves in an over-friendly way
- curses at the server's slow service
- complains that drinks are getting weaker
- insists on singing with the band

RED LEVEL – loss of coordination, customer:
- spills a drink
- sways when walking
- has slurred speech
- asks for a double
- is unable to pick up change
- annoys or argues with other customers
- becomes tearful or drowsy
- has difficulty focusing
- falls or stumbles

With thanks to the National Restaurant Association, Washington, DC

BAR

CUSTOMERS CAN:

18 — **Buy and drink alcohol**

14 — **Be in the bar**

0 — **Be in a bar which has a children's certificate**

RESTAURANT · FAMILY ROOM · LOUNGE · GARDEN

18 — **Buy and drink alcohol**

16 17 — **With a meal, buy and drink beer, cider and perry and in Scotland, wine**

5 — **Drink alcohol, but not be served**

0 — **Be present**

Draught beer and whisky are two of the drinks that can only be sold in certain measures.

Who can and cannot consume alcohol on the premises

No one under the age of 18 can drink alcohol in a bar. Nor, as explained above, can they buy it. A bar is defined as 'any place exclusively or mainly used for the sale and consumption of intoxicating liquor'.

But in other areas of licensed premises young people below the age of 18 (but not less than 5) can legally drink alcohol provided it has been bought for them by an accompanying parent or guardian. This includes restaurants, the restaurants and eating areas of pubs and hotels, since they are mainly used for the service and eating of food (and where, as noted, 16 and 17 year olds can buy beer, cider or perry).

In Scotland, 16 and 17 year olds can buy wine with a table meal (as well as beer, cider and perry). It must be a substantial meal.

When young people are allowed in bars

Young people are allowed in bars from the age of 14, even though they have to be 18 before they can buy or drink alcohol. Youngsters below the age of 14 can go through the bar if there is no other convenient way of getting to the restaurant, toilets, garden, family room, etc. The children of the licensee and anyone staying in the pub, inn or hotel can be in the bar.

There is no age restriction for parts of the premises that are not a bar.

Pubs which have a Children's Certificate can allow youngsters below the age of 14, and in the company of an adult, to be in bars where meals and non-alcoholic drinks are available. The certificate may apply to a particular bar or bars, and not beyond a certain time (9 p.m. typically, or 9.30 p.m. if the child or someone with the child is finishing a meal). In Scotland the latest time is 8 p.m., and the children must be eating a meal.

A card like this is available to young people aged 18 and over. It carries their name, photograph, date of birth and signature, to help them prove their age. It is issued free of charge by The Portman Group, 2d Wimpole Street, London W1M 7AA. Many pubs and bars stock application forms.

What measures of alcohol can be sold

Pubs and bars have to comply with the requirements of the weights and measures and trade descriptions legislation in the same way as shops and other suppliers. Customers must be served the quantity they pay for. But some drinks can only be sold in particular measures.

Trading standards officers visit the pub or bar from time to time to check that the law is being followed. Sometimes the officers make purchases as a customer before saying who they are.

Prepackaged drinks

If the customer is buying the whole content of a bottled, canned or otherwise prepackaged drink, there is no need to measure what is served. This includes bottled beers and ciders, bottles or cans of soft drink or mineral, and bottles of wine (when the customer is having the whole bottle). Some hotels sell spirits in miniatures when customers order from room service.

The producer or bottler has responsibility for the accuracy of the contents, and for complying with EC regulations on how these are stated on the label.

Whisky, gin, rum and vodka

These spirits can only be sold in measures of 25 ml or 35 ml, or as multiples of these, e.g. 50 ml or 70 ml for a double. The publican must decide which base measure to use, either 25 ml or 35 ml, and display a notice stating what it is.

The spirit must be dispensed through a spirit measure into the customer's glass, or poured into a thimble measure, and then into the glass. Measures have to carry the government stamp certifying their accuracy (see page 107).

These requirements do not apply when whisky, gin, rum or vodka is sold as part of a mixed drink, e.g. a cocktail, containing two or more other liquids (even if these are spirits).

Draught beer and cider

These can only be sold in measures of a half-pint and multiples of a half pint (i.e. 1 pint). (A one-third pint measure is also allowed, but rarely used.) There are no plans to replace pints/half-pints of beer and cider with metric measures.

The beer or cider must be measured through a metered dispense system, or by serving it in a glass of the right size. The dispense system or glass must carry the government stamp to show that the quantity is accurate. It is no longer illegal to serve over-measures.

Customers must be able to see the beer or cider being dispensed from a metered system. It should be dispensed into an unstamped, over-sized glass to avoid confusion with brim-measure glasses.

A brim-measure glass holds the legal quantity when filled to the brim. With beers that form a head of froth, the amount of liquid left after the froth has collapsed must be at least 95% of the measure sold (pint or half-pint). If at the time of service the level of liquid beer (i.e. not froth) in the glass does not meet the customer's requirements, a top-up can be requested and should be served. You should not serve the beer until you are satisfied with the measure – so if the beer forms an excessive head, leave it to subside before topping up and serving.

The third type of glass has a line marking the level to which it must be filled. With beers that form a head, the amount poured has to be judged carefully. Once the head has collapsed, the top of the beer should be level with the line on the glass. If not, you have served an under-measure.

When beer or cider is sold as a mixed drink of two or more liquids, e.g. a lemonade shandy, the measures do not apply. But when a customer asks for a pint of beer with a splash of lemonade, and is charged the cost of a pint plus extra for the mixer, the full measure of beer must be dispensed into the glass before the lemonade is added. The same must be done for requests for a pint of lager plus lime. So that this is possible, serve the drink in an over-sized glass.

Drinks served from a bottle or can do not have to be measured, provided the customer is paying for all the contents of the bottle or can.

Other drinks

Measures are not specified by law for other drinks sold in pubs, nor do the quantities have to be stated on price lists. To be seen to be giving good value and to avoid a charge of misleading customers, many pubs and bars serve brandy in the same quantity as whisky and the other spirits. Martini and similar aperitifs are often served as 50 ml measures, while liqueurs, sherry and dispensed soft drinks and minerals are usually served in a particular size of glass (see Section 10).

Advertising the price of drinks

The price of drinks (and food) must be on display in the bar. Customers should be able to see what each drink will cost before they order, although when more than 30 drinks are sold, only a selection need be shown. Prices must include VAT (but not in small bars, hotels, guesthouses, etc. which do not have a sufficiently high turnover to register for VAT).

The prices you charge customers must be those on display. For a spirit and mixer, the price has to be the same as if buying the two separately.

Wine by the glass

Wine can only be sold by the glass in measures of 125 ml and 175 ml, and multiples of these (e.g. 250 ml and 350 ml). Unlike spirits, both measures can be used in the same bar.

There is no requirement on how the wine must be measured, nor for the dispense system or glass to carry a government stamp. The method chosen must give the customer at least the advertised measure. Many pubs and bars do this by serving the wine in a glass which has a mark to show its capacity.

Weights and measures *Bass* ▲ TAVERNS

There are two main priorities to be considered when serving behind the bar regarding the law on weights and measures and you.

First is the service of draught beer. Second is the service of the four main spirits.

If these are incorrectly served, the licensee and the bartender are liable to prosecution.

Finally, there are legal obligations when being asked for brand names. If a customer asks for a specific brand, and the bartender serves something different, the bartender is liable for prosecution. This is called 'passing off'.

1   Tick the type of licence your bar has. Briefly explain the other types of licence.

❑ On-licence
❑ Public house licence†
❑ Hotel licence†
❑ Restaurant licence
❑ Residential licence
❑ Restaurant and residential licence
❑ Restricted hotel licence†
❑ Off-licence
❑ Refreshment licence†

† for Scotland

2   Tick the drinks your bar is licensed to sell.

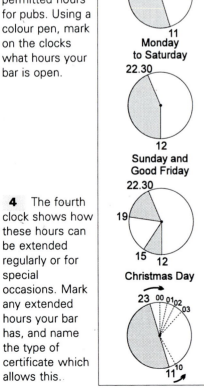

3   The three 24-hour clocks show the usual permitted hours for pubs. Using a colour pen, mark on the clocks what hours your bar is open.

4   The fourth clock shows how these hours can be extended regularly or for special occasions. Mark any extended hours your bar has, and name the type of certificate which allows this.

23

11
Monday to Saturday

22.30

12
Sunday and Good Friday

22.30
19
15   12
Christmas Day

23 00 01 02 03
11 10

5   Mark on this clock the drinking-up time allowed in your bar. What should you do if customers are still drinking after this time?

0   5
10
45   15
20
30   25

6   What age does this youngster have to be? What is the minimum age before the drink can be an alcoholic one?

ARFALAGER BAR

7   This group of customers come into a bar where food is not served, and sit down. What should you say to them?

8   In what circumstances can these drinks be sold to 16 and 17 year olds?

9   What should you do if you think a customer ordering alcohol is below age?

10   If your pub has a Children's Certificate, where would you suggest this group should sit? What is the latest time they could be served?

11   Write on each glass the quantity in ml for these measures of whisky sold in your bar.

Single   Double
Triple

12   What other spirits must be sold in these measures, by law? Tick or cross those shown.

Bacardi
Armagnac   Gin
RUM   MALT WHISKY
VODKA
Cognac
Brandy

13   Which method(s) are used in your bar to serve a legal measure of beer? Identify the other methods available.

Press
Ice Beer 330ml
Premium Lager 440ml

14   Write the minimum quantities for serving wine by the glass. How is this measured in your bar?

What pubs and bars offer

Pubs, like any business, aim to offer what customers want and what will make a reasonable profit. Like a clothes shop, pubs have to hold stock ahead of what customers may buy – influenced by fashion and the weather, as well as advertising. Like a food shop, pubs have to judge carefully what level of stocks to hold, so that nothing spoils in quality or goes out-of-date before it has been sold. The stock requires storage space and ties up a lot of money while it is waiting to be sold.

As customers expect to be able to get certain basic items from a general food shop or supermarket (bread, milk, butter, etc.), so most customers expect even the smallest pub to sell beer, whisky and probably gin.

Like supermarkets, most pubs give their customers quite a wide choice of products: several varieties of beer, different brands of whisky, gin, vodka, brandy and rum, as well as wine, other spirits, and various mixers and soft drinks. The brands sold will depend on who owns the pub. The equivalent of a supermarket's own brands are the controlling brewer's selection of bitters and lagers, and preferred brands of spirits – preferred because they provide good profit margins.

Some pubs have a wider range of particular lines: draught bitters, imported lagers, draught ciders, malt whiskies, etc. Some bars specialise in cocktails. Wine bars often only sell wine and a small range of soft drinks. Bars in hotels, especially where there is an upmarket restaurant, have a wider range of aperitifs, cocktails, sherries, wines, Champagnes, spirits, liqueurs and ports.

The products sold reflect the identity or image of the pub or bar. In turn that reflects the interests and preferences of the customers it attracts. When a pub's customers follow the latest trends in their choice of drink, the publican will try to keep pace with changing tastes. New brands may be taken into stock in expectation of their success.

Some pubs and bars feature the specialities of the area. Malt whisky from the nearby distillery, the local brewery's cask-conditioned ales, draught ciders made from apples grown on surrounding farms.

Showing the customers what is available is an effective way of promoting sales.

What all pubs and bars sell

Alcohol is what pubs and bars sell. This is why they must have a licence. The reason a licence is needed to sell alcohol is because of the effect it has on the drinker.

Many people enjoy an alcoholic drink. It helps them relax.

The negative effects of alcohol

But alcohol affects different people in different ways. The problems occur when people have had too much. Some become violent. Others loose control over their emotions and behaviour. They can become offensive to others, perhaps violent, perhaps damaging or removing property which is not theirs.

Although alcohol may give the drinker a powerful feeling of being in control, more alert and sensitive than usual, this is deceptive. There is a strong link between the risk of an accident when driving a car or operating machinery and the amount of alcohol drunk.

A very high proportion of traffic accidents are alcohol related. Each year, many people lose their lives because they have been driving after drinking. Many more innocent people are injured or killed because these accidents involved passengers, other cars and pedestrians.

Illustration with thanks to Toby Restaurants

How alcohol enters the body

Most of the alcohol is immediately absorbed into the bloodstream, from there it passes to the liver where most of it is broken down. The body gets rid of the rest via sweat and urine.

How much alcohol is in the body depends on how much has been drunk. Drinking on an empty stomach increases the rate at which alcohol is absorbed. Men, because they have more water (which dilutes the alcohol) in their bloodstream, are less affected by alcohol than are women. The weight and height of the drinker are other factors; bigger people being less affected.

Measuring alcohol

As you can see by comparing the information on the label of bottles and cans, the alcohol content of spirits is much higher than that of beers. But if you look at how people normally take their drinks in a pub, the alcohol in a single measure of spirit is about the same as that in a half-pint of beer, or a glass of wine. This is one unit of alcohol.

The body takes one hour to expel each unit of alcohol.

The level of alcohol in the body

With each drink, the level of alcohol in the body goes up: two units for a pint of beer, one unit for a single whisky, etc. Everyone takes about one hour to expel each unit of alcohol from the body. So it takes six hours to burn up the alcohol from drinking three pints of beer. People who have had a heavy drinking session the previous night may well be over the legal limit for driving to work in the morning.

Strong coffee or similar 'remedies' to lessen the effect of alcohol may make the drinker feel sober. However, they do not speed up the rate at which the alcohol is lost from the body.

The other drinks pubs and bars sell

An increasing number of customers do not come to pubs and bars for alcohol. This may be because they don't like it or can't drink it for health reasons, or because they will be driving or going back to work. To meet this demand, a standard range of mixers and soft drinks is available – soda, lemonade, cola, ginger ale, bitter lemon, etc. Interesting combinations can be made with these, perhaps with garnishes of fruit and fruit syrups.

Many pubs add to this range with low-alcohol beers and wine, mineral waters, fruit juices, herbal fruit drinks, coffee and tea.

Bar snacks and food

Most pubs sell crisps, salted nuts and similar products which are conveniently packaged for sale, and which are popular nibbles to enjoy with a drink. The majority offer food, from sandwiches, rolls and meat pies to a full-restaurant style meal prepared and cooked on the premises. In some places, food sales are more important than drink sales, even though a large investment is required for kitchen and restaurant equipment and additional staffing.

Tobacco products

A few pubs and bars sell cigarettes over the counter. But because the profit is low, and entirely disappears if just a few packets go missing, it is more usual to let a cigarette vending company place a machine in the pub. The publican gets a proportion of the money taken.

Where there is a demand, pipe tobacco and cigars are sold over the bar counter. It is an offence to sell or to allow anyone aged under 16 to purchase tobacco products.

Knowing what customers like to drink

Customers are pleased if you know a little about the drink they are ordering. When they ask your advice on their choice, the more you know, the more helpful your answer will be.

But for a newcomer to barwork, especially if you have not often been in pubs, or know only one or two of the drinks, the challenge may seem big.

No one expects you to become an instant expert – few people achieve this. You may find that the publican and your colleagues, in the quieter moments of the day, enjoy sharing their knowledge. So do many customers, if you get into conversation with them, if it's their favourite drink you are asking about, and if the right opportunity arises!

The drinks sold in pubs fall into a few main groups, each with key characteristics. Start with these, and with the more popular sellers in your bar, before getting too deeply into descriptions of the taste of individual drinks. Then if a customer asks for a bitter, a lager, a pint of special, a cocktail, a liqueur, a Martini, a stout, etc., you will know:

- what sort of drink they want
- what brands you can offer if the one requested is not sold in your bar
- what sort of glass it should be served in (covered in more detail in Section 10).

What customers might ask for

When ordering a drink, customers might ask for:

- the brand, e.g. 'a pint of McEwan's', 'a large Gordon's', without mentioning what the drink is (bitter and gin in these examples) – when the customer has said 'pint' or 'large' this is a clue about the type of drink: beer, lager or cider, and a spirit
- the drink, e.g. 'a pint of bitter', 'a large gin' – no problem if you have only one type of bitter, or one gin, or there is a preferred brand which should be served when the customer doesn't specify a different brand – otherwise you should name the choice available
- the drink by its local name, e.g. 'scrumpy' (in Somerset and Devon, among other counties in south-west England, for rough cider), 'rye' (by an American, meaning rye whiskey). If you haven't come across the name before, ask a colleague, or use charm and humour to persuade the customer to give you more clues

- a mixed drink by a name which is traditional or has become popular, e.g. 'black and tan' (half Guinness, half bitter), 'spritzer' (half white wine, half soda or sparkling mineral water) – ask, and show that you are interested in tradition and keen to keep up with drink fashions
- details that are important to them, e.g. 'is the tonic low-calorie?', 'is the house wine from country X?' (because they do, or don't want to buy products of that country)
- advice, e.g. 'what imported lagers do you sell?' – a great opportunity to share your knowledge, and help promote bar sales (see Section 5).

Beers

British customers usually ask for the type of beer they want, e.g. real ale, lager, bitter, special, mild, pils, etc. They may also ask for 'a pint of draught' meaning they want a beer dispensed from the keg or cask, not a bottled beer.

The majority of pubs and bars sell the beers of the brewery they are owned by or have business links with, plus one or a few 'guest beers' decided on by the publican. Many brand names are so well known that customers identify the taste with the brand rather than the type of beer, and use the brand name, e.g. 'half of Director's'.

Visitors from Europe and the Far East may ask for 'beer', rather bewildered by the choice or because they do not know there is more than one type. Visitors from Africa, America and Australia may be used to getting a chilled lager when they ask for 'beer' – because in their home country 'all' beers (as far as they are concerned) are lagers, drunk ice-cold.

All beer is brewed. Although the main ingredients are similar – malt (produced from barley, and sometimes other cereals), sugar, hops and water – the flavour, colour and alcohol content vary widely. There are differences too in the way they are packaged for sale and the serving temperature (see also Section 7).

Cider

Cider is made from the fermented juice of apples. Much of the cider sold is carbonated (to add sparkle) and pasteurised (to give long life). It varies from being quite sweet to dry. In pubs where a lot of cider is sold, it is dispensed from kegs in a similar way to draught beer. Pubs specialising in traditional cider sell it as scrumpy. This has neither been carbonated nor pasteurised, and because of the high sugar content of the apples used contains up to twice as much alcohol as most beers.

Premium ciders (bottled and canned) have become fashionable. These have a high alcohol content, around 8% compared to 4.5% for the standard brands.

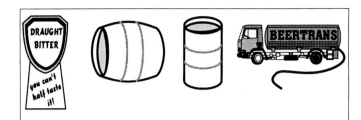

The term **draught beer** is used in a general way to cover all types of beer which come from the brewery in casks or kegs, or in bulk tankards from which they are pumped into tanks in the pub's cellar. Pipes connect these to the dispense points at the bar counter.

Cask conditioned beers – called real ales by many customers – complete their maturing in the cask. Before they leave the brewery, 'finings' are added so the various solids settle at the bottom of the cask after positioning in the pub cellar, leaving the beer 'bright' (i.e. clear). As the beer is 'living' (i.e. not pasteurised), it must be kept at the right temperature and not for too long.

Keg beers come from the brewery ready to drink. There is no sediment. Some are pasteurised. Customers usually ask for the type of beer, e.g. bitter, export, premium or special ales (i.e. heavy, high quality, bitter ales with a high alcohol content), lager, premium or special lager.

Most **bottled beers** are produced in a similar way to keg beers, and keep well. Some mature in the bottle. They are a good way of adding to the range of draught beers, providing premium bitters and lagers, high in alcohol, and imported beers.

Canned beers are easy to handle at bars serving outdoor events. Also the indoor occasions when it is difficult to collect empties, and breakages are both likely and particularly dangerous.

Some canned beers have a capsule of nitrogen in them (a widget), which releases bubbles of gas into the can when it is first opened. This simulates the slightly cloudy appearance (because of the many, tiny bubbles) of draught beer.

Low alcohol beers are made to have similar taste and character to lager and ales. The alcoholic strength is less than 1.2%. Some are made in the normal way, the alcohol being reduced after fermentation. Others are specially brewed to have little alcohol.

Non-alcoholic beers have the alcohol removed after fermentation (to less than 0.05%).

The brewing of beers.

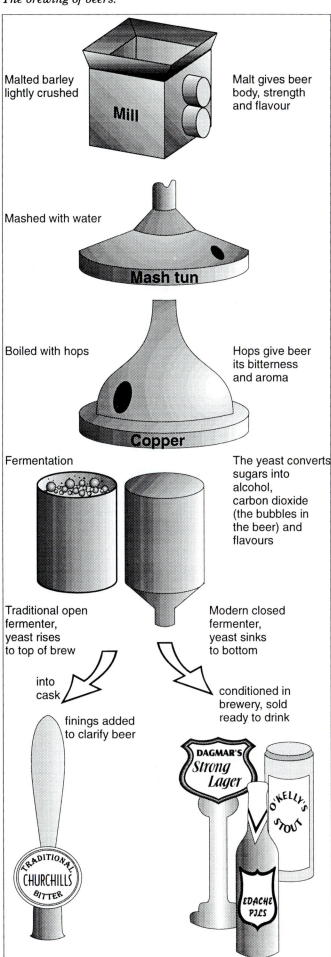

Malted barley lightly crushed

Mill

Malt gives beer body, strength and flavour

Mashed with water

Mash tun

Boiled with hops

Copper

Hops give beer its bitterness and aroma

Fermentation

The yeast converts sugars into alcohol, carbon dioxide (the bubbles in the beer) and flavours

Traditional open fermenter, yeast rises to top of brew

Modern closed fermenter, yeast sinks to bottom

into cask

finings added to clarify beer

conditioned in brewery, sold ready to drink

Spirits

Spirits are made by distilling. The fermented liquid is heated to the point where the alcohol evaporates. The alcoholic vapour – which has taken on the flavours of the ingredients (grains, grapes, fruits, herbs, etc.) – is then cooled, forming a liquid high in alcohol.

The process is very adaptable, as shown by the many spirits on the market, each with distinct characteristics:

* *whisky* – from Scotland, this is the type British customers expect when they ask for 'whisky'. It is a blended whisky, made from the products of different distilleries, including grain whisky (made with barley and maize, usually unmalted). To be sold as Scotch whisky, it must have been matured in casks for at least three years

* *malt whisky* – also from Scotland, and more expensive than blended whisky, with distinctive characteristics. It is a complex blend of whiskies from different casks and of different ages, but all from the one malt distillery. The finest ones are 10 or more years old (this being the age of the youngest malt used in the blend)

* *Irish whiskey* (note the different spelling) – from Ireland; the brands best known to British customers are the ones which have been matured for several years

* *rye whiskey* – from Canada and the USA, at least half the basic ingredient is rye

* *Bourbon* – takes its name from Bourbon County, Kentucky, now made throughout the USA and quite well known on the British market

The distilling of spirits.

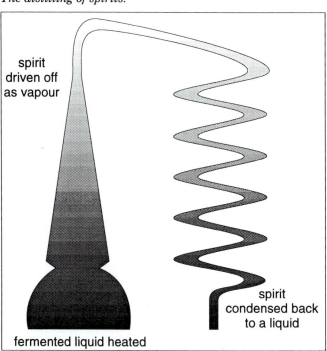

spirit driven off as vapour

spirit condensed back to a liquid

fermented liquid heated

45

- *brandy* – although French brandy dominates the market (and is what most British customers expect when they ask for 'brandy'), Spain, Greece and most of the other wine-growing regions of the world make brandy (from the fermented juice of grapes). The longer it matures in the cask before bottling, the finer the quality and the more expensive the price

- *Cognac* and *Armagnac* – superior quality brandy exclusive to the regions of that name in France. Discerning customers may check whether the brandy is 3-star, Napoleon, VSOP, etc., or ask for these specifically. These classifications denote the age and thus the quality and price of the brandy

- *Calvados* – a French brandy made from apples, which customers may ask for by name – as they might for brandy made from other fruits, e.g. cherry brandy (or Kirsch)

- *gin* – most of the gin sold in pubs is London dry, as the style is known, although it is produced throughout the UK and the world. Made from fermented grain, malted barley, maize or rye and flavoured with juniper berries, gin is not aged or matured, and is colourless. Most customers drink gin with tonic or another mixer. Plymouth gin (distilled in Plymouth, Devon) has a fuller flavour, and Dutch gin (from The Netherlands) is a richer, heavier drink, usually drunk neat (i.e. on its own) and ice cold

- *rum* – made in the world's main sugar cane producing countries. Jamaican rum is dark and full-bodied, but Jamaica, like Puerto Rico and Cuba, also produces white rum. Light rum producers include Barbados and Trinidad

- *vodka* – originated in Russia and Poland, now produced widely. Made from sugar cane spirit or grain spirit, the western European brands are colourless and flavourless, with premium brands being very high in alcohol. Some eastern European brands retain the character of the original grain. Some are flavoured with fruits.

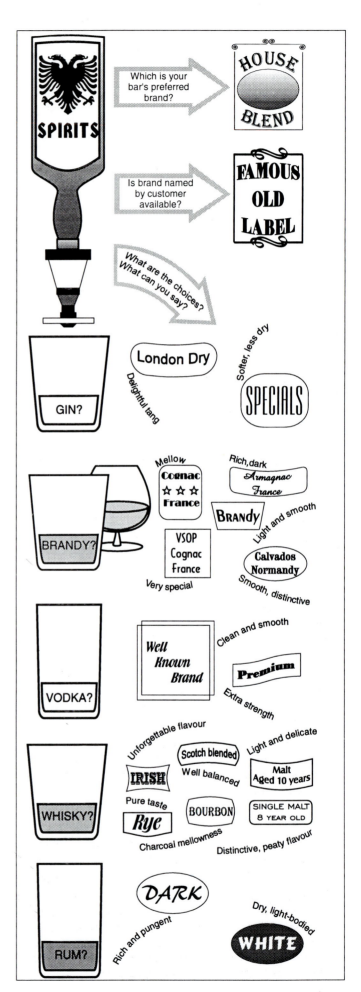

Low-alcohol and alcohol-free drinks

Much of the appeal of low-alcohol and alcohol-free drinks is their similarity to the original product, beer or wine. Yet the customer does not have to worry about going over the limit if driving, and can avoid alcohol if medical or other reasons require.

Low-alcohol drinks must not contain more than 1.2% alcohol. Non-alcoholic drinks must not contain more than 0.05% alcohol.

Soft drinks, mixers, minerals and other non-alcoholic drinks

These are increasingly drunk on their own, combined to make more interesting, non-alcoholic drinks, or mixed with spirits and sometimes beer. Customers and bars call them by different names, but they fall into different groups according to how they are made and their use:

- *carbonated waters* – the bubbles are from carbon dioxide gas. Soda water is colourless and flavourless, tonic has a quinine flavour. Other examples of flavoured types are: ginger beer, dry ginger, bitter lemon, lemonade, orangeade, and cola

- *mineral waters* – from natural water springs and containing natural minerals found in the soil. Some are charged with carbonated gas to make sparkling water

- *fruit juices* – sometimes freshly squeezed at the bar, more often the fresh variety which must be kept chilled, or the long-life product which requires chilling once opened; also bottled and canned varieties are available, which do not require special storage, and frozen versions (usually concentrated)

- *squashes* and *cordials* – made from fruit juices and other flavourings; diluted with water or lemonade to drink, e.g. orange, lime, blackcurrant, peppermint

- *syrups* – made from a fruit base with no artificial flavours; a finer flavour but more expensive than squashes and cordials, and used in making cocktails, for long drinks, and to add to wines, e.g. cassis (blackcurrant), grenadine (pomegranate), framboise (raspberry), gomme (white sugar syrup).

47

Sherry

Sherry comes exclusively from Spain, although similar products (but these cannot be called 'sherry') are produced in Cyprus, South Africa, Britain (from imported ingredients) and other countries. Sherry is made from fermented grape juice, fortified with spirit to increase the alcohol content. It is mostly drunk on its own. The dry varieties (e.g. the pale, straw coloured *fino*) are best chilled. More popular with British customers are *cream* (smooth, rich and fairly sweet), *pale cream* (lighter) and *amontillado* (amber colour, with nutty flavour).

Port

Port comes exclusively from Portugal, although other countries produce port-type wines. It is made from grape juice and fortified, like sherry, although most port is red, fairly sweet and quite heavy. The exception is white port, which is drunk chilled, and quite dry. *Ruby* and *tawny* ports are examples of blended ports, made from the wines of various years and vineyards. These are sometimes drunk as a long drink with lemonade: 'port and lemon'.

Vintage ports are expensive, for enjoying after a special meal perhaps, with a very full red colour and fine bouquet. They are made from the wine of one year of exceptional quality, and left in the bottle to mature for 10 to 15 years. They continue to improve for up to 40 years.

Vermouths

Spice and herb flavoured, these are fortified wines mostly produced in Italy and France. Red vermouth is sweet, white may be dry or sweet, and rosé is medium dry.

Liqueurs

Liqueurs are mostly high in alcohol, mostly sweet, and for drinking after a meal or at the end of an evening, or as part of a cocktail. There are many different varieties. Some of the herbal and fruit-based ones have been produced by monks from the same secret recipe for hundreds of years (e.g. Chartreuse). Newcomers on the market include the dairy liqueurs, with cream, coffee or chocolate as the predominant flavour.

Fashion (often stimulated by clever advertising) plays a large role in influencing what customers ask for.

Other alcoholic drinks

Many customers try different drinks when they are on holiday abroad, and when they are eating out at non-British restaurants in Britain. They may just like to try new things, or perhaps are persuaded by enthusiastic bar and serving staff who know and like the drinks. Examples include:

- ouzo from Greece – with a strong aniseed flavour, colourless until water is added when it goes milky
- Pernod and Ricard from France – also aniseed flavour, yellow and turns milky with water
- Campari from Italy – red, flavoured with herbs and spices, usually drunk with soda
- saki (also spelled saké) from Japan – a rice wine, served warm
- schnapps from The Netherlands, Germany and Denmark – colourless, very strong, made from grain or potatoes
- aquavit from Scandinavia – colourless, similar to schnapps but flavoured with caraway seeds
- tequila from Mexico – colourless or sometimes golden, made from the juice of a cactus-like plant.

The main liqueurs we serve

Cointreau and **Grand Marnier** – brandy-based, flavoured with oranges, both from France

Drambuie – Scotch whisky-based, flavoured with a secret blend of herbs

Benedictine – made by the monks of the French abbey of this name, using secret herbs

Kummel – made in The Netherlands and Germany, flavoured with caraway seeds

Pernod – flavoured with aniseed, turns milky-white when water is added, made in France

Midori – bright green Japanese liqueur flavoured with melon

Southern Comfort – Bourbon-based, flavoured with peaches, often mistakenly classed as a spirit

Kahlua – made from Mexican coffee beans and rum

Tia Maria – made from Jamaican rum and coffee beans

Amaretto – from Italy, made with apricot kernels

Malibu – UK-produced, made from coconut milk

Bottled soft drinks

Always shake juices before opening.

	glass	accompaniment
Orange juice	Slim Jim	ice, orange slice
Orange juice & soda	Half pilsner	ice, orange slice
Orange juice & lemonade	Half pilsner	ice, orange slice
Pineapple juice	Slim Jim	ice
Grapefruit juice	Slim Jim	ice
Tomato juice	Slim Jim	ice, lemon slice, offer Tabasco and Worcestershire sauce

Wine

Wine is made from the fermented juice of freshly picked grapes. It is the choice of more and more customers in British pubs, sold by the glass (from bottles, bulk containers or even tanks), by the bottle (especially in wine bars, or for pub customers who are having a meal), or sometimes in carafes (decanted from a bulk container).

Customers will say (or expect to be asked) whether they want red or white wine, and if it is white whether they want sweet, medium or dry. Rosé wines (pink-coloured) may add to the choice, especially in summer. Sparkling wines (mostly white, but some rosé and a few red) and Champagne (mostly white, some rosé, and usually the most expensive of the choices) are favourites for special occasions.

Most pubs offer one or two of each of these types, choosing wines that have a wide appeal and offer good value. They may be from one of the traditional wine growing countries of Europe – France, Germany, Spain, Italy and Portugal. But they are as likely to be from Australia, Bulgaria, Hungary, the USA (California), Chile, England and South Africa – just a few of the countries whose wines customers have got to know and enjoy because they are affordable, do well in wine tastings, and are widely sold at supermarkets.

A pub, bar or restaurant specialising in wines is more likely to have a list of 20 to 50 wines, perhaps even a few hundred. Customers in these places will expect you to know more about the characteristics of the different wines, perhaps comment on the vintage (the date on the bottle indicating the year when the grapes were harvested), the wine growing region it came from, the grapes it was made from, the producer or shipper, the quality grading, etc.

The bottle label will usually give a description of the wine, which will help you answer questions or give advice to customers. Be prepared for those customers who have a very limited experience of wine, and really only enjoy something sweet – suggesting a red wine will not be helpful.

You may also come across customers who do not know as much about wine as they would like you to believe. They can easily draw you into confusing comparisons about the grape variety, or the maturing process.

1 Tick the products your pub/bar offers, and put a ? against those you need to find out more about to answer customers' questions.

❏ Real ale
❏ Imported lagers
❏ Special bitter
❏ Premium lager
❏ Low-alcohol beers
❏ Cider
❏ Cocktails
❏ Spirits
❏ Liqueurs
❏ Sherry
❏ No-alcohol drinks
❏ Coffee/tea
❏ Crisps/nuts
❏ Snacks
❏ Meals
❏ Children's menu
❏ Special parties
❏ Cigars

4 When a customer asks for 'whisky', what choice (if any) do you offer? Name each of the whiskies sold in your pub/bar.

7 Match the name of each drink with its alcoholic strength.

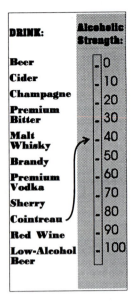

2 Write the number of units of alcohol in each of the drinks illustrated, and how long it would take for the body to expel the alcohol.

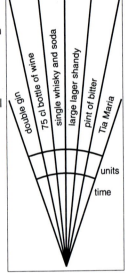

5 Briefly say how you would explain the difference to a customer between each of the beers shown.

8 Say what you would offer a customer asking for each style/type of drink.

3 Say what sort of drink(s) you would expect to serve when a customer starts his/her order with each of the words illustrated.

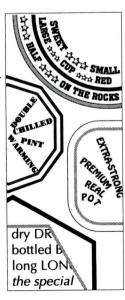

6 Match the drinks shown with what they are made from.

DRINK:	MADE FROM:
Beer	Hops
Port	Cereals
Gin	Apples
Cider	Pears
Kirsch	Grapes
Saki	Sugar cane
Perry	Cherries
Vermouth	Rice
Calvados	
Rum	
Vodka	
Sherry	
Cognac	
Wine	

9 Do the same for these customer requests.

How you can promote bar sales

The contact you have with customers gives you many opportunities to promote bar sales. There are the opportunities that happen anyway – every time you take a customer's order or answer a question about the drinks or food available. And there are the opportunities that you can create. For example, asking if customers would like another drink after the call for last orders, or enquiring when you clear the meal plates from their table, if they would like a dessert or coffee.

Being a good salesperson in the bar means taking advantage of and creating these opportunities. It means developing your knowledge of the products your bar offers. It also means developing your understanding of why customers come to your pub or bar, and what influences their choice of drink and food.

You do not have to learn high pressure selling. No one wants you to intrude on customers' time, or to harass them into buying something they don't want.

Instead, you are fine tuning your customer care skills (Section 1) to help your customers enjoy their visit more, and at the same time to increase the amount they spend at your pub or bar.

Why customers buy

Customers buy drinks and food in pubs (and bars) for a number of reasons. These can be a straightforward need, 'I must have something to eat', or a complex mix of feelings. Think of the advertisements for beers, spirits, soft drinks, etc. on the TV and radio, in the papers and magazines. The images and messages these use to persuade people to buy are likely to be similar to the reasons your customers choose those products (or react well when you suggest they try the product).

Fashion, pride, desire

Some drinks enjoy popularity because they are seen as fashionable. Younger customers are especially influenced by what their friends are doing, and by the desire to be seen drinking the 'right' drink. They want to impress and to be admired. They want to enjoy the lifestyle presented in the advertisements.

At some social events, certain drinks are regarded as fashionable, e.g. Pimms at the Henley Regatta. Champagne or sparkling wine is the accepted drink for weddings and other celebrations.

Professional, friendly bar staff are one of the main reasons why customers choose a particular pub or bar.

Pleasure

The appeal is based on the taste, appearance and aroma of the drink, e.g. the refreshing sparkle, the tangy taste, the full bouquet, or the depth of flavour. There may be a subtle link to the fact the drink is alcoholic.

Health

Many of the advertisements for non-alcoholic drinks and soft drinks highlight the health benefits, e.g. 'packed with Vitamin C and real fruit goodness'.

Tradition and quality

Mostly used for drinks made by traditional methods and secret recipes passed down over many generations. The drinker is invited to share in an experience which has been enjoyed by countless numbers over the years.

Strength of brand name

Some advertising skilfully builds awareness of the drink name. Little or nothing is said about the taste, etc. of the drink. You will be able to think of some examples.

Value for money

These are often linked to promotions and special incentive deals from suppliers, e.g. extra large cans for the price of a regular size. Publicans and bar managers can have their own value-for-money offers, e.g. 'happy hour' when certain drinks are reduced in price or double measures are served for the price of a single.

5 Your role in promoting bar sales

Sales opportunities

Sales opportunities occur quite naturally during your contact with customers. You learn to spot these quickly and can then decide how best to take advantage of them. You may decide that it is not an opportunity to sell, because of special circumstances. What you are not doing is to let the chance slip by, unnoticed.

Commonplace opportunities to sell

These are when a customer asks you:

- about the drinks or food available, e.g. 'What soft drinks have you got?', 'Do you do bar snacks?'
- for a type of drink, but not the brand, e.g. 'I'd like a large brandy', 'Orange juice please'
- to make the final choice, e.g. 'A medium dry or pale cream sherry, please', 'Ice beer or premium lager'
- for a drink or food item that doesn't exist, e.g. a tourist, muddled over the 'useful phrases', asking for a pint of hop beer, or someone asking for a glass of sweet red wine
- for a drink or food item that is not available – because it is not sold at your bar, or because supplies have run out temporarily.

Clarifying what the customer wants

To turn situations like these into greater customer satisfaction and more profit for the pub:

- listen to what the customer is saying, e.g. 'soft drinks' indicates a drink without alcohol; 'bar snacks' suggests the customer does not want the formality or expense of a restaurant meal, nor to eat a large meal
- watch for clues about what the customer wants, e.g. if the customer asking about soft drinks has come into the pub with a child, the drink is probably for the child; if you do not have the item requested by a customer who looks very hot, offer a cooling, refreshing alternative
- consider why the customer is buying, e.g. if the customer asking for a soft drink is carrying car keys, it is probably to avoid drinking and driving; if the customer asking for ice beer/premium lager is trendily dressed, this indicates an awareness of fashion
- ask questions to get more information and to check your understanding, e.g. whether it's the colour or the sweetness of the wine that is more important to the customer; whether the large brandy should be the regular one, or a quality cognac
- do not patronise or give offence, e.g. by saying that there is no such thing as a sweet red wine; or that all beer is made from hops and you sell 20 beers, so which one does the customer want?

CHECKlist: Why customers are buying

- ✔ need – to drink, to eat
- ✔ pleasure – I love everything about this place, particularly the friendly staff and the decor
- ✔ comfort – you can get a place to sit
- ✔ value for money – the bar snacks are really tasty, generous portions, and cost not much more than buying sandwiches from the takeaway
- ✔ health – these wines are organic
- ✔ convenience – if we eat now we won't have to break the journey again
- ✔ fashion – everyone drinks Pimms
- ✔ tradition and quality – the brewery's been making that bitter for a century
- ✔ strong brand name – I always have Martell
- ✔ pride – they are having cocktails, so we must
- ✔ desire – just fancy a very dry sherry
- ✔ anxiety – if the children don't eat now they'll be impossible

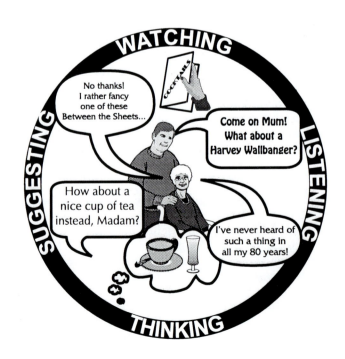

52

Creating sales opportunities

Now consider how other contacts you have with customers might present an opportunity to promote sales.

First, there are the occasions when customers ask for a specific drink or food item, but might spend more money if told of alternative or related products. You must judge whether it is appropriate to do this, and your suggestion should be relevant to the customers' needs.

For example, when a customer orders salted crisps, do you tell the customer about:

- other flavours of crisps? If the customer cannot see the full range, this might be helpful but, otherwise, and unless you are selling a more expensive variety, this would not boost sales

- the delicious range of sandwiches and filled bread rolls? This would be welcome if the customer hadn't realised that more substantial food was available. But it would be wrong if the same customer had earlier asked you to reserve a table in the restaurant for lunch

- the new range of cocktail drinks? This would be interesting to the customer you had earlier served with cocktails, and was in the mood for trying other varieties. But to the customer drinking pints of bitter, it may seem a silly suggestion.

Second, there are the occasions when you have a reason or the opportunity to talk to customers (see also page 54):

- when they are studying the menu – telling them what the dish of the day is, and how other customers have really enjoyed it

- emptying ashtrays at their table – asking if they would like another bottle of wine or some coffee

- in conversation at the bar – when the subject has a connection with drinks or food, e.g. police crackdown on drink driving, telling the customer of a new no-alcohol beer that has a good beer taste

- answering a question about activities in the area – mentioning other information, e.g. that your pub has live entertainment every Friday and Saturday evening

- when customers mention how much they have enjoyed their drink/food/time in the pub – telling them of the new menu/happy hour on Fridays/a popular winter drink.

Remember, you can influence sales in your bar.

CHECK**P** list
Promoting your bar

✔ know what products and services your bar offers

✔ keep up-to-date with the latest products

✔ take an interest in the popularity of different drinks

✔ follow any rules on serving preferred brands

✔ listen and watch for clues to what customers want

✔ use your knowledge of why customers are buying

✔ ask questions to clarify customer needs

✔ remember, customers need to know the why or how

✔ make what you are saying personal to the customer

Your role in selling

- you can confidently recommend all the products we sell, be they liquor, food, facilities, entertainment, etc.

  WHITBREAD INNS

- have a positive approach and thorough knowledge of products stocked

- make sure that all products are ready for sale, including the new and unusual lines

- customers appreciate the extra attention to their needs

- guide customers in their choice if they appear doubtful. Suggest an alternative if what they ask for is unavailable

- answer questions from customers and show a lively interest in what they say – even if you have heard it (many times) before

- use open questions to give customers a choice, e.g. 'What else would you like with your drinks, nuts or crisps?'. Other words which start open questions are: 'Why', 'How', 'Where' and 'When'

5 Your role in promoting bar sales

Converting an opportunity into a sale

Sometimes all that customers need from you is information about the drinks or food available. You do not have to describe the drink, because it is one of their favourites. You do not have to point out the good value of the buffet lunch, because they often eat at your pub. What they want to know from you, or be reminded of, is that you sell that particular drink, and that the buffet lunch is served on Mondays.

The big challenge is pin-pointing the benefits of the product for the customer, and expressing them in such a way that the customer decides to buy.

Building on some of the examples given earlier:

* *asking about soft drinks* – 'We have most flavours of sparkling and still drinks: raspberry, blackcurrant, orange and lemon.... And of course we have (name a favourite brand with children), as well as the new drink like it, which has less sugar.' You provide a fashionable choice for children, and a healthier option which parents might consider more suitable

* *asking about snacks* – 'You might like to try one of our pizzas. They come in two sizes, small and large, with a choice of toppings. They have proved a very popular, good-value snack since we started doing them.' This gives the customer the option to have a large pizza, establishes that there is a good range of toppings, and that the price is reasonable

* *the request for medium dry or pale cream sherry* – 'We have a medium-dry sherry full of character which our wine merchants import direct from Jerez. It won a gold medal in the *Wine Magazine*. Or there is ...' and you name one of the recognised sherry names, e.g. Harvey's. This makes the choice interesting to the customer, shows that your bar is careful with the selection of sherries it offers, and that the barstaff are knowledgeable about the products

* *conversation at the bar* (about a wedding) – 'Our doubles bar upstairs is very popular for stag parties. We close it to other customers, and provide snacks and nibbles free. We can also arrange entertainment...' You are showing what a good deal the customer gets: a venue people like, privacy, free food, and no hassle over special arrangements.

Don't get carried away with your knowledge of the product. You want to convince the customer that the experience of having the drink or eating the food will be pleasant. Many customers enjoy wine without knowing which year is a good vintage, or the variety of grape, or how many years it has been in oak barrels.

When you are talking to a customer who knows a lot about whatever the drink is, you have a chance to give more detailed information. But if you get out of your depth, admit this – the customer will think no less of you.

Good presentation encourages customers to buy.

Bar merchandising

Effective product displays boost business.

YOUR BAR IS YOUR SHOP WINDOW

REMEMBER YOU ARE IN BUSINESS TO SELL DRINKS

Products are divided into two types:

DEMAND PRODUCTS	IMPULSE PRODUCTS
products asked for by name	products purchased on the spur of the moment after being seen on display

Customers usually notice price changes in demand products but not in impulse products. Impulse products are generally more profitable.

HOT SPOTS

All back bars contain 'hot spots' to which the customer's eye is drawn. These include: • till area • the centre of the bar • the area of the bar most likely to be visited in the path from the door. High profit products should be displayed in hot spot areas.

EYE LEVEL IS BUY LEVEL

* use eye level shelf space for high profit brands
* use normal shelf space in hot spots for high profit brands and products of the month
* place demand products on lower shelving

Extracts from Service for Sales, a training package which helps the staff of Scottish & Newcastle Retail gain their NVQ/SVQ

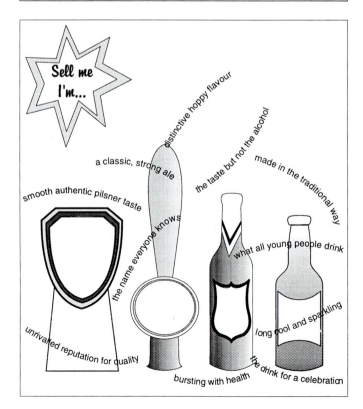

Only sell what you know to be available. If a cask is being changed, suggest one of the other cask conditioned beers.

When you should not attempt to sell

Customers do not want to feel pressured into buying something they do not really want, or spending more money than they intended. There is little risk of doing this if you remain thoughtful in your approach, and take note of what customers say and how they respond.

Do not try and sell to the customer who:

- always has the same type and number of drinks

- has already said no

- has earlier said no to a similar request, e.g. declined wine or any alcohol with the meal, or is not likely to want a brandy or liqueur after the meal

- is very familiar with what your pub or bar offers, and likes to decide without help

- has had too much to drink already – it is against the law to serve more alcohol to someone who is already drunk (see page 37)

- you know or suspect should not drink alcohol (e.g. driving, with a drink problem, on medication) – but there is no reason not to sell non-alcoholic drinks and food

- you have been warned is a troublemaker, and the publican is considering banning.

CHECK**W**list **hen you can sell**

- ✔ you are asked for advice
- ✔ customer is not sure what to order
- ✔ customer asks for either/or
- ✔ brand, style or strength not specified
- ✔ product/brand asked for is not available
- ✔ customer may not know what is available
- ✔ clearing the table
- ✔ presenting the menu
- ✔ serving or clearing away food (to sell drinks)
- ✔ serving drinks (to sell food)
- ✔ opportunity arises in conversation
- ✔ responding to compliment

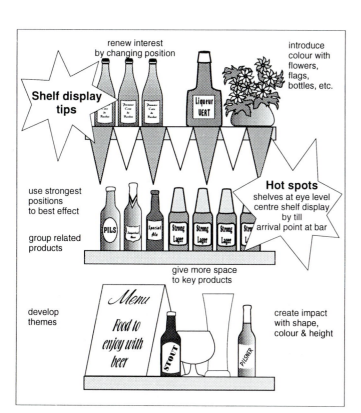

Shelf display tips

renew interest by changing position

introduce colour with flowers, flags, bottles, etc.

use strongest positions to best effect

group related products

Hot spots
shelves at eye level centre shelf display by till arrival point at bar

give more space to key products

develop themes

create impact with shape, colour & height

Advice on chalkboards

fancy printing is hard to read

even space between letters

even space between words

even space between lines

JULIE'S SPECIAL

PLAIN, CLEAR LETTERING SIMPLE AND BOLD

LAYOUT PLANNED CAREFULLY

WATCH THAT SPE L LING

names give a personal touch

light bright colours give impression of fun

deep colours give impression of quality

let one or two people read what you have done before customers arrive

Promoting bar sales

1 Name some of the things that attract customers to your pub/bar.

Pub quiz

Happy hour

Hallowe'en party

Darts match

Good food

4 What would you sell to each of these customers?

I'd really like a long drink.

Goodness, it's hot today!

What crisps have you got?

What's the cider that's very strong?

Something low in alcohol, please.

We got engaged today...

7 What dishes could you promote to these customers? Describe the dish as you would to the customer.

We're vegetarians

This is our anniversary

Something very light and tasty

I can't eat anything with garlic

I'm on a low-calorie diet

I'm famished

2 Name a drink which customers buy because it is fashionable. Name two other drinks bought because of their strong brand names.

5 Say something about the customers and the sort of occasion when you could promote these products.

8 What questions would you ask to clarify what these customers want?

Do you do food

Do you have accommodation

Do you serve special pâté

Do you have entertainment

3 What would you say are the favourite drinks of a) male customers and b) female customers in your pub/bar?

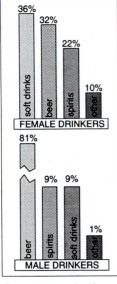

FEMALE DRINKERS — soft drinks 36%, beer 32%, spirits 22%, other 10%

MALE DRINKERS — beer 81%, spirits 9%, soft drinks 9%, other 1%

6 What would you say to these customers to promote these products?

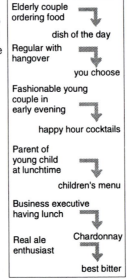

Elderly couple ordering food → dish of the day

Regular with hangover → you choose

Fashionable young couple in early evening → happy hour cocktails

Parent of young child at lunchtime → children's menu

Business executive having lunch → Chardonnay

Real ale enthusiast → best bitter

9 Say when you should **not** try to sell an alcoholic drink.

NO ALCOHOL SERVED

NO THANKS I'M DRIVING

NO ALCOHOL SERVED

NO THANKS

From a survey by the Brewers and Licensed Retailers Association

Working in the bar

Working relationships with other staff

You will enjoy your time at work if you get on well with the people there. You do your job better.

Good working relationships require effort to develop. You need to respect the points of view of others, and be willing to sort out problems before they become major difficulties. It also helps to have a polite, good-tempered attitude to everyone, even when working under pressure.

Doing what's asked of you

You're part of a team. The standards of service your customers get depend on the contribution of everyone involved. Standards are highest when:

- the efforts of everyone in the team are coordinated – this is mainly the job of your managers and the publican, but they can't do it without your cooperation

- everyone is clear about their roles and responsibilities – this depends not just on being given information, but also on taking notice of it.

When you start a new job, you are guided about your role and responsibilities. You have an up-to-date job description, and questions will be encouraged as you settle into your job.

In a busy place, you may find yourself doing a wider range of tasks, especially when other members of the team change, or there are staff shortages. Some of these may involve more responsibility – this is a valuable way of developing your skills, getting experience and proving your readiness for promotion.

Fitting into the team

Good teamwork depends on people knowing how they contribute, and on thinking of the needs of others. Where does your work tie in with that of other people? How can you make your colleagues' jobs easier? Do you do what your manager asks of you? Do you meet your commitments to others within the agreed time?

House rules

Telephone calls – incoming personal calls will not be accepted unless of an emergency nature. You may make personal calls on the public phone during break times.

Smoking – you must not smoke in public areas of the bar.

Drinking – alcoholic drinks must not be consumed while on duty or before coming on duty.

Socialising – when off duty, you may use the pub's facilities during opening hours (as a customer).

Complimentary food and drink – you may not offer or supply complimentary drinks or food at any time.

Handbags and personal belongings – keep personal belongings in the lockers provided in the staff room. Please do not bring valuables to work. If you have to, for some reason, please ask a manager to lock them in the safe.

Absence – should you fail to arrive for work you will not only burden your colleagues with extra work pressure, but the standard of service to our customers may suffer. If you are unable to attend due to sickness or other personal problems, contact your manager in person or by telephone urgently, so that alternative arrangements can be made.

With thanks to J D Wetherspoon

Acceptable working practices

Get to know your workplace rules on timekeeping, accepting drinks from customers, dealing with complaints, etc. When you undertake a new task, check the right way to do it: by asking your manager or from workplace instructions.

Don't rely on your own sense of what is right and wrong. In a hygiene or health and safety prosecution, an employer's main defence is that their procedures prevent safety problems – if so, why have you not followed them? When you handle a complaint by telling the customer the drink or meal will be free, when this is against your pub's policy, you make the situation worse.

If you have a grievance

A grievance is an employment-related matter that troubles you, e.g. hours of work, overtime payments, training opportunities, promotion prospects, or holiday entitlement.

Even if you work for a very small pub, your employer will have a procedure for handling grievances. This is usually set out in your employment contract or the staff handbook, stating who you should approach, and what you can do if the outcome is still not satisfactory.

6 Working in the bar

Your rights in a disciplinary situation

If you are doing or not doing something that gives your employer dissatisfaction, this is a disciplinary matter, e.g. deliberately ignoring an instruction that relates to licensing laws, health and safety or hygiene. Your action puts the business at risk, and puts in danger the well-being of all those in your workplace.

Similarly, being drunk on duty or under the influence of drugs, violent or abusive behaviour and theft are serious disciplinary matters. If your guilt is established beyond reasonable doubt, you can expect to be dismissed without notice. Your employer will have a procedure (set out in your contract of employment or the staff handbook) covering such matters.

There will also be a sequence of verbal and written warnings which follow timekeeping offences, poor standards of work, or other problems that do not justify immediate termination of your employment.

The disciplinary procedure protects your rights, and establishes what action your employer can take.

Passing on information

Your job is made easier if you know, before you take the customer's order, that one of the bitters is off, while the cask is changed. In the same way, kitchen staff appreciate being told that a large party has just arrived, and asked for menus. They can warn you about any dishes that are running low.

Other examples of how you can help by passing on information are:

* telling a new colleague that a regular likes to add the ice and water to his whisky himself

* mentioning to the manager that a variety of crisps is not selling, and its best-before date is near.

Handling and passing on compliments

WHITBREAD INNS

Compliments can be a great motivator and a valuable clue to improving the success of the business.

1 If customers want to compliment you, listen to what they have to say.

2 Thank them for their support and show you are pleased to hear their comments.

3 Find out what else they feel about the operation and other areas for improvement.

4 Use the opportunity to promote other services or products. Take positive action, e.g. ask if you can book a table for next week.

5 Thank them for their custom.

6 Keep the compliment to yourself – but tell others!

It is not only your efforts that are being complimented. You will have had the support of many others in the team, some of whom never come into direct contact with the customers, so they rely on feedback from front line staff.

Requesting assistance

If in doubt, ask. You don't help yourself or anyone else by struggling on.

When everyone is under a lot of pressure, it may be difficult to find the opportunity to ask. But people know you are learning, and realise they have a duty to help you. When your request is politely made, and quite clearly a genuine one, you should not be rebuffed.

Building better working relationships

There will be occasions when:

* you can help a colleague contribute more fully to the team, e.g. by being friendly and supportive

* your influence has to be directed to the whole team, e.g. saying things at staff meetings, in order to make the work easier for everyone

* you want to persuade your boss, for example, to let you try out some new cocktail recipes.

In deciding how to do this, do learn from the effects of other people's actions (at work and outside work) on you. In your mind, run through your friends, tutors, trainers, bosses, etc. How do they make you feel more significant, more confident, more positive – in other words, encouraged? Perhaps by:

* asking your opinion and taking your ideas seriously

* letting you take the lead

* trusting you to make decisions

* encouraging you to try new skills and techniques

* telling you what you have done well

* supporting you in front of other people.

Now try out these suggestions with colleagues.

Contributing ideas and making proposals for change

As you would like your idea listened to, think about the best occasion to explain it. In a small pub, the most effective time can be during a quiet moment in the day, when your boss is in a relaxed mood.

In larger organisations, there is usually a mixture of informal and formal channels of communication. Staff meetings are a useful forum, free from pressures and distractions. Meal breaks can be a chance to share ideas. Other opportunities may arise in a training session or during an appraisal interview. Written methods include responding to a questionnaire, putting a note in the suggestion box, or writing a memo.

Discussing ideas face-to-face may require more courage, especially if you are shy. But you do have a chance to explain yourself more fully, and to answer questions as they are put to you.

Prepare for the questions you might be asked. Plan your answers from the point of view of your audience. Your boss will like ideas that are going to increase sales, or reduce costs. Your colleagues may focus on the impact it will have on their jobs. Will it save them time? How will their customers benefit?

If your ideas and proposals are rejected

Rejection of your proposals can be a disappointment. Knowing the reasons helps, and a personal presentation will give you the chance to ask. If opinion is going against you, try to be detached, presenting your responses calmly but firmly. Getting angry will not help. Nor will it if you appear weak, giving way without comment.

Your proposals may have to be taken to others in the company, perhaps by your boss. If rejection follows, your boss will give you some feedback. When this is not possible, or the reasons seem weak to you, try to:

- understand the pressures that management is under

- accept that management is paid to make decisions

- not take rejection of your ideas personally, or to dwell on it.

How well you do your job has a direct impact on the work of your colleagues, and on the success of your bar.

Dealing with difficulties

There are two aspects here: doing your best to play a positive and full role in the team yourself, and doing what you can to help colleagues overcome difficulties.

Calm discussion may help clear the air, and enable each person to express points of view. Often the team leader or manager can provide the necessary authority.

Understanding how difficulties can arise, willingness to listen, and sensitivity are strong healing forces. It does no good to dwell on disagreements, or build up grudges.

Telling your manager about problems

Not all managers are easy to approach with a problem, and you might be afraid of wasting their time. But your manager is human. It is part of a manager's job to recognise the help that an outsider can give.

You also have to weigh up the consequences of keeping silent. Someone else may say things which are not true, or only part of the story. You don't want to lose the trust of your manager, nor leave the problem to develop to the stage where the manager can't do much to help.

When problems affect your timekeeping, concentration at work, or your relationship with your colleagues, your manager will soon notice. You need help. You are more likely to have this when your manager knows the reason is not laziness, or lack of interest in the job.

If you become aware of a work colleague's problem, think first what you can do to help as a friend or fellow team-member. Try and get the person concerned to take the lead.

CHECK **H** list
andling disagreement or conflict with colleagues

- ✔ have the discussion when interruptions are less likely

- ✔ be courteous, polite, and even-tempered

- ✔ listen to the other person's point of view

- ✔ ask the other person to explain the objections, point by point

- ✔ go for points where you can get agreement, restate what these are, then move on to the other areas, one step at a time

- ✔ if your point has not been accepted, say you can understand the objection, but ... and proceed to explain your point of view

- ✔ make a joke, or introduce another subject to lighten the atmosphere, before returning to tackle the argument from a different angle

- ✔ suggest another person (who you think will see both points of view) is brought into the discussion

Using suitable methods of communication

Good teamwork and getting a clear understanding of your job role depend to a large extent on effective communications. In the sort of work you do, the spoken word will be the most used method of communication. But there may be forms and documents to complete (e.g. requisitions for bar stock) and written messages to leave for colleagues on duty at a different time from you.

Choosing the best methods

If you need to ask your manager for a day off to go to a friend's wedding, would you do so in the middle of a busy session, or interrupt a conversation? Almost certainly not. Instead, you might decide to write a note.

In this example, you would be choosing the timing and method of your communication to increase the prospect of a 'yes' answer. You want to avoid anything which distracts from your message. In deciding whether to speak or write to your manager, you will balance the advantages:

- speaking gives the chance to answer questions and explain further

- writing gives your manager more time to think about the reply

and the disadvantages:

- speaking carries the risk that your manager will tell you off for being late recently, an incident you do not intend to repeat and would prefer not to discuss

- a written message might not be dealt with soon enough.

Choosing the best way to communicate extends to all areas of your work. It is not helpful to mention that the lid is missing from one of the outdoor waste bins as the manager rushes out to a meeting with the area manager. A scruffy note for the person on the next shift 'Don't sell the draught cider' is not enough. Does the cask need changing (the later shift might have time to change it), or has there been a complaint about the quality (which the publican is checking)?

Communicating to colleagues with special needs

Some colleagues – if not now, then in a future job – may have difficulties hearing, a speech impediment, sight problems or a combination of these. Similarly, colleagues whose first language is not English may find it hard to communicate with you. These situations require patience, and the use of some simple skills (see checklist on right and page 63).

Respecting the confidentiality of information

Some information that you get during your work could cause problems if you reported it in a conversation, or answered a customer's questions too helpfully. For example:

- to know the number of bar meals served, or how much discount is offered to attract large parties, would help a competitor to undermine your employer's business

- a freelance journalist who overhears you telling friends in the pub about the environmental health officer's recent inspection (exaggerating to make the story more interesting) could result in bad publicity in the local newspaper.

Your legal responsibilities

The law makes it illegal to discriminate in work-related matters on the grounds of sex, race or marital status. Behaviour towards a colleague could contribute towards a charge of discrimination, e.g. by unfairly picking on someone of a different ethnic group.

CHECK list
Communicating to those with special needs

✔ move away from loud noises

✔ look directly at the person

✔ speak slowly and clearly

✔ keep your hands away from your mouth

✔ use plain language

✔ avoid standing with your back to a window or bright light (which make it difficult for the person to see your face)

With speech difficulties

✔ avoid correcting the person or trying to take over what the person is saying

✔ ask short questions that can be quickly answered or only require a nod of the head or other simple gesture

✔ be honest if you don't understand something

✔ repeat what you do understand, checking from the other person's reactions whether or not you are right

Greeting and assisting visitors

Most of the visitors to your pub or bar are customers, people coming for a drink and perhaps something to eat, to meet friends, etc. (see Section 1). There will also be representatives from a whole range of companies calling to sell their products and services. Officials from local authority and government departments and agencies will also visit from time to time.

Visitors get a good impression of your pub or bar when they are greeted promptly and courteously. Just as you do when you take your purchases to the shop counter to pay for them. You appreciate a friendly greeting, not being kept waiting and a thank you for your custom. You expect to be charged the right price, and to be given the correct change.

Safety, security and hygiene

There is another aspect to visitor and customer care: safety and security. If a stranger comes into the pub kitchen or cellar, one of your first thoughts will be: what's this person doing here? There are the risks of an accident, e.g. the visitor could get in the way of a colleague carrying a heavy case of drinks.

For hygiene reasons, there may be rules regarding overclothing and head covering for everyone entering the kitchen. There is a possibility that the visitor is not who she or he claims to be: e.g. a trickster, posing as a health inspector, with plans to blackmail your employer, or a thief, watching for a chance to take something valuable – a bottle of spirits, a wallet left in a hanging jacket, even a valuable painting. Such things regularly get stolen because of lack of attention to security.

Greeting styles

You will often be the first person to greet a visitor, face-to-face or on the telephone:

- remember that you represent the pub, the publican, the brewery, etc.: those first few moments of contact with a member of the barstaff generally form a powerful impression on the visitor – when it's a good one, that helps everyone

- overcome any shyness you feel: you shouldn't hang around hoping that someone else will look after the visitor or answer the telephone

- follow any house rules

- politely greet the visitor – this has as much to do with your tone of voice and the look on your face (even if you are on the telephone) as it does with the words you use: a warm smile and 'hullo' are more effective than a long form of words said without feeling.

Rights of entry

The following have the right to enter a pub:

- Police Officers
- Environmental Health Officers
- Customs and Excise Officers
- Trading Standards Officers
- Fire Officers.

They may do so at any reasonable time. The Police and Customs and Excise have the right to entry at any time, if they suspect the law is being broken.

When answering the telephone, don't be afraid to say who you are. It wastes time if the caller proceeds on the assumption you are the bar manager. Be accurate when you are giving the name of your pub's owner – know the correct pronunciation, spelling, style, etc. A lot of thought goes into the names of pubs, breweries and businesses, and the messages they give to customers.

Helping visitors (who are not customers)

The next step is to establish how you can help the visitor. Usually this means finding the right person to take the matter over. Obtain, politely, the information which will help you do this:

- name of the visitor

- company or organisation he or she represents

- reason for the visit and confirmation of who the visitor wants to see.

It helps when you are offered a business card. Most representatives from suppliers will do this, while government or local authority officials, the police, engineering contractors, etc. will be happy to show their identity cards. This is a widely accepted security precaution.

You may find yourself being asked questions. Be wary when you answer these not to give away information which is no business of the visitor, and not to say things which might cause difficulties for your employer. For example, someone anxious to get the contract for pest control on your premises might try and find out who currently does the work.

Knowing your workplace

If visitors don't know who can help them, or the person they want is unavailable, offer alternatives. In a small place, the publican may be the only person who can help. If he or she is absent, you might offer to take a message. But should you suggest another time for the visitor to call? Do you know when the publican will be back, and if so can you tell the visitor? These decisions, which have to be taken quite quickly, are much easier if you take an interest in what goes on around you at work, and have a good grasp of who does what.

Security systems

At some conference centres, hotels, leisure centres and other premises with bars, there are special security procedures. This will also be the case even when your workplace's main activity is not catering (e.g. the armed forces, a commercial office such as a bank or insurance company, or a hospital). Visitors are required to sign in at the security officer's desk or reception, and to wear an identity badge while they are on the premises. Your own responsibility will be clear, e.g. to call security immediately if you see anyone not wearing a badge.

Security may also require that visitors are met at reception by the person they are seeing, or escorted to the bar or catering area by you or one of your colleagues. In other situations, you will need to decide on a waiting area, where the visitor will be comfortable, not in the way of people who have work to do, and safe.

Some hotels and large catering firms have an office at or near a goods or staff entrance. Visitors for the bars and catering departments may have to report and sign in there, including anyone making a delivery, or engineers calling to repair or service equipment.

Routing procedures

There are usually places where visitors should not go – for safety and security reasons, or because it might give them a wrong impression. Find out where suppliers should be taken, e.g. to the office or to one of the bars? Some visitors, e.g. an environmental health officer, have a right to go to many areas, but usually they should be accompanied by a manager or the proprietor.

Explaining delays

Visitors will have a poor impression of your workplace if they are kept waiting for a long time without explanation or apology. Ask for an indication from your manager, or the person the visitor has come to see, of how long the delay might be. The visitor will appreciate being offered suitable refreshment (e.g. tea or coffee).

When, at the end of this time, the visitor is still waiting, try and get an update from your manager and pass the information on, with renewed apologies. At some stage, the visitor may decide not to wait any longer, and you could find yourself acting as a go-between. Potentially awkward situations like this, and a visitor who gets cross with even a five minute wait, can usually be overcome by an apology, and an offer to do what you can to help.

Dealing with aggressive visitors

Try and contain the situation while you get help from a manager or security officer:

- keep calm, or at least give that impression to the visitor – inwardly you might be very angry or very nervous. Becoming awkward or aggressive yourself only raises the temperature higher still. Try and control your body language so that you appear relaxed. Maintain a careful distance. Avoid prolonged eye contact

- gently encourage the visitor to move away from any other people who might be disturbed or provide an audience, preferably to a room where he or she can be comfortable and from which you can phone for help. Stress that it's their comfort and convenience you are considering

- when the matter is related to security (e.g. a stranger you have accosted in the corridor, who probably shouldn't be in the building at all), try and get him or her to an area where other people can keep a watchful eye, or remain with the person yourself until help arrives. But don't put yourself in danger.

Dealing with emergencies

In an emergency, you have the advantage over visitors – you know what to do. Re-check your workplace procedures specifically on how you can help visitors, e.g. escorting them out of the building, helping to calm them, helping those with vision or hearing difficulties, or special mobility needs.

Special mobility needs

When a person depends on a wheelchair to get around, or uses crutches or walking sticks, what others take for granted can become potential obstacles. Stairs can be difficult or impossible to manage. Doors which are on a strong spring – as many fire doors are – can be very hard to deal with.

You can help by being aware of these difficulties. Some businesses which provide for those with special mobility needs get their staff to use a wheelchair and experience for themselves the journeys customers and visitors might make.

Don't make assumptions about the help the person needs: some wheelchair users do not want to be pushed. Ask if and how you can help (see pages 16 to 18).

Communicating with visitors

On the occasions you found visitors difficult to deal with, what do you think went wrong? Did you misjudge some aspect of their visit, which caused problems?

Verbal and non-verbal communication

Communicating with visitors must have an element of uncertainty. You won't know the visitor as well as you know colleagues. This means you have to listen very carefully to what they say. But you can also pick up valuable clues from how they say it, their facial expressions and what they are doing with their arms and hands, or how they are standing. For example:

- someone bright red in the face might be angry – perhaps after a bad journey and thus not your fault, but you know this is not a person to keep waiting

- fidgeting with a briefcase – could indicate nervousness, in which case you can help put the person at ease.

These non-verbal forms of communication, which can be very powerful, are described as body language (see page 14).

Paging systems

Some people move around quite a lot during their job, e.g. the brewery's area manager. In these situations you may find yourself using a paging system:

- sending a signal to a bleep which the person carries (the unit to do this will be at reception or some other convenient place)

- broadcasting a message through the bars, other public and work areas over the loudspeaker system.

When using a public address (PA) system, don't shout. Keep your mouth at the right distance from the microphone and speak slowly and clearly. Ask the person concerned to contact security (or whatever), without giving more details than you need to. Some places have messages for particular situations, e.g. 'Duty manager call 9' means go to the club entrance urgently.

Special communication needs

Find out the best method of reaching an understanding with visitors who have special communication needs (see page 16).

A combination of words and gestures may work: pointing to show a direction, nodding to indicate 'yes', shaking your head for 'no', shrugging for 'don't know', etc. If the visitor is non-English speaking, you may be able to call on a colleague who speaks the other language.

NVQ SVQ — Skills check — Develop effective working relationships — Unit 1NG4 — level 1

Use this to check your progress against the performance criteria.

Element 1

Create and maintain effective working relationships with other members of staff

Promptly and cooperatively action requests from colleagues ☐ PC1

Pass on information to colleagues promptly and accurately ☐ PC2

Politely request assistance when required ☐ PC3

Discuss or resolve difficulties, or report them to the appropriate person ☐ PC4

Use methods of communication and support suited to needs of colleagues ☐ PC5

Element 2

Greet and assist visitors

Promptly and courteously greet visitors and identify their needs ☐ PC1

Give visitors only disclosable information ☐ PC2

Direct or escort visitors to destinations as required ☐ PC3

Explain politely reasons for delay or unavailability of information ☐ PC4

Refer situations outside your responsibility to appropriate person ☐ PC5

Use methods of communication and support suited to needs of visitors ☐ PC6

QUIZ – workplace rules

1 What is the policy regarding the wearing of jewellery, cosmetics and perfume when on duty?
2 What clothing should you wear at work? Where should it be kept when you are off-duty?
3 Where can you smoke on duty? What are the other rules regarding smoking?
4 What sickness must you report to your manager?
5 Why must sickness and infection be reported immediately?
6 What accidents must be reported? Where do you record these accidents?
7 What is the procedure for lost property?
8 What is the procedure for dealing with trouble?
9 Who is it an offence to serve alcohol to?

Extracts from Service for Sales, *a training package which helps the staff of Scottish & Newcastle Retail gain their NVQ/SVQ*

Create and maintain effective working relationships

1 How can you help to build work relationships? Why should you?

2 How can you improve communications with a) your colleagues, b) managers, c) someone with special needs?

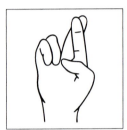

3 What can you do to persuade someone that an idea of yours is good?

4 How do you try and sort out a problem a) with a colleague, b) with your boss?

5 What can you do to help a new colleague at work? What helped you when you started this job?

6 List six rules you must follow at work.

7 Besides customers, who might visit your workplace? Who would they be coming to see?

8 Say what you do when you are the first person to greet a visitor.

9 When answering visitors' questions, what rules should you follow?

10 Describe some ways that visitors to your pub/bar might be a security risk. What can you do to prevent such problems?

11 What do you do if the person the visitor has called to see is not available? If the visitor gets angry at this stage, how do you react?

12 If you come across someone in a part of the pub/bar where customers are not allowed, what do you do?

Use this to check your progress against the performance criteria.

Element 1

Establish and maintain working relationships with other members of staff

Take appropriate opportunities to discuss work-related matters with staff ☐ PC1

▲ Staff: line managers, immediate colleagues, other members of staff with related work activities

Promptly and accurately pass on essential information ☐ PC2

Maintain effective working relationships with individuals/teams ☐ PC3

Meet commitments to others within agreed time-scales ☐ PC4

Use methods of communication and support suited to needs of other staff ☐ PC5

Element 2

Receive and assist visitors

Greet visitors promptly and courteously ☐ PC1

Identify the nature of the visit and match visitors' needs to products, personnel or services ☐ PC2

Receive and direct visitors in accordance with procedures ☐ PC3

Describe and promote services, etc. to visitors ☐ PC4

Use suitable methods of communication and support ☐ PC5

Openly acknowledge communication difficulties and seek help ☐ PC6

Acknowledge difficulties in providing support to visitors and seek help ☐ PC7

Make complete, legible and accurate records ☐ PC8

Follow procedures for dealing with awkward/aggressive visitors ☐ PC9

Receiving drink deliveries

Drink stocks and bar equipment are high-value items. If mistakes go unnoticed at the time of delivery, and your supplier is paid for items that were never received, the profits are damaged. There is also a risk that poor checking systems encourage dishonesty – then everyone is under suspicion and working relationships are harmed.

Preparing for deliveries

The people making the delivery want to get on their way again quickly. The unloading, checking and moving to the cellar or storage area need to be done safely. You want to be able to check each item properly, without risk of muddling new stock with old, or stock that is waiting to be returned.

In good time before the delivery is expected:

- clear the delivery area of anything which is not needed

- put returns and empties aside for collection, counted

- collect trolleys, etc. to help with the moving of stock

- check for safety risks and get these put right, e.g. burnt-out light bulbs replaced, tripping or slipping hazards removed

- prepare safety barriers and warning signs if delivery is through a hatchway

- have ready your record of what was ordered and any other documentation needed.

Safety during deliveries

You will be trained in safe methods for handling (see page 26). During a delivery, pay special attention to:

- keeping the area safe to move around in – so there is minimum risk of you or the delivery crew falling, tripping or slipping

- cellar flaps and hatches – when open these must be properly secured, a safety barrier in place and someone in attendance to warn passers-by

- leaving the specialist tasks to the trained delivery crew – stand well away, and do not help move casks or kegs

- using the equipment that is provided, e.g. trolleys and lifts.

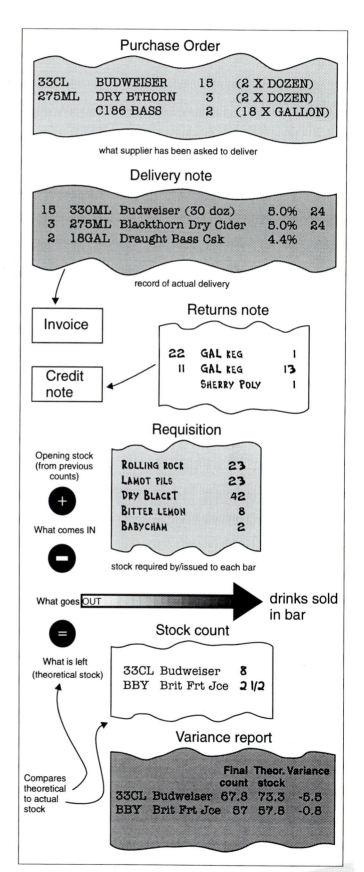

Examples of documents with thanks to Bass Taverns

Checking and signing for deliveries

Do not take short cuts. Even if you know the delivery staff well and find them reliable, it is your responsibility to check the delivery. Most suppliers refuse to consider claims for missing or faulty items if the problem is not identified at the time of delivery.

1 If it is not provided, ask for the delivery note (sometimes this is the invoice).

2 Check that the items listed agree with your record of what was ordered.

3 Tell your manager immediately if the supplier has not delivered the quantity, brand or size requested, so that a decision can be made on what items to accept. Arrangements may have to be made urgently to get the correct stock.

4 When you are satisfied that the delivery can proceed, check as each item is unloaded that the quality is acceptable. Examine the date mark, packaging and appearance of each item – that crates and boxes have the stated contents, bottles are full, seals intact, fittings on kegs, casks and gas cylinders undamaged, glasses not chipped, cracked or broken.

5 Put aside any items which cannot be accepted, or which you are unsure about and need to check with your manager.

6 Count the number of each acceptable item, and tick off against the delivery note.

7 If you get a different total for any item, recount the delivery. If there is still a discrepancy, tell the delivery person. Usually he or she will check.

8 When all is well, sign for the delivery – the delivery person will tell you where to sign if it is not obvious. You will be given a copy of the signed delivery note. Make sure this gets to your manager, the control office or appropriate place without delay.

Dealing with problems

When items are not acceptable – wrong brand, size or a quantity or quality problem – the delivery note has to be altered so that the supplier and the people paying the invoice in your company know what has happened. Usually the delivery person will do this, make a note of the reason, and sign against the changes. You can then add your signature for the items which have been accepted.

Some suppliers use a returns note for items not accepted on delivery. The delivery person will complete it with the quantity and description or code number of each item, the reason for the return, and customer details (your pub).

If you disagree with the delivery person over quality or quantity or some other aspect of the delivery (e.g. dangerous unloading of kegs), politely ask the person to wait while you call your manager.

Storing and issuing drinks

An efficient system for storing and issuing drinks is a priority for publicans and bar managers. This is because:

- drink stocks are valuable – tight control reduces the risk of items being stolen, and of privately-purchased stock being sold from the bar (a dishonest practice to take profits away from the business)

- most drinks spoil in quality if they are stored for too long – stock which has passed its expiry date cannot be sold

- some drinks need a particular temperature and humidity to get them into condition to be drunk, and to keep their condition for a reasonable time

- most drinks are enjoyed cool or chilled, and less energy is required to get them to the right serving temperature if the cellar is cool

- all drinks are regarded as food under food safety law (see page 21), so the cellar and drinks storage areas have to meet the requirements for food premises. They must be kept clean and hygienic.

Drink storage

Many pubs keep the main stocks of drinks in basement stores (often known as the cellar). The temperature below ground is cool throughout the year. A disadvantage is the handling required to move barrels, crates, etc. down to and back up from the cellar, and in older buildings stock for the bars may have to be carried up steep and narrow stairs.

In modern buildings, drinks will be kept at a level which is convenient for deliveries, for the bars and for security. In large bar and restaurant complexes and hotels, the main storage area is usually in the same part of the building as the food stores. Each bar might have its own mini-store or cellar where kegs and casks can be kept within easy reach of the dispense point. Temperature control equipment is used for draught beers and ciders, as well as for wines and soft drinks dispensed from bulk containers.

Keeping the right storage conditions

Good *lighting* is necessary so that you can see what you are doing, keep the storage area and cellar clean, and work safely. To avoid wastage, turn the lights off when you leave the cellar. Report any lights which are not working.

If your bar specialises in good wines, these prefer darkness. The lighting in that part of the cellar will not be as bright, and you should not leave it on any longer than you need to. Sometimes wine – particularly if it is a table wine, or a wine which is going to be sold within a few weeks or months – is kept in its original box in the cellar, rather than being put on racks. This protects the wine from light. Bottles closed with a cork should be lying on their side so that the cork remains moist.

Good *ventilation* reduces the risk of dampness in the cellar (which encourages mould and the growth of harmful bacteria). To increase air circulation, you may be asked to open the cellar door, hatchway and windows (if any) at particular times (e.g. five minutes each morning and evening). This also prevents a build up of carbon dioxide gas (which can kill) – see page 75.

The *temperature* of the parts of the cellar or rooms where the following drinks are kept should be carefully controlled:

- *cask conditioned beers* – the final stage of maturing (which takes place while the casks are in the cellar) depends on the temperature: too high and the process happens too quickly so the beer becomes very lively and quickly spoils; too low and the beer will be flat and lose its clarity. The best temperature range depends on the beer and the part of the country it has been brewed for. A typical range is between 9°C and 11°C for the north of the UK, between 11.5°C and 13.5°C for the south

- *keg beers* – although these are more tolerant of temperature variation, being fully matured when they arrive from the brewery, for practical reasons they are best kept in a cool cellar so they are at, or near to, the right serving temperature

- *wines* – these keep best at a temperature of 9°C to 10°C, but up to 13°C will not harm the quality

- *bottled and canned drinks* (including beers, cider, spirits, fortified wines and soft drinks) – cool conditions are best, around 15°C.

Tell your manager as soon as possible if you find the temperature has gone outside these ranges. Your duties may include recording the readings of the thermometers hanging in different areas of the cellar.

High standards of *cleanliness* are required in the cellar, as in any food storage area (see page 72):

- wash away any spills at once, so that you leave no traces of the spilled drink to breed bacteria or cause smells

- follow cleaning schedules and instructions carefully, e.g. floors should be washed daily and scrubbed weekly, using a cleaning agent that will not taint the beer because of its strong smell

- remove any cobwebs or mould as soon as you notice them (or tell your manager where you have found them) and report any signs of pests such as mice

- follow safety instructions when cleaning. Many of the substances used are hazardous. Take care not to let water or cleaning fluids come into contact with electrical equipment or plug sockets.

Storing gas cylinders

These hold the carbon dioxide or mixed gas required in beer and drink dispense systems, and for concentrated mixes of soft drinks. Because the gas is held under great pressure, the cylinders must be handled with care and kept away from heat sources or the direct rays of the sun. Cylinders waiting to be used must be kept upright, and clamped or chained to the cellar wall.

Cylinders are regularly tested by the suppliers to ensure their safety. But misuse and poor storage or handling can cause the safety disc to burst. There is then a rapid release of the highly poisonous gas and the cylinder becomes frosted up. The release of gas cannot be stopped until the cylinder is empty and the force of it escaping will propel a cylinder around the room (if it has not been fixed securely).

Never touch a cylinder which has frosted up. Tell your manager immediately.

Stock rotation

Old stock should be used before new – you can remember this as FIFO: FIRST IN FIRST OUT. By doing this, there is less risk of stock getting out-of-date because it has been kept too long.

With cask conditioned and keg beers, you should always check the date on the label. Casks should be put into their final position on delivery. Kegs can be moved from one area of the cellar closer to the dispense point as stock is used, if this improves efficiency.

With bottled drinks a typical system for rotating stock is:

- place the most recent delivery at the back of the shelf

- move the bottles already on the shelf to the front

- take bottles as required from the front of the shelf.

Issuing drinks

Pubs and bars need good security and an effective system of stock control. This is because bottles of spirits, liqueurs, etc. are high-priced items. Once removed from the premises, it is very difficult to prove that they have been stolen.

To prevent problems like this, and to ensure the business runs efficiently, management controls are likely to include:

- rules on who is allowed in the cellar and drink stores, and when

- access to the cellar keys being tightly restricted (often only the publican will have the keys to the stores where spirits are kept)

- a system for recording every item that is issued from the cellar to the bars for sale

- stock-takes at regular times (and also without warning) so that the value of the stock can be checked against records of receipts and issues.

In some premises there are carefully-placed security cameras to discourage crime, and other systems such as marking stock in a way that cannot be seen in normal light.

Typical procedure for recording stock issues

1 The bar manager (or sometimes barstaff) completes a *requisition* with details of what is required (see example on page 65). This might be in a duplicate book with the pages numbered in sequence, or on a company form (also numbered and self-carbonated to produce copies).

2 If required, the requisition is authorised by a manager.

3 The top copy of the requisition goes to the cellar. One copy is kept in the bar as a record of what is on order.

4 There may be rules on when requisitions must be received by, and times set aside for you to gather together and issue the items required. This helps avoid clashes with deliveries and your other duties.

5 You tick against each item on the requisition to indicate that the quantity stated has been issued. If the quantity is different, e.g. because stocks are not available, write clearly the actual quantity issued.

6 When the stock is collected by the barstaff (or you deliver it), the person taking collection checks that each item is correct and, when satisfied, signs the requisition.

Breakages or faulty stock

When issuing stock, you may come across broken bottles in the crate or box, or other problems such as items that have passed their best-before date, or which have developed faults (e.g. a leaking bottle of wine).

Put these aside to check with your manager what should be done (see also page 69). Whatever the reason, the faulty stock has to be properly accounted for – otherwise it will show up as missing stock, putting you and colleagues under suspicion of being dishonest.

When the fault is the supplier's, your manager will be able to claim a replacement or credit note.

Controlling stock levels

So that stock does not run out, and to avoid over-stocking (which ties up money and leads to wastage), it is usual to have a system of minimum and maximum stock levels. An order is placed when the minimum level has been reached. This is worked out so there is time for new stock to come in. The quantity ordered should not take the stock above the maximum level.

Computer-based stock control systems are used in some pubs and bars, to highlight what needs ordering quickly. Or there may be *bin cards* or a *cellar book* to record in coming and outgoing stock for each item, and the balance at any time.

Often the person responsible for ordering will back up the information from such systems with a physical check to see what is running low – and in a small pub, a physical check may be the main method of deciding what to order. There may also be a board on which you and colleagues can note items that need ordering.

CHECK list
Safe storage

- ✔ remove empty cartons and packaging

- ✔ keep walkways unobstructed

- ✔ clear up breakages and spills immediately

- ✔ use trolleys and other equipment provided to help handle stocks

- ✔ stack cases and boxes to no more than shoulder height

- ✔ avoid stacking kegs and casks

- ✔ keep gas cylinders upright, clamped in position

- ✔ pay attention to no-smoking and hazard warning signs (e.g. for low beams)

- ✔ report any hazards to your manager promptly

Returning unsaleable items and containers

Pubs and bars, like any business, expect suppliers to take back goods which are faulty and provide a credit note, refund or replacement. There are also the various containers in which gas, beer and other drinks are supplied, which for cost and environmental reasons are returned to the supplier to be reused.

Your pub may have arrangements for taking cans and non-returnable bottles to a recycling centre.

Drinks unsuitable for consumption or service

This may be a problem that you or barstaff become aware of before the drink is served, e.g.:

- the leaking bottle of wine (mentioned earlier) which is the result of a faulty cork – this must be a recently delivered bottle, otherwise the supplier would argue that the problem was caused by poor storage

- bottles which have not been filled to the correct level – because of a fault at the bottling plant.

Other faults only show up when the drink is served or the customer complains, e.g.:

- a bottle of lager which is flat, or foreign substances in a soft drink

- the drink has developed off-flavours, even though it is well within the best-before date, or it is a wine which should be in drinking condition.

There are other reasons for returning drinks:

- wrong item delivered (not noticed at the time)

- arrangement made at the time of purchase that the supplier would take back surplus stock, e.g. drinks purchased for a promotion, or sparkling wine for a special function

- the supplier has recalled stock because of a quality problem.

Returnable kegs, casks, containers and cylinders

Kegs, casks and gas cylinders are expensive to make and are built to be reused many times. The brewery or drinks supplier does not sell the container, but the contents. Checks are made to ensure that containers delivered to pubs and bars are returned. Sometimes gas cylinders are only supplied on a one-in, one-out basis.

Suppliers expect to get back the crates in which bottles are supplied (but not usually cardboard containers).

Other returnable containers include: flagons, jars, polycasks and polykegs (for cider), pre-mix tanks (for cordials) and syphons (for soda).

Returnable bottles

Your manager will tell you what these are. The supplier has charged a deposit on the bottles as an incentive for them to be returned in good condition. Do not put damaged bottles among other bottles to be returned to the supplier.

Returnable and damaged bar equipment

This includes equipment which has been:

- hired or loaned from the supplier and is no longer required, e.g. a cigarette vending machine

- purchased recently but is faulty and the supplier will be replacing or repairing it, or refunding the purchase price (under the terms of the warranty)

- hired, loaned or purchased and has been damaged or developed a fault and requires repair or replacement.

Storage ready for return

Items which are to be returned must be suitably packed, labelled if necessary, and stored, so they can be quickly and correctly identified by the people who have come to collect them, counted and checked, and loaded into the vehicle.

Remember, you may know who should collect what, but if you are not present at the time of collection or too busy to supervise every detail, mistakes can easily be made, e.g.:

- bottles on which there is a deposit are collected with the waste

- kegs are taken by the wrong brewery

- valuable equipment goes missing – putting suspicion on cellar and delivery staff alike

- faulty bottles of drink are thrown out, or taken back into stock.

For safety reasons, empty gas cylinders should be clamped or chained in an upright position against a wall. If this cannot be done, they should be laid flat on a dry floor, and wedged firmly.

Dispatch documentation

A record must be made of everything that is returned to the supplier. For drinks, kegs, casks, gas cylinders and returnable containers and bottles, this is usually a *returns note* (see example on page 65):

- tell the delivery staff what is to be taken back and the quantity (they will usually do their own count)

- the delivery staff will complete the returns note with the appropriate details

- you will be asked to sign on behalf of your employer: check that all details are correct before signing

- you will be given a copy of the returns note: keep this safely and ensure it goes to the right person in your company without delay.

With equipment, you should get a receipt or other, similar form which provides evidence of what was returned, when and to whom (including the signature of the person taking the equipment).

NVQ SVQ

Skills check
Receive, store and
return drinks
Unit 2NC6

level **2**

Use this to check your progress against the performance criteria.

Element 1

Receive drink deliveries

Prepare receiving and storage areas ready for delivery ☐ PC1

Check drink deliveries against delivery and order documents ☐ PC2

⚠ Deliveries: crated and boxed bottled drinks, beer kegs, gas cylinders, bar equipment, glasses

Check deliveries are undamaged, good quality and within date mark ☐ PC3

Goods remain undamaged during transportation to storage ☐ PC4

Keep receiving areas clean, tidy, free from rubbish and secure ☐ PC5

Accurately complete delivery documents and retain copies for records ☐ PC6

Deal with unexpected situations and inform appropriate people ☐ PC7

Prioritise & carry out your work in an organised, efficient & safe manner ☐ PC8

Element 2

Store and issue drinks

Rotate stock and maintain correct storage conditions ☐ PC1

Keep accurate records of drink items received, stored and issued ☐ PC2

⚠ Drink items: crated bottled drinks, bottled wines, bottled spirits, keg beers, gas cylinders

Issue drink items ☐ PC3

Report low stocks to appropriate person ☐ PC4

Keep storage areas clean, tidy, free from rubbish and secure ☐ PC5

Deal with unexpected situations and inform appropriate people ☐ PC6

Prioritise & carry out your work in an organised, efficient & safe manner ☐ PC7

Element 3

Return unsaleable items and containers

Pack and store unsaleable drink items and containers ☐ PC1

⚠ Drinks unsuitable for consumption or service; returnable kegs, casks, containers and cylinders; returnable and damaged bar equipment; returnable bottles

Complete dispatch documents correctly ☐ PC2

Keep dispatch areas clean, tidy, free from rubbish and secure ☐ PC3

Deal with unexpected situations and inform appropriate people ☐ PC4

Prioritise & carry out your work in an organised, efficient & safe manner ☐ PC5

1 What do you do to prepare for a delivery? Why is this important?

2 What happens when the quantity or quality delivered is not correct?

3 What is the purpose of the delivery note? What do you check on it?

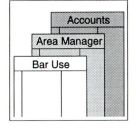
```
what was orDered
         typE
      controL
         s I z e
            Verify
        agrEe
       recoRd
     quantitY
```

4 What happens to copies of orders and delivery notes after you have checked the delivery?

5 What does FIFO stand for? Describe how you put this into practice when a) storing new stock and b) issuing stock.

6 What do you do if you find stock in the cellar which is damaged or faulty?

7 Why is it important that there is not too much, nor too little stock of any item?

8 Describe the procedures for issuing stock from the cellar.

CELLAR

All requisitions must be signed.

Stock issued 9-10am ONLY

9 List the types of items which are returned to the supplier in your pub/bar, why and to whom.

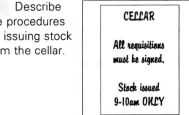
RETURNS
☐ KEGS
☐ SPLITS
☐ FLAGONS
☐ GAS CYLINDERS

10 What are the safety risks if items to be returned are not stored (and labelled) correctly?

Dr Algy Pan Back Specialist

11 What would you do: a) if you found the wrong items had been collected, b) items which should have been taken away when a delivery was made were not? How can you prevent such problems?

RETURNS

BREWERY & CO
3 KEGS
1 GAS CYLINDER

BAR SNACKS INC
1 BOX DAMAGED
CHEESE 'N' CHIVE

VINTNERS SUPPLIES LTD
2 DOZEN
PARIS GOBLETS-
WRONG SIZE

Illustration for question 1 with thanks to De Vere Hotels

Maintaining cellars

Draught beer, cider and other drinks dispensed from bulk containers are kept in the cellar. The storage of spirits, bottled wines, beers, cider and soft drinks which may be kept in other rooms or areas of the cellar, was covered earlier in this section.

The cellar also contains the dispense equipment (including cylinders of carbon dioxide or mixed gas) which propels the beer, cider and sometimes wine from the cask, keg or tank to the service point in the bar (which is typically one floor higher than the cellar, or on the same floor). Some soft drinks can be dispensed from the cellar, from concentrated mixes.

High standards of hygiene are necessary to protect the quality of the drinks, and because the cellar is a food room under the food safety regulations (see page 21). Nothing should be stored in the cellar which might taint the drinks, give off strong smells, introduce dirt or bacteria, encourage dust to collect, or bacteria and mould to grow. Cleaning materials, non-work clothing, food, stocks of china, glassware, etc. must be kept elsewhere. Smoking is forbidden.

Environmental conditions

The cellar must be adequately lit and ventilated, and maintained at the right temperature and humidity for the drinks kept there (as explained on page 67). If you find the cooling system is not working, or has been turned off without explanation, tell your manager immediately.

The compressor units of temperature control equipment (for chilling drinks on their way to the dispense point) are usually outside the cellar, otherwise the heat they give off warms the cellar. Refrigerators, freezers and ice-making machines should not be located in the cellar, for the same reason.

Cleaning procedures

Refer to the cellar cleaning schedule in your workplace for details of the equipment, cleaning agents and methods to use, and how often to clean. Always:

- pay careful attention to safety instructions and the warnings given on the labels of cleaning agents – many are harmful if used in the wrong way, if they come into contact with your skin or eyes, or if you breathe in the fumes

- use safety steps to reach high surfaces – do not stand on kegs, casks or other equipment

- keep water away from electrical equipment – tape over plug sockets before washing walls, relocate equipment which can be moved away from the area to be cleaned, and never spray water into or near electrical appliances

- use a push-and-pull action when mopping floors – avoid stretching too far, or trying to cover too large an area at once, as this can put a strain on your back

- close off the area you are cleaning or place warning signs

- mix cleaning agents accurately – adding too little water reduces the effectiveness of cleaning, adding too much may harm surfaces, adding another agent may produce harmful gases

- prepare a fresh solution as necessary and dispose of the old – do not top up a cleaning solution

- rinse well when instructed, and change the rinsing water frequently

- clean in a logical order – so that you do not make surfaces you have just washed dirty. Clean the walls before the floors. Clean the floor last, in time for it to dry before anyone walks over it

- pay special attention to areas where spills occur (e.g. under kegs and casks) – get the help of a colleague when heavy items have to be moved in order to clean under and around them.

Clean the equipment after you have finished each task, and put it away in the correct place. Mops should be washed and rinsed thoroughly, and then hung up or placed on a rack to dry. After washing and rinsing mop buckets, leave them upside down to dry, so they can drain completely. Do not store brushes resting on their bristles, as this will cause them to become mis-shapen.

Drains, gullies and sumps

Drains and gullies collect and carry away waste water (and major spills). Sumps are found in cellars that are below the level of the main drainage system. They collect waste water, etc. which is then pumped up into the drains.

Regular cleaning (usually weekly) will prevent dirt from accumulating, and the water in sumps from giving off unpleasant smells (which harm the drinks). Sometimes cleaning contractors will be called in (e.g. once a year). Their powerful equipment gets rid of the more stubborn deposits.

Equipment and machinery

The grilles of cellar cooling equipment require regular cleaning (e.g. with a soft brush) to remove dust, dirt and fluff which has gathered there. Hot air generated by the equipment needs to escape freely, otherwise the efficiency of the machine is reduced.

Racks, shelves, cradles (on which gas cylinders sit) and stillages (on which kegs of cask conditioned beer rest) should be cleaned from time to time, and kept dry.

Safety with cleaning agents

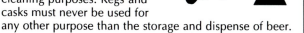

1 Never use beer containers for cleaning purposes. Kegs and casks must never be used for any other purpose than the storage and dispense of beer.
2 Never mix cleaning agents with one another or with other products.
3 Never use a cleaning agent for any purpose other than that for which it was supplied.
4 Never put cleaning agents into containers designed for other products, food or drink, in case they are mistakenly used for the wrong purpose or drunk.
5 Never use a drinking glass for measuring cleaning agents.
6 Always wear gloves and follow instructions on use of eye protection.

Element 2

Preparing kegs and gas cylinders for use

Keg is the name for the large cylinder-shaped aluminium or stainless steel container in which brewery-conditioned (i.e. ready-to-drink, see page 44) beers and ciders are delivered. The keg is stored in the cellar, standing upright, with the *spear well* (also called *keg closure valve*) at the top (see illustration, page 74).

The *coupling head* (also called *tapping head*) fits into this well, making the connection to the beer line (which takes the beer or cider to the dispense point in the bar) and to the carbon dioxide or mixed gas (nitrogen and carbon dioxide) supply. As the contents of the keg are drawn off, the gas:

- fills the air space left above the beer or cider – otherwise there would be a vacuum

- helps the beer or cider keep its condition – if air were let into the keg, this would cause harm

- prevents the carbon dioxide which is in the beer or cider from escaping – it is this gas which gives the drink its sparkle (from the thousands of very tiny bubbles).

The gas usually has another purpose, which is to provide sufficient pressure for the contents of the keg to reach the dispense point in the bar. When the distance and/or height to the bar is too great, a pump system is used.

Kegs come in various sizes, the most common being 50 litres and 100 litres – which, because beer is still sold in pints, would serve 88 and 176 pints respectively, if there were no wastage.

The most popular size of gas cylinder is 14 lb (about 6 kg). This holds sufficient gas to dispense a few thousand pints!

Two-part kegs have their own, integral gas chamber. If for some reason this is insufficient to dispense all the beer in the keg, the brewery should be told. Never attempt to refill with gas, or connect the beer chamber to a gas cylinder.

At the end of service

The gas supply to kegs should be turned off overnight, after the last drink has been served, and for the afternoon if the bar closes then. This is a safety precaution. It also reduces the risk of the beer absorbing too much carbon dioxide, leading to excessive foaming when it is dispensed into the glass. Known as *fobbing*, this problem can also be caused by other factors such as dirty beer lines (see page 76).

Changing a keg

In small pubs, or for the beers which are less popular in very busy pubs, only one keg at a time is connected to each dispense point in the bar. When the keg runs out, barstaff will ask customers to wait, or offer them another beer while you connect a fresh keg.

Larger and busy outlets have a system which allows several kegs of the same beer to be connected. When one keg is empty, the system automatically draws beer from the next one in line. The other method for fast-selling beers is the large tank connected to two or more dispense points at the bar and refilled from the brewery's bulk tanker (like those that deliver petrol and diesel to garages).

Kegs must be connected to the dispense system in date order, the oldest first. Depending on the brewer, each keg is marked with the date it was brewed on, or a brew number, or a best-before date (after which it should not be used).

The maximum storage life of keg beers and ciders not marked with a best-before date depends on the brewer, the product, cellar conditions and even the part of the country you are in. Examples are:

* until connected to the dispense system, keg beers up to 42 days from the date brewed, keg ciders about 6 months

* once connected to the dispense system, about 3 days.

General procedure for changing a keg

1 Locate the keg to be connected. Even in a well-organised cellar, you should confirm that you are connecting the right beer or cider, that it is the oldest (for stock rotation), and that it is at cellar temperature (kegs need 1 to 3 days to reach cellar temperature, depending on the size and time of the year).

2 Turn off the gas supply to the empty keg. The tap is near the *reducing valve*, which controls the gas pressure as it leaves the cylinder, or as it is fed from a ring mains system (where a large cylinder of gas supplies pressure to several kegs).

3[†] Pull the lever on the coupling head out and upwards until it clicks. Turn the coupling head anti-clockwise to unlock it from the keg.

4 Take off the protective seal which covers the spear well of the new keg. Check that the fitting is clean and undamaged.

5[†] Check that the coupling head is clean, insert into the spear well and turn clockwise. Do not over-tighten.

6[†] Pull the level on the coupling head out and push downwards until it clicks. This opens the beer flow.

7 Check the connection to the gas supply, and turn on.

8 Check there are no leaks at the coupling head – of beer, which you would see, or gas which you would hear hissing.

† Some kegs have a different locking system: check steps 3, 5 and 6 against the supplier's instructions.

Safety when changing kegs

It is very dangerous to tamper with the fittings on kegs, or to try and remove the extractor tube. They are designed to let gas in and beer out. If you suspect there is a blockage, connect another keg to the dispense system and tell your manager. The faulty keg will be returned to the brewery.

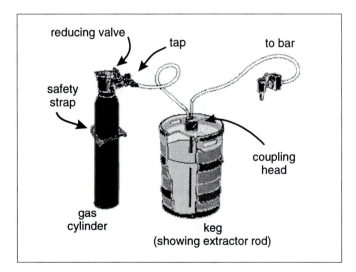

reducing valve
tap
to bar
safety strap
coupling head
gas cylinder
keg
(showing extractor rod)

Changing a gas cylinder

Between the gas cylinders and the keg is a *pressure-reducing valve* (see diagram, page 74). This will be pre-set by the brewery or on-site by a technical services fitter/engineer. Each type of beer has its own pressure requirement to keep it in the best possible condition. When the gas is supplied through a ring main, there is one reducing valve at the cylinder, and another at each connection to a keg, called *secondary reducing valves* (see illustration on page 76).

General procedure for changing a gas cylinder

1 Close the main valve of the empty cylinder by hand (hand tight). Have a look at the gauge to make sure the cylinder is empty.

2 Using the spanner designed for this purpose, undo the nut on the reducing valve of the empty cylinder, and pull it free.

3 Place the empty cylinder to one side (see below).

4 Clamp the new cylinder in position (it should be upright and against a wall).

5 Remove the protective cover or tape from the outlet valve.

6 Standing to one side, open and immediately close the outlet valve. The jet of gas will blow out any dust or moisture which may be in the valve. *Snifting* or *cracking*, as this is called, also checks that you are not, by mistake, about to replace an empty cylinder with another empty cylinder.

7 Connect the reducing valve to the new cylinder by hand, ensuring the washer is in place and in good condition. The nut should go on quite easily; if not, remove it and start again (to avoid damaging the thread which can happen if you force it on). Tighten the nut with the spanner, but do not over-tighten.

8 Fully open the main valve of the new cylinder.

9 Check for minor leaks. The gas is invisible and has no smell, but makes a hissing sound if it is escaping (e.g. because of a faulty washer or connection). If you can't hear hissing but suspect there is a leak, squeeze some liquid soap (or detergent and water) over the joint – bubbles mean there is a leak.

Safety when changing gas cylinders

If you find a minor leak, turn the gas off at the main valve, and get your manager to investigate. The cellar will need to be ventilated. It also helps to spray the floor with water, as carbon dioxide is heavier than air and readily soluble in water.

Do not touch a gas cylinder which is leaking from its main valve, or because the safety disc has burst. The casing becomes extremely cold (hence the frosting) and will burn your skin. Leave the cellar immediately and get urgent help. Do not return to the cellar until someone in charge says it is safe to do so. It will need to be thoroughly ventilated by opening cellar flaps, doors and windows from the outside. Even then a second person should be within calling distance.

Remember the gas in the cylinder is under great pressure, and very harmful if breathed in – a concentration of more than 5% in the air can be fatal. Follow the instructions on the safety notice in your cellar:

• never leave full or empty cylinders unattended in the cellar unless they are clamped to the wall in an upright position (if cylinders have to be stored horizontally for some reason, they must be wedged)

• do not adjust the setting of the pressure-reducing (also called *pressure-regulating*) valve yourself

• never use the main valve at the cylinder to control the flow of gas

• never connect the gas supply to a coupler which is not suited to the keg

• never connect cylinders which have been damaged or exposed to very high temperatures (e.g. left near a boiler).

If there is no one else in the cellar at the time you are changing a keg or gas cylinder, let someone in the bar or your manager know where you are, and how long you expect to be. Then if you get into difficulty or have an accident, it should not be too long before help arrives.

Get advice when you are not sure what to do, and report any problems immediately.

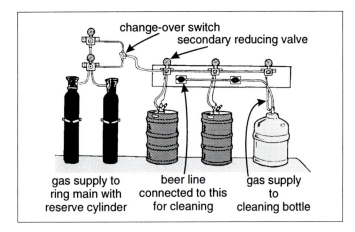

change-over switch
secondary reducing valve

gas supply to ring main with reserve cylinder

beer line connected to this for cleaning

gas supply to cleaning bottle

Dealing with empty kegs and gas cylinders

These should be in a different place from full containers, so there is no risk of confusion. Besides the time that would be wasted if you had to look for a new keg or gas cylinder among an assortment of empty ones, there is a risk of back injury. Attempting to lift something you expect to be heavy, when it is not, puts considerable strain on your muscles.

Throw away the plastic cover which protects the spear well of a keg. Do not transfer it to the empty keg, as this may give the impression that it is full.

Empty kegs and gas containers should not be left where they might be stolen, get wet or be exposed to extremes of hot or cold (which can damage the fittings). Empty gas cylinders should be stored upright, clamped or chained to a wall, or lying flat on a dry floor, wedged firmly.

Moving a keg

1 Wear sturdy shoes and gloves to protect against metal splinters.

2 Stand in front of the upright keg, feet apart to give you balance. Place hands at 'ten to two' position on top rim of keg.

3 Use your body weight to tilt the keg slightly towards you so that it is balanced on the rim. Move smoothly, do not jerk!

4 Use your hands to turn the keg so that it moves on its rim to the required position. Move your feet as you go to avoid twisting your body. Allow to return to the upright position.

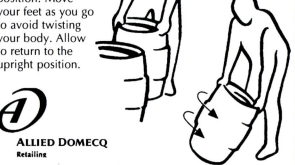

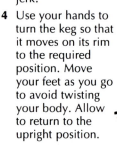

ALLIED DOMECQ
Retailing

Cleaning drink dispense lines

The pipes which carry the drink (beer, cider or soft drinks) from the keg, tank or container in the cellar to the bar are called *dispense lines* or *beer lines*. They have to be cleaned regularly (at least every seven days for beers) otherwise the appearance and taste of the drink is harmed. There is also a risk of bacteria breeding in the pipes.

The cleaning is done by running a detergent solution through the system in much the same way as the beer or drink is run through. This is followed by water to remove all traces of the detergent. Finally some beer, cider, etc. is dispensed at the bar, until the product arriving from the cellar looks, smells and tastes as it should. Inevitably, there is a small amount of wastage, as there is when the detergent is first drawn through.

Cleaning method and equipment

The most commonly used method is to connect a cleaning bottle to the dispense line and to a gas cylinder or the cellar gas ring main. The bottle is large, made of plastic, and designed to take the coupling head (which normally connects the beer and gas lines to the keg). The bottle is filled in turn with:

* water to flush the beer out of the line (sometimes this step is omitted)

* beer line cleaner – a detergent made for the purpose, and diluted before use with water

* water to rinse the cleaner out of the line.

Do not use separate cleaning bottles for beer line cleaner and rinsing water. The beer line cleaner ensures that the bottle is properly clean before the rinsing water is added. Emptying it between each step means that both beer line cleaner and rinsing water are fresh.

A bucket is required to collect the run-off from the dispense point in the bar, e.g. beer, cleaner, rinsing water, and beer. Another bucket is needed in the cellar to:

* collect the beer which drains from the drinks line after it is disconnected from the keg

* hold the coupling head while the contents of the cleaning bottle are changed

* collect the rinsing water which runs out of the drinks line before it is reconnected to the keg.

Use the stainless steel buckets reserved for cleaning drinks lines – stainless steel is durable, can be properly cleaned, and will not react chemically with the beer line cleaner (see below). After each use, thoroughly clean the bucket – with beer line cleaner, and following instructions on diluting the cleaner and standing time – then rinse and dry before storing away.

Cleaning a beer line

	gas connected to:	cleaning bottle filled with:	dispense tap to drain:
in the cellar			**in the bar**

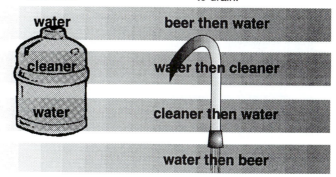

Disconnect beer and flush out with water (steps 1 and 2)	bottle	water	beer then water
Fill with cleaner and soak (steps 3 to 5)	bottle	cleaner	water then cleaner
Rinse with water (steps 6 to 9)	bottle	water	cleaner then water
Reconnect and test beer (steps 10 and 11)	keg		water then beer

General procedure for cleaning a beer line using gas

1 In the cellar:

- fill the cleaning bottle with water
- turn off the gas to the keg and beer line that you are cleaning
- remove the coupling head from the keg
- let the beer in the pipe drain into the bucket
- connect the coupling head to the cleaning bottle
- turn on the gas.

2 In the bar:

- place the second bucket under the dispense tap
- open the dispense tape and let the beer run until it is replaced by clean water
- dispense another two or three pints of clean water – to rinse any loose sediment out of the system.

3 In the cellar:

- turn off the gas
- release the gas pressure from the cleaning bottle
- remove the coupling head from the cleaning bottle and place in the bucket
- empty any remaining water out of the cleaning bottle
- pour into the cleaning bottle sufficient beer line cleaner for the length of line to be cleaned, diluted with water according to the instructions – your manager will advise on quantities
- connect the coupling head to the cleaning bottle
- turn on the gas.

4 In the bar, open the dispense tap and let the rinsing water run out of the pipe until it is replaced by the beer line cleaner.

5 Continue with your other duties, while the cleaner stands in the pipes for the time stated on the instructions of the beer liner cleaner (typically 20 minutes). During this standing time, it may be recommended that you draw off small quantities from the dispense tap in the bar, until the detergent runs clear.

6 In the cellar:

- turn off the gas
- release the gas pressure from the cleaning bottle
- remove the coupling head from the cleaning bottle and place in the bucket
- pour away any remaining beer line cleaner – it will lose its effectiveness if topped up, or if kept until the next time the lines are cleaned
- rinse the cleaning bottle with water, then fill with fresh water
- connect the coupling head to the cleaning bottle
- turn on the gas.

7 In the bar, open the dispense tap and let the beer line cleaner run out until it is replaced by the rinsing water.

8 Continue with your other duties, if the rinsing water has to stand in the pipes (some products recommend 20 minutes).

9 In the bar, open the dispense tap and let more water run out – the equivalent of 24 pints or 3 gallons is recommended to rinse the beer line thoroughly.

10 In the cellar:

- turn off the gas
- release the gas pressure from the cleaning bottle
- remove the coupling head from the cleaning bottle and reconnect it to the keg
- turn on the gas.

11 In the bar:

- open the dispense tap and let the rinsing water run out until it is replaced by undiluted beer
- hold the beer against a good light – it should be clear and bright
- smell it, and taste a small sample – there should be no trace of the beer line cleaner.

Safety when cleaning drink lines

Beer line cleaner is corrosive. In contact with:

- acids it creates a toxic (poisonous) gas – do not pour used cleaning solution into the cellar sump. Follow the instructions for disposal on the label

- aluminium it can form a highly flammable gas – this is why beer line cleaner should never be mixed or stored in an aluminium bucket

- your skin or eyes, or if breathed in or swallowed, it will cause great harm – wear rubber gloves and eye protection.

Measure quantities accurately before use when adding water to the beer line cleaner. Never store cleaning agents in containers used for food or drink, or leave them in a place where they might be taken for a non-harmful substance.

Always read the warnings on the container label and follow your workplace instructions for using hazardous substances. (See also industry example on page 73.)

Beer quality: fault finding

To produce a perfect pint is a great skill. From time to time problems arise. When they do, finding the solution can be time consuming.

Cloudy beer – the beer lines have not been cleaned properly or often enough. The cellar cooling system may not be working properly or there is a problem with the gas supply. The sparklers at the dispense point may be too tight, or the beer on service too long.

Poor head retention – the beer lines are not clean or the sparkler too slack. The cellar may be too warm, affecting the temperature of the beer in the glass. The beer may have been on service too long, or cask-conditioned beer has been used before it was ready.

Fobbing – may occur in hot weather if the cellar gets too warm because the cooling motor is over-working. If the temperature is not a problem, the beer lines are probably at fault. Check that the gas supply is working properly.

Check the sparkler to ensure it is not too tight, or that the beer is dispensing too fast. The beer may be over-carbonated: check the racking date.

Use this to check your progress against the performance criteria.

Element 1	**Element 2**	**Element 3**
Maintain cellars	Prepare kegs and gas cylinders for use	Clean drink dispense lines
Keep cellar floors free from dirt, rubbish and spillages ☐ PC1	Change keg/gas cylinder at appropriate time ☐ PC1	Prepare drink dispense line for cleaning ☐ PC1
Keep drains, gullies and sumps free from blockages ☐ PC2	⚠ Beer, cider or lager kegs, carbon dioxide gas cylinders	⚠ Beer/lager/cider dispense lines; post-mix syrup dispense lines
Keep ceilings and walls free from dirt and mould ☐ PC3	Disconnect and remove used keg/gas cylinder ☐ PC2	Use cleaning agents and equipment correctly ☐ PC2
Keep racks, shelves, cradles and refrigeration units clean, and in good working order ☐ PC4	Prepare and connect new keg/gas cylinder ready for use ☐ PC3	Cleaned pipes and taps free from debris, detergent and water ☐ PC3
Use correct cleaning equipment and materials, and store after use ☐ PC5	Store used keg/gas cylinder ready for dispatch ☐ PC4	Cleaned dispense line free from damage, and in good working order ☐ PC4
Maintain cellar environmental conditions ☐ PC6	Deal with leakages effectively and inform appropriate people ☐ PC5	Drink of correct quality for service ☐ PC5
⚠ Humidity, ventilation, lighting, temperature	Prioritise & carry out your work in an organised, efficient & safe manner ☐ PC6	Deal with unexpected situations and inform appropriate people ☐ PC6
Keep cellar secure from unauthorised access ☐ PC7		Prioritise & carry out your work in an organised, efficient & safe manner ☐ PC7
Deal with unexpected situations and inform appropriate people ☐ PC8		
Prioritise & carry out your work in an organised, efficient & safe manner ☐ PC9		

1 Give the safety rules you must follow when cleaning the cellar.

2 Describe how you store your cleaning equipment after use.

CLEANING EQUIPMENT ONLY

3 What is meant by 'environmental conditions' and how are these controlled in your cellar?

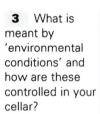

FORECAST: Cool fresh breezes

4 Why is good security important? Describe the arrangements for your cellar.

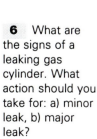

5 Why is it wrong to throw or drop a gas cylinder? How should gas cylinders be stored before, during and after use?

6 What are the signs of a leaking gas cylinder. What action should you take for: a) minor leak, b) major leak?

7 What do you check before connecting a new keg? Describe how the coupling head is fitted.

8 Describe the safe way of moving a keg into position.

9 Why must rubber gloves and eye protection be worn when using beer line cleaner?

10 What should you do if you spill beer line cleaner?

CORROSIVE

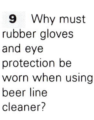

Wash away with plenty of water

11 Why is it important to use the same cleaning bottle for both rinsing water and beer line cleaner?

clean fresh

12 Checking the drink after the lines have been cleaned, you find an unpleasant taste and smell. What has gone wrong? What should be done to correct the problem?

wrong dilution? insufficient soaking? not adequately rinsed?

13 Identify the following in the photograph above: a) beer line, b) gas line, c) coupler, d) fob detector, e) gulley.

14 Say what might go wrong if the advice on this poster is not followed.

⚠ WARNING ⚠

1	ALWAYS	connect CO_2 or gas cylinder to **REDUCING VALVE.**
2	NEVER	try to connect cylinder directly to beer container.
3	NEVER	connect cylinder to any equipment not provided by brewery.
4	ALWAYS	secure cylinder upright whilst in use.
5	ALWAYS	keep cylinder away from heat.
6	NEVER	drop or throw cylinders.
7	NEVER	try to unscrew fittings from containers.
8	ALWAYS	ventilate cellar after CO_2, nitrogen or mixed gas leakage.

MORLAND

This safety poster, originally published by the Brewers and Licensed Retailers Association, has been adopted throughout the industry.

Storing and preparing cask conditioned beer

Cask conditioned beer is not ready to drink when delivered by the brewery (see page 44). It requires a few days in the cellar for fermentation to be complete and the sediment to settle at the bottom of the cask.

There is no one correct way of preparing cask conditioned beer. What is right for one product is not necessarily good for another. What suits one cellar is not so good in another. Tradition also plays a strong part, with some of the pieces of equipment being called by two or three different names.

Conditioning equipment

The cask is made of aluminium, stainless steel or sometimes oak. The delivery team usually put each cask into position so it can lie undisturbed until ready to drink. This is done by hand, or using *raising equipment*. The cask rests on a raised platform called a *stillage*, *thrawl*, *stillion* or *gantry*. The cask lies on its side, held in position by a wooden wedge on either side, called a *scotch* or *chock*.

Some stillaging is higher at the back, and the chocks are fixed to the back bearer to stop the cask rolling. When the cask is first put in position, a block has to be put on the front bearer, so that the cask is level. Later, the cask can be tilted by pulling out the front block.

At one end of the cask – and this should be the end facing into the cellar so you have access to it – is the fitting which will take the *cask tap* from which the beer is dispensed to the bar. When the cask is delivered, this fitting is closed by a wooden or plastic *keystone plug*. Later the tap will be hammered into this plug with a *mallet* (wooden or plastic) so that the connection can be made to the beer line. The cask should be positioned with the keystone plug at the bottom (i.e. in the 6 o'clock position).

On one side of the cask – at the top when the cask is resting horizontally, with the keystone plug in the 6 o'clock position – is the *bung hole*. This is closed with a wooden plug or bung called a *shive*. The shive has a small hole in the centre to take a *spile* or *vent peg*.

Depending on the brewer, the hole in the shive:

- is only partially bored so that the cask is sealed until the spile is tapped into place

- must be fully opened using a venting punch, and then the spile is tapped in

- is fully open but plugged with a wooden, cork or plastic peg called a *tut* or *tit*. When the shive hits this, the peg goes through into the cask (but will not harm the beer).

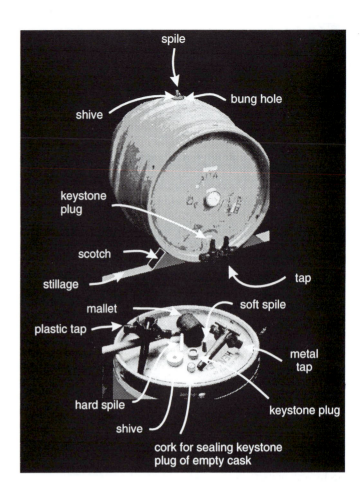

cork for sealing keystone plug of empty cask

The spile is used to open or shut the hole in the shive. There are two types of spile. The *soft spile*, usually made of cane, is porous, so it does not make an air-proof seal. It is used until the beer stops fermenting, and replaced as necessary, so that carbon dioxide can escape. Once this stage is complete, the soft spile is replaced by a *hard spile*, usually made of hard wood or plastic. This is either pushed home firmly, to make an air-proof seal, or pulled loose to allow some air into the cask.

Wooden spiles should only be used once and then thrown away. Other types can be reused provided they are thoroughly cleaned between use (usually by soaking in beer line cleaner).

The hole in the shive:

- allows gas out of the beer during the final fermentation – when the soft spile is used

- admits air into the cask as the beer is drawn off – the hard spile is pulled loose (or sometimes removed, or sometimes replaced by a soft spile)

- is used sometimes to connect the gas supply to the cask – as beer is drawn off, it is replaced by gas (rather than air). The gas helps keep the condition of the beer. A metal spigot is screwed into the spile hole to take the gas line.

Sometimes the gas is used to drive the beer along the drinks line to the dispense point in the bar – instead of using traditional hand pumps at the bar, or an electric pumping system.

Conditioning the beer ready to use

Conditioning takes place in the pub or bar cellar, under the right conditions of temperature and humidity, lighting and ventilation (see page 67). The process takes between 1 and 3 days, depending on the type of beer. During this time, the beer is *vented*, so that carbon dioxide created by the fermentation can escape. The beer also needs time for the sediment to settle.

The cask is placed in position on its stand as soon as possible after delivery. It will remain there until empty. The only time the cask is moved is to slightly raise the end furthest from the tap after about a third of the beer has been drawn off (see page 83). Great care is needed to avoid disturbing the sediment, which would make the beer cloudy and unpleasant to drink.

Some cask conditioned beers are *tapped* on delivery, some when the beer has quietened down and the soft spile is exchanged for a hard spile, and others on the day before the beer is served.

The condition of the beer is checked by drawing off a little into a clean, straight, half-pint glass. Once any sediment caught in the tap has cleared, the beer should be bright and palatable.

General procedure for venting the beer

1 Scrub and rinse the shive clean with water.

2 With the mallet, tap a soft spile into the hole in the shive.

3 Leave the beer to complete its fermentation (usually 12 to 24 hours). Froth will form around the spile.

4 Each morning and evening, wipe away the froth and replace the spile with a new one (if this is not done, the spile can become blocked).

5 When, after wiping away the froth, no more bubbles appear, this means the beer has stopped fermenting (or *working* or *fretting*). Remove the soft spile with pliers or *peg easers*.

6 Tap a hard spile into the shive. This allows the carbon dioxide to build up inside the cask, until the beer has cleared and is ready to drink. To prevent too much gas building up during this time, gently ease the hard spile once a day.

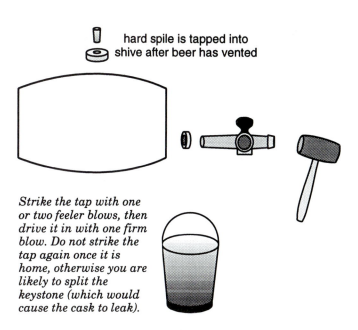

hard spile is tapped into shive after beer has vented

Strike the tap with one or two feeler blows, then drive it in with one firm blow. Do not strike the tap again once it is home, otherwise you are likely to split the keystone (which would cause the cask to leak).

General procedure for tapping the cask

1 Scrub and rinse the keystone plug clean with water.

2 Check that the keystone is flush with the cask. If not, gently tap it into position.

3 Partially open the cask tap – this avoids pressure building up in the cask as the tap is hammered into place. Some brewers recommend keeping the tap closed.

4 Place a stainless steel bucket under the keystone plug – to catch the beer which runs through the tap while it is open.

5 With the mallet, hammer the end of the tap into the keystone plug. Do this in one stroke, to avoid disturbing the sediment or splitting the plug. The plug is forced into the cask.

6 Close the tap.

Changing a cask

The aim is to have a new cask ready for connection to the dispense system at the same time as the old cask is empty. This is not easy, unless business follows a well-established pattern.

1 Turn the tap off at the empty cask, and disconnect the beer line.

2 Allow any beer in the line to run into a bucket (see page 83 for dealing with waste beer).

3 Test that the beer in the new cask is ready to serve (see above).

4 Check that the hop strainer (if used) on the beer liner is clean and in good condition.

5 Connect the beer line to the tap on the new cask, but only do up the nut up loosely.

6 Half open the tap to allow any air in the line to escape through the loose connection.

7 Hand-tighten the connection.

8 Open the tap fully.

9 Loosen the spile.

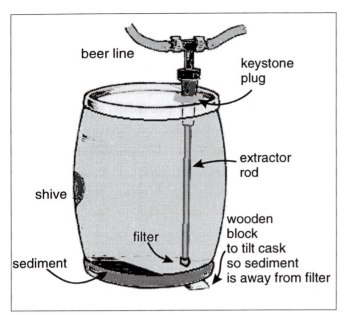

beer line

keystone plug

extractor rod

shive

filter

wooden block to tilt cask so sediment is away from filter

sediment

In some cellars where space is limited, the casks are stood on their ends (as kegs are). The beer is vented through the keystone plug. When ready, an extractor rod is driven through the plug, to reach almost to the bottom of the cask.

Illustration with thanks to Courage Ltd.

Cleaning cask taps

COURAGE

1 Remove front and rear cleaning eyes with a screwdriver. Turn tap to open position.

2 Put on rubber gloves.

3 Flush the tap out with clean cold water. Brush thoroughly and rinse again with water.

4 Carefully, so as not to splash, place tap and screw eyes in a bucket containing beer line cleaner (mixed to the correct strength). Leave for 20 minutes.

5 Carefully pour away cleaner, so as to avoid spills or splashes.

6 Thoroughly rinse the tap and screw eyes with clean cold water. Test by feel and smell that all traces of cleaner have disappeared.

cleaning eye

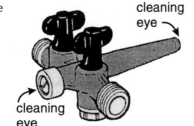

cleaning eye

7 Reassemble the tap. Check that it operates freely.

8 Store the tap in a plastic bag until required.

Maintaining cask conditioned beer

Cask conditioned beer begins to spoil quite quickly. Ideally the contents of the cask should be sold within 24 hours, once the beer has reached drinking condition. However, the quality usually keeps for 3 to 4 days provided the cellar is kept at the proper temperature and humidity (see page 67). Replacing the space left as the beer leaves the cask with carbon dioxide or mixed gas, not air, can also improve the keeping quality.

Conditioning the beer during use

Looking after the beer during use helps keep it in better condition for a longer time. The main concerns are to slow down the escape of carbon dioxide from the beer, otherwise the beer becomes flat, and to avoid disturbing the sediment, which would cause the beer to be cloudy.

The beer lines from cellar to bar must be cleaned regularly (see page 76) – at least every seven days is the usual rule.

Checking beer levels

You need to check the amount of beer left in the cask regularly to:

- avoid drawing sediment from the bottom of the cask to the bar, and dirtying, perhaps blocking the beer line in the process

- judge when the cask can be tilted – this helps get as much from the cask as possible (see below). If this is left until too late (i.e. after half the beer has gone), the sediment will be disturbed.

The level of beer is checked using a dipstick (the process is similar to checking the oil level in a car). Each size or type of cask requires its own dipstick, and the dipstick must be absolutely clean – otherwise you risk contaminating the beer.

Remove the spile, carefully push the dipstick through the shive until it just touches the bottom of the cask, withdraw the dipstick and note the mark left by the beer.

Do's and Don'ts

W WETHERSPOON

ALWAYS	NEVER
clean lines once a week	use vent pegs more than once
swill away spilt beer	use disinfectants for cleaning cellar floors
use hop filters	use cellar as a food store
keep all utensils clean	disturb casks once gantried
keep cellar floors clean	leave waste beer in open containers

General procedure for conditioning the beer during use

At the end of every session, push the hard spile firmly into the bung hole. This protects the beer from contamination (the air in the cellar is likely to contain bacteria and dust). It also slows down the release of carbon dioxide from the beer.

Before every session, loosen the hard spile, so that air can be drawn into the cask as the beer is drawn off. If this is not done, the sediment will be disturbed. Some brewers recommend that the hard spile is replaced by a soft one.

Before the first session of each day, drawn off a small amount of beer, sufficient to clear the lines of beer which may have fermented overnight.

Once about one-third of the cask has been drawn off, raise the end of the cask furthest from the tap by 60 to 80 mm. This helps get more of the beer from the cask. Tilting is done at the end of the evening session, to give the beer as much time as possible to resettle should some of the sediment be disturbed.

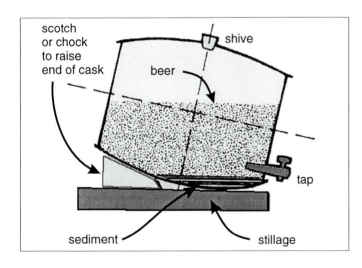

Returning beer to the cask

The only beer that may be returned to the cask is that:

- drawn from the cask to check its quality
- drawn off the beer line before cleaning, before changing a cask, and at the start of a session.

The return of any other beer (e.g. from drip trays) may result in prosecution under food safety legislation.

The beer may only be returned to the cask from which it was drawn. This cask must not be less than two-thirds full. The filter equipment must be clean and sterilised, and the process must be done gently to avoid disturbing the beer already in the cask. It is a task which should only be attempted by an expert.

Some pubs never return beer to the cask.

Preparing and storing empty casks

As soon as possible after a cask is empty, make it airtight:

- drive a hard spile into the bung hole
- remove the tap – gently tap it on each side to loosen it
- block the keystone with a cork.

Sealing the cask keeps out insects and stops bacteria spreading. The sediment is left in the cask, as it is much easier for the brewery to wash out wet sediment.

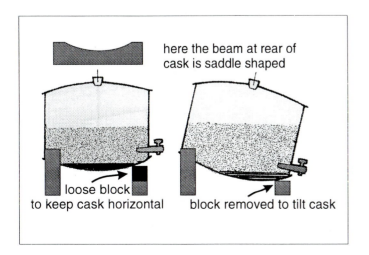

1 How is the storage of cask conditioned beer different from keg beer?

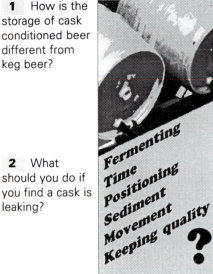

2 What should you do if you find a cask is leaking?

Fermenting
Time
Positioning
Sediment
Movement
Keeping quality
?

3 Describe how the cask can be safely moved into position on the stillage. Why is it important to wear sturdy gloves and shoes?

4 On the lower illustration, mark these:
a) stillage,
b) keystone,
c) the scotch or chock,
d) position of the shive.

Reproduced from the poster in Backbreakers, a video-based training package published by Whitbread Inns

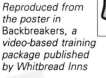
WHITBREAD
INNS

84

5 How do you prevent the sediment in the bottom of the cask being disturbed?

6 Give two reasons why care must be taken when tilting a cask. When should this be done?

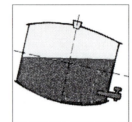

7 Describe how to check the level of beer in the cask. When and why is this done?

right dipstick?
dipstick clean?
avoid sediment
when to tilt?

8 Match each of the following faults with its possible cause (there may be more than one):
a) cloudy beer,
b) sour beer,
c) flat beer,
d) too much froth/excessive foaming.

- ❏ cellar too cold
- ❏ cellar too warm
- ❏ cask not had time to settle
- ❏ cask on service too long
- ❏ end of cask
- ❏ first drink from new cask
- ❏ first drink of session
- ❏ hard spile left in when beer is dispensed
- ❏ hard spile not pushed in at end of session
- ❏ cask tilted too soon or too late
- ❏ beer lines not clean
- ❏ beer lines not rinsed properly
- ❏ acid smells in cellar

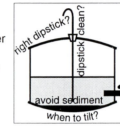

NVQ
SVQ
Skills check
Store, prepare and maintain cask conditioned beers
Unit 2NC11
level
2

Use this to check your progress against the performance criteria.

Element 1

Store and prepare cask conditioned beer ready for service

Handle and position casks correctly ❏ PC1

Use clean, undamaged conditioning equipment to prepare casks ❏ PC2
⚠ Equipment: stillage/gantry, keystone, shive, soft spile, hard spile, cask tap, mallet, chocks/raising equipment

Maintain correct storage conditions for casks ❏ PC3
⚠ Humidity, ventilation, lighting, temperature

Check conditioned beer is correct quality for service ❏ PC4
⚠ Service: cask tap, manual beer engine

Deal with unexpected situations and inform appropriate people ❏ PC5

Prioritise and carry out your work in an organised, efficient and safe manner ❏ PC6

Element 2

Maintain cask conditioned beers

Check beer levels regularly ❏ PC1

Reposition casks as appropriate ❏ PC2

Use correct conditioning equipment between service sessions ❏ PC3
⚠ Equipment: hard spile, soft spile, bungs, mallet, chocks/raising equipment

Prepare and store empty casks ready for dispatch ❏ PC4

Maintain storage conditions according to service style ❏ PC5
⚠ Conditions: temperature, lighting, humidity, ventilation
Service style: cask tap, manual beer engine

Deal with unexpected situations effectively & inform appropriate people ❏ PC6

Prioritise and carry out your work in an organised, efficient and safe manner ❏ PC7

Before and after service
routines in the bar

Preparing customer and service areas

Customers say cleanliness and comfort – along with the friendliness of the barstaff – are their main reasons for liking a particular pub. To help your pub or bar create the right impression – the impression that brings customers back – be ready to make that extra effort.

Train yourself to notice what customers notice, to see things through their eyes. The attention to small details really makes a difference – chairs neatly arranged, ashtrays where they should be and clean, curtains hanging tidily, pictures straight, etc.

Much of the cleaning – vacuuming carpets, polishing furniture, etc. – is probably done before you come on duty. In your pre-opening preparations, you are checking that everything is as it should be and making the final adjustments. You are also getting ready what you need to serve customers' orders.

Stocking up

The stock is kept behind the bar, on the shelves and in the drink cabinets, to help you serve orders quickly. It also tells customers what is available. A neatly arranged display, making good use of colour and shape, looks good. It is also a way of promoting particular drinks. In pubs, like supermarkets, the position and amount of shelf space given to each product can make more sales.

If you are responsible for receiving stock ordered from the cellar or stores, check that you have the correct items, and the correct quantity. The details should agree with the requisition (see page 65).

General procedure for stocking up

1 Check the date mark on stock. Remove any items which have passed their best-before or use-by date. Your manager will tell you what to do with them.

2 Place new stock at the rear of shelves, and move old stock to the front. Rotating stock like this reduces the risk of items getting beyond their date. It also gives drinks a chance to reach the right serving temperature.

3 Position bottles and cans in neat rows, with the product label facing towards customers. Wipe away any dust or dirt with a slightly damp cloth. Put aside

---

Golden rules on stocking shelves

Shelf and fridge displays have greater impact when products are at the front of the shelf.

Good display: lots of impact on customers

Poor display

Always pull products to the front of the shelf.

Make sure labels face the front.

When you group products tightly together in rows on shelves, this gives the product lots of impact on the customer.

Put products which are bought on impulse (see page 54) in the strongest position. These are also high-profit products.

Stacking the shelves as shown here gives equal space to products A, B and C, all high-profit items.

Products D and E are those customers ask for by name (demand products).

Extracts from Service for Sales, *a training package which helps the staff of Scottish & Newcastle Retail gain their NVQ/SVQ*

---

to return to the cellar any items which are damaged, e.g. chipped top on a bottle, dented can, or leaking bottle.

4 Check with your manager what should be done with nearly-empty bottles of spirits, cordials and wine which is served by the glass.

5 Put away empty cases, boxes and cartons. Take care while you are stocking up that packaging is not a safety hazard, e.g. left where someone might trip over it.

8 Before and after service routines in the bar

Preparing drink accompaniments

These fall into three groups, those that:

- customers expect to be offered – ice and sliced lemon with a gin and tonic, ice and water with whisky, Worcestershire sauce and freshly ground black pepper with tomato juice, milk or cream and sugar with coffee, etc.

- customers expect to be available if requested – ice with soft drinks, sliced lemon or orange with mineral water, etc.

- form part of the presentation of cocktails and other drinks – angostura bitters with gin, twist of lemon rind with a Martini, paper umbrellas, stirrers, sugar to frost the rim of the glass, cherries, fresh mint, olives, sliced lemon, orange and lime, etc.

Check that you have adequate stock of the items that do not spoil – sugar, jars of cherries, pre-sliced lemons, paper umbrellas, etc.

Until you know the routine of your bar, ask your manager what fresh fruit should be sliced in advance, and how much. It helps in the busy periods to have fruit ready, but you waste time and fruit preparing too much, since at the end of service any that has dried up will have to be thrown away.

Do not put out too many buckets of ice at the beginning of service if the bar is only busy later in the day. In hot weather, ice melts quite quickly. Try and match the supply with the demand.

Promotional displays and signs

By law, all pubs and bars must display the prices of drinks, or at least a sample. Restaurants and hotels have to meet similar requirements, so that customers, if they wish, can work out how much their drinks, food or room will cost before making a commitment.

It makes good marketing sense to tell customers what is available. Ways to do this include drink lists, menus, boards for describing guest beers, new cocktails, dishes of the day, etc., and promotional material supplied by the brewery, distillery, wine producer, etc.

Your responsibilities may include inserting the day's menu in folders for the bar counter and tables, tidying promotional displays, and writing details of dishes and drinks on the board (see page 55).

Plan these tasks into your pre-service routine, so that nothing is overlooked and you have enough time to check all the details, including spelling. Customers get a poor impression when they find yesterday's dish of the day in the menu folder, or the menu cards torn and stained. They won't bother to look at a display board if the writing is hard to read or the spelling wrong.

Preparing the bar for service

Back bar – clean, no clutter, mirrors sparkling, adequate supply of glasses, skips clean and tidy and out of view of customers if possible

Bar counter – clean and polished, bar towels and ashtrays clean, lights on beer founts switched on

Bar fruit and sundries – freshly prepared, ice bucket clean and full, water jug clean and full, accessories clean

Display shelves – stocked and attractively arranged, supply of bar snacks if required

Chilled drinks cabinets – temperature correct, promotional range displayed, labels facing outwards, stock rotated, lights working

Customer areas – lights on and working, extractor fans on and working, curtains open/drawn depending on time of day, amusement machines switched on and tokens replenished, furniture clean and neatly arranged, price lists, menu boards and notices up-to-date, neat and tidy

Getting customer and services areas ready

What has to be done will depend on the after-service routine, perhaps on how busy the bar has been in the previous session and on how responsibilities in your workplace are arranged. You may need to:

- check the temperature of cold shelves, chilling cabinets and refrigerators

- check that drip trays under dispense taps are in position, empty and clean

- put out drip mats and/or coasters on the bar counter and tables

- polish and put away glasses

- return ashtrays to tables and the bar counter in the correct position

- clean and polish the bar counter fittings – founts become sticky with use

- put out thimble measures, pourers, cork screws, knives, chopping boards, ice tongs, cocktail shakers and similar items of bar equipment

- position bottle skips and containers (for storing empties so that returnable and non-returnable bottles are kept separate) and waste bins

- fill dishes with crisps, nuts, olives and similar bar snacks when these are provided free

- switch on display lights for beer founts, drink cabinets and shelves

- turn on the glass washer

- adjust the ventilation and heating, turn on lights in customer areas, the toilets, entrance, etc., for vending and amusement machines, and turn on the sound system and cash tills

- put tables and chairs in position – special arrangements may be required for competition nights, when there is entertainment, and, if the weather is suitable, for sitting in the garden.

Element 2

Clearing customer and service areas

Customers may not be anxious to go at closing time, but everyone else is! And your colleagues won't appreciate being left to clear up what you should have done just because you have a bus to catch!

The aim is to leave the bar safe and secure, reasonably tidy and clean. Details of the closing routine differ from one bar to another, and there is usually less to do if the bar is closing for an afternoon break. Certain tasks may be the responsibility of your managers or the publican, such as locking the bar, turning off heating and ventilation systems, doing a final check that windows, etc. are secure, and that there is no one left on the premises (e.g. in the toilets).

Drink stocks and drink accompaniments

Sometimes cold shelves, chilling cabinets and refrigerators are restocked at the end of service, so that bottles and cans have plenty of time to get to the right temperature. Move the stock that is already there to the front so it will be used first.

Check that the tops are firmly on jars of cherries and containers of pre-sliced lemon, etc. Cover with cling wrap and put in the refrigerator sliced fresh fruit and similar garnishes for drinks which will keep, otherwise discard them.

Cleaning and storing service equipment

Wash and put away glasses and ashtrays (see pages 89 to 91). Empty and clean ice buckets and water jugs. Wash thimble measures, chopping boards and knives and put back in place, ready for use.

Clean all drip trays and service trays. Collect drip mats, glass cloths and other items ready to go for laundering.

Electrical equipment

Follow specific instructions on what should be turned off, what should also be unplugged and what should be left on (e.g. refrigerators and chilling units). Damage to equipment and wastage of food and drink may result from doing the wrong thing.

If you find something still on when you believe it should be turned off, check with your manager before taking further action. There may be a reason it was left on (a note left by the switch helps avoid such situations).

Closing down checklist

Always make sure you leave the bar clean and tidy, ready for the next session. At the end of the session, remember to:

- re-stock shelves and drink cabinets
- wash and put away glasses
- collect and wash ashtrays, first emptying the contents into a fire-proof container
- put away lemons, cherries, etc.
- empty water jugs and ice buckets
- empty and wash drip trays
- clean sinks
- wipe back counters
- sweep and mop the floor behind the bar
- switch off amusement machines, display lights, etc.
- tidy customer areas, and leave ready for cleaners

Security and safety checks

- any broken glass disposed of correctly
- no cigarette ends on carpets, seating, etc. or in waste bins
- cash tills empty and left open
- no one remaining in the toilets
- windows and doors locked

Tidying customer and service areas

Clear glasses, ashtrays, empty bottles, crisp packets, etc. from tables and other places customers might leave them, e.g. window sills, behind curtains, under chairs, dropped on the floor, in flower beds in the garden. Wipe up spills. Check that smouldering cigarette ends are not trapped in the joins of upholstered furniture or behind cushions.

Place empty bottles in the correct skip or container, returnables in their own container. Waste left in the wrong place is a safety, hygiene and fire hazard. Broken glass is particularly dangerous if not stored properly (see page 91).

Return tables and chairs to their usual position, or back into storage (e.g. furniture put outside when the weather is suitable).

Wipe clean the bar counter, worktops and shelves. Thoroughly wash cleaning cloths and brushes, and leave to dry. Rinse out the sink and wipe down the draining board.

1 What do you do about each of the problems illustrated?

Problems to sort out

✳ *Crisps passed 'best-before' date*

✳ *Dented can*

✳ *Broken bottle of lager in crate of full bottles*

✳ *Mouldy lemon*

✳ *Fruit juice off*

6 For each of the items shown, say what action you would take and why, if you found them when clearing customer areas of the bar.

forgotten item of clothing
signs of drug abuse
smouldering cigarette
briefcase left behind
wallet with money and cards

2 How is the bar stock and equipment kept secure?

7 Why is it important to check that no one is left on the premises before locking up?

3 When you are stocking shelves and cabinets, what rules must you follow?

FIFO
Group like items
Labels to front
Safe handling

8 How can you make easier the work of those who clean the bar?

PUT THINGS IN THEIR PLACE

4 What must you do to ensure that drinks are at the right temperature for service?

°C
service temperature reached
hours

9 Identify the electrical equipment which should be a) left on, and b) turned off while the bar is closed.

display lights
music system
extractor fans
AWP machines

chilling units
refrigerators
security alarms

5 List the items of service equipment you should have ready, and state where each should be.

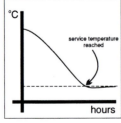

open
pour
measure
garnish
present

NVQ
SVQ

Skills check
Prepare and clear areas for drinks service in licensed premises
Unit 1NC5

level
1

Use this to check your progress against the performance criteria.

Element 1

Prepare customer and service areas

Store, rotate and replenish stocks for drinks service   ☐ PC1

△ Bottled beers, wines and spirits; soft drinks; minerals/juices; hot drinks; sundry items

Prepare and store drink accompaniments ready for service   ☐ PC2

△ Ice; cordials; food garnishes for drinks; decorative items for drinks; accompaniments for hot drinks

Get service and electrical equipment ready for use   ☐ PC3

△ Service equipment: bottle openers, cork screws; optics, measures, pourers; glasses, ashtrays; drip trays, drip mats; ice buckets, tongs; knives, chopping boards; coasters, drink mats
Electrical equipment: refrigerated units, washing machines

Prepare signage and promotional material correctly   ☐ PC4

△ Drinks menus, promotional displays

Check that customer and service areas are ready for service   ☐ PC5

△ Floors; counters and shelves; waste bins and bottle containers; tables and chairs

Check and secure service areas from unauthorised access   ☐ PC6

Deal with unexpected situations effectively & inform appropriate people   ☐ PC7

Prioritise and carry out your work in an organised, efficient and safe manner   ☐ PC8

Element 2

Clear customer and service areas

Store and replenish or dispose of drink stocks and accompaniments   ☐ PC1

Clean and store service equipment   ☐ PC2

When appropriate, turn off electrical equipment and machines   ☐ PC3

Leave customer & service areas tidy, free of rubbish & ready for cleaning   ☐ PC4

Secure customer and service areas   ☐ PC5

Deal with unexpected situations effectively & inform appropriate people   ☐ PC6

Prioritise and carry out your work in an organised, efficient and safe manner   ☐ PC7

Cleaning glassware

Sparkling, clean glasses add to the enjoyment of the drink. They tell customers that hygiene standards are high and that the barstaff take pride in their work.

A good quality glass shows the colours of a drink to best advantage. A thin rim is more pleasant against the lips than is a thick one. For drinks like wine and brandy, a narrowing top concentrates the bouquet so that the aromas of the drink can be better appreciated.

But these advantages come at a price. The finer the glass, the more delicate its shape, the more expensive it is to buy and the easier it is to break. Many of the glasses used in the bars of luxury hotels have to be hand-washed, and even then a high percentage of breakages are expected – one reason why customers at these places pay three or four times more for their drinks than they would at the local pub.

Handling glassware safely

All glasses should be handled carefully. Dropping or knocking a glass against any hard surface may break it, or cause a crack or chip, so that the glass has to be thrown away. Sometimes the damage is not visible to the eye, but internal weaknesses lead to the glass cracking when you would not expect it to, e.g. when washing up (the change of temperature) or polishing (the extra pressure).

To reduce the stress to glasses, do not pick them up in handfuls with the fingers, overload trays or stack them one inside the other (unless they are the type made to be stacked). Glasses should never be used to scoop ice, or to store steel cutlery, even if this is only for a short time while you are drying up.

The edges of broken glass are very, very sharp. Use a dustpan and brush to clear up breakages – no matter how careful you are, picking up a broken piece in the fingers can cause a cut. Much more serious injuries can result from contact with broken glass that you have not seen, e.g. hitting your hand against a glass which has broken in a too-full sink of items to be washed.

When a glass drops on the bar counter or a hard floor, the tiny pieces of broken glass scatter over a wide area so that it is very difficult to be sure you have cleared up completely. When the broken pieces might have got into uncovered food or drink, this must be thrown away. Get your manager to the scene immediately. If the accident has happened in view of customers, they will be very concerned to see that their safety is protected. It may be necessary to prove that the proper procedures have been followed if customers threaten or take legal action.

Handling glassware hygienically

Keep your fingers away from the rims of glasses, which have contact with customers' lips, and the insides of glasses, which have contact with the drink. Hold glasses at the base, by the stem or the handle.

If it is necessary to polish glasses, use a dry, clean cloth, of the type that will not leave fluff or smears.

To prevent the very strong smell of nicotine from spreading, and contamination from ash and the ends of cigarettes and cigars, wash ashtrays separately from all other glassware, cutlery, or china. Dry with paper towelling or leave to air-dry.

Cleaning glasses

The busier the bar, the more pressure there is to get glasses washed and back into use quickly. If there is little space, or a shortage of glasses, the difficulties increase. Nevertheless, the task must be done properly and with care so that:

- harmful bacteria are prevented from spreading
- breakages and accidents are less likely to occur
- glasses look sparkling and clean
- drinks taste and look good – their flavour and appearance can be ruined by a glass which is not clean. Traces of detergent or grease stop the head forming on a glass of beer.

Pour drink and ice which customers have left in the glass down the sink. If you can't do this, e.g. because the sink is full with fresh washing-up or rinsing water, use a plastic bucket or bin to collect it, or a large glass which you leave to last. Putting a very cold glass (because it has contained ice) into hot washing water or the glass washer harms the glass (see checklist on page 91). If possible, let it stand for a few minutes to reach room temperature.

Remove cocktail sticks, lemon pieces, cigarette ends and other rubbish, and rinse out remaining debris from the glass before you wash it or place it in the dish washer. Wipe off lipstick with paper towelling.

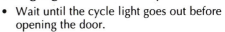

Using a glasswasher safely
- Wait until the cycle light goes out before opening the door.
- Load racks carefully to prevent glasses knocking against each other and cause breakages.
- When cleaning, watch for broken glass in the bottom of the machine.

By hand

The best arrangement for hygiene reasons is a double sink or two wash basins – one for washing, the other for rinsing – and a large draining board or nearby work surface so that glasses can be left to air-dry.

If left-over drink has been poured down the sink, or it has been used for washing ashtrays, etc., clean the basin and draining board before starting on the glasses.

Wear rubber gloves – over time, contact with detergents makes your skin very dry, aggravates small cuts and sores, and can cause dermatitis. This is a painful, unpleasant looking condition which, until it is cured, would stop you from doing bar work or handling food. Gloves also protect your hands against the very hot water – if you are able to put your hands in the washing or rinsing water without gloves, the water is probably not hot enough.

Let the water from the hot tap run very hot before you fill the rinsing basin – it should be about 80°C. This means the glasses will dry quickly, and helps kill any bacteria. You may be asked to use a rinse or polishing aid – to leave the glasses shiny and to disinfect them. The washing water may need some cold water added with the hot, so that it is at about 55°C.

Use the detergent provided, and, if available, a dispenser to measure the quantity accurately. Too much is wasteful and some is likely to remain after rinsing, so spoiling the drink. Too little will not clean the glass. Change washing and rinsing water frequently.

Wash and rinse glasses one at a time. Never stack the water full of glasses as they will knock into each other causing damage and probably breakages. When you return to washing up from doing something else, feel with your hand (of course, you should be wearing gloves) that there are no glasses lying in the water before you start again.

If the rinsing water is the right temperature, the glasses will dry quickly when left upside down on the draining board. Before using or putting them away, check and if necessary give them a polish with a dry, clean cloth.

When you have done the glasses, clean the sink and its surrounds, and wipe all the surfaces to leave them dry and shiny. Some sinks have stationary brushes on which glasses are inverted and agitated. Wash and rinse the brushes after use, making sure there are no bits of lemon, etc. trapped in the bristles.

> ### Faults with drinks – finding the reason
>
> Glasses which have not been washed or rinsed properly may be the reason for a fault with a drink – fobbing when draught beer is dispensed, beer which is cloudy, or does not keep its head, an off-taste with spirits, soft drinks, etc., sparkling drinks which go flat quickly.

By machine

Most bars have a cabinet glass washing machine. The glasses are loaded in the machine (in a special basket), the door shut and the start button pressed. In a few minutes, the machine washes and rinses the glasses and a light shows that the glasses can be removed.

In smaller bars there may be a brush-operated glass washing machine. These sit on a work surface. Glasses are cleaned one at a time, by holding them against the revolving brushes in the detergent solution. Each glass has to be cleaned in two moves: the bottom, then the top.

Very large bars have a conveyor machine. The glasses, loaded in trays, move slowly through the machine as the water changes from washing to rinsing mode.

Using a cabinet glass washing machine

Turn the machine on a little in advance, to give it time to get the washing and rinsing water up to temperature. A light will show when it is ready for use.

Check and if necessary replace the containers of detergent and rinse aid. Wear gloves and follow your workplace rules for hazardous substances (see also page 73).

Put the glasses upside down into the basket, and spaced slightly apart. If you are washing glasses of similar size, it is easier to use a basket with divisions to take individual glasses.

When you lift the tray of glasses in or out of the machine, plan your movement so that the weight is evenly balanced between both hands, and so as to avoid twisting and bending at the same time. This reduces the strain on your back (your manager or trainer will give you advice on manual handling).

Shut the cabinet door before you turn the machine on. Remove the glasses when the light shows that the wash/rinse cycle is complete.

Follow instructions for cleaning and draining the machine at the end of the session. The filters at the bottom of the machine, where any debris left in the glasses is trapped, need to be cleaned regularly.

Storing glassware

When you come to serve a drink, you and your colleagues don't want to waste time looking for the right glass, or checking that every glass is clean. And any customers seeing you do this would get a poor impression.

Checking glasses before storage

The efficiency of the bar depends on glasses being in their proper place, ready for use. Check glasses carefully before putting them away:

- polish if the glass looks dull or has smears
- return to the washing-up any glasses that are not clean
- put aside any cracked or chipped glasses, or check with your manager that they can be thrown away.

Storage of glassware

How the glasses are stored depends on the space available, the design of the bar and the type of glass. Where possible, glasses for a particular drink – beer, spirits, soft drinks, wines, sherry, liqueurs, etc. – are kept near the dispense point. Glasses in which the top selling drinks are served have the most accessible position.

Sometimes glasses are stored resting on their rims, sometimes standing upright, and sometimes hanging from the handle or by the stem. When stored resting on the rims, the shelf must be kept very clean. Sometimes a plastic mat is used, to protect the rims and to allow some air circulation in the glasses.

When storing glasses:

- hold them by the base, the handle or the stem – for hygienic reasons
- put them in place gently – to avoid knocking other glasses or the shelf or bracket

and check the glass is safe before letting go:

- hanging securely by its handle
- away from the edge of the shelf
- tall, thin glasses not likely to topple over.

CHECK list Handling glassware

✔ take chipped or cracked glasses out of service immediately

✔ dispose of broken or damaged glasses safely – use the bin provided for this purpose, or wrap them in lots of paper

Care of glasses

✔ avoid banging or knocking glasses together

✔ keep glasses slightly apart on shelves, on trays or in the hand and not stacked – unless they are of the type designed to be stacked

✔ after washing, allow glasses to cool before filling with a cold drink

✔ for hot drinks, warm glasses first under hot running water

Safety first

✔ spread the weight evenly on trays and do not overfill the tray

✔ watch where you are going when carrying a tray, so that you do not trip or bump into colleagues or customers

---

Handling glasses and bottles

- never use chipped or cracked glasses
- use a clean glass for each drink served – if the customer insists on the same glass explain it is our hygiene policy to give a clean glass for each drink served
- do not put broken glasses or bottles in the bottle skip. Wrap in strong paper and place into strong waste bin. Never put broken glass into a plastic bin sack
- do not pour bottled drinks if you notice that the collar of the bottle is chipped when you remove the crown top
- always make sure that the catching tray is in place when using a crown top opener – bottle caps are a slipping hazard if they get on the floor

Glass washing

- always check the machine/sinks for broken glass before use
- always use the correct detergent at the recommended dilution
- regularly change water when sink washing
- always use a rinsing sink when washing glasses by hand
- do not leave glasses in the sink unattended

1 What would you say to someone who thinks that rinsing a glass in warm water is sufficient to clean it.

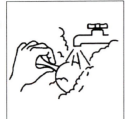

6 How can you prevent rubbish left in glasses from blocking the sink outlet?

Use this to check your progress against the performance criteria.

Element 1
Clean glassware

Empty and assemble glassware ready for cleaning PC1 ☐
⚠ Glasses, ashtrays, water jugs

Get glass washer/sink and cleaning materials ready for use PC2 ☐

Clean glassware by machine/hand PC3 ☐

2 How do you dispose of broken glasses? Also say what you should not do and why.

7 If you cut yourself on a broken glass (not seriously), how can you stop the bleeding and protect the wound? To whom and why should you report the accident? Where is the first-aid box kept?

Dispose of damaged or broken glassware correctly PC4 ☐

Dispose of waste or dirty water correctly PC5 ☐

Leave glass washer/sink ready for future use PC6 ☐

Deal with unexpected situations effectively & inform appropriate people PC7 ☐

Prioritise and carry out your work in an organised, efficient and safe manner PC8 ☐

3 Give the do's and don'ts for looking after glassware.

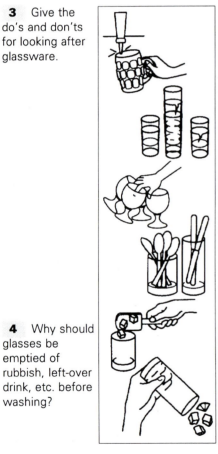

Element 2
Store glassware

Handle glassware carefully at all times PC1 ☐

Store glassware which is clean, dry, undamaged, polished if appropriate PC2 ☐

Keep storage areas clean, tidy and free from rubbish PC3 ☐

8 If the edge of a water jug or ashtray has a chip on it, what should you do and why?

Dispose of damaged or broken glassware correctly PC4 ☐

Deal with unexpected situations effectively & inform appropriate people PC5 ☐

9 What might damage or break glassware when putting it back into storage?

Prioritise and carry out your work in an organised, efficient and safe manner PC6 ☐

4 Why should glasses be emptied of rubbish, left-over drink, etc. before washing?

5 Which is better and why: to let glasses air-dry, or to use a drying cloth?

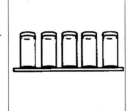

10 How should you hold a clean glass and why?

Illustrations with thanks to (questions 1 to 5 and 8 to 10)

RAVENHEAD
GLASS

and Whitbread Inns (question 7)

Taking payment
for drinks and food

Maintaining a payment point

The payment point in a bar is the cash till. The till is placed conveniently for barstaff, but also for customers to see what is rung up. It is usually on the back bar counter rather than the front, so a customer is not tempted to steal money from the cash drawer when your back is turned.

In busy bars there will be a number of tills. Sometimes each member of staff will have a separate till, or his or her own cash drawer. Any errors can be sorted out with the person responsible for that till or cash drawer.

Cash tills make a record of every transaction. At its simplest this is a printout (on the till roll) of the price of drinks and food ordered by the customer, and the total the customer was asked to pay. By operating a special key, your manager can get a total for all the transactions during the session. This is used to check the amount of cash taken, and to provide information for the accounts of the business.

It is not usual in pubs to give customers a receipt for drinks. Customers see their order rung up and totalled on the till display, and know (or can easily find out) the price of what they have ordered.

If they are entertaining, business customers may ask for a receipt. It is usual to give a receipt when customers are served their drinks in the restaurant, or at the table in a cocktail or wine bar. This reassures customers that they are being asked to pay the correct amount. In some bars, customers paying at the bar counter are also given a receipt. Presenting this on a plate, as happens in restaurants, is a feature of the type of service offered.

Cash security

1 All monies must be placed in the safe after each trading session. All safes are to be kept locked. The house licensee is responsible for the keys.
2 All tills must be checked at least once per day.
3 The licensee is responsible for the cash in accordance with the till readings and house float as designated. Spot checks may be carried out at any time.
4 IOUs to customers are forbidden.
5 The policy on cashing cheques is decided by the house licensee. Any cheques not honoured will be the responsibility of the house licensee.
6 All personal money and/or valuables kept in the safe must be properly labelled. The company accepts no responsibility for such items.

With thanks to CCC Leisure

Cash handling is closely supervised to safeguard:

your **customers** so that they:
- are not overcharged
- get the correct change

you and your **colleagues** so that you are not:
- blamed for losses which were not your responsibility
- suspected of being dishonest without reason
- put in danger in the course of a robbery – thieves often target cash-rich businesses such as pubs

your **employer**:
- so that customers are not undercharged – which would have a bad effect on profits and lead to problems under trading standards legislation
- so that customers are not overcharged – when they would be likely to complain and unlikely to return
- to reduce the risk of cash being stolen by outsiders, or employees
- to prevent the acceptance of forged bank notes or dud cheques and credit card payments
- to prevent claims (not always genuine) by customers that they have been given too little change (e.g. for £10 when they said they handed over a £20 note).

Security procedures

The money that customers pay belongs to the business. The amount they pay should be exactly the advertised selling price of what they have been served.

As in other aspects of security (see page 29), you can do much to discourage dishonesty by:

- being alert to the unusual – the customer who is undecided on which credit card to offer, possibly a genuine reason, possibly because the card is stolen

- promptly reporting suspicions to your manager – the customer who as you are handing over the change for a £20 note, says he or she meant to give you £10, could the £20 be given back, possibly a genuine muddle, possibly a ploy to confuse you

- promptly telling your manager of problems – the regular customer whose payment by credit card is not authorised, possibly a temporary problem, possibly a sign of serious financial difficulties

- reducing the opportunity for problems – keeping the cash drawer shut at any time you are not using it, locking your till if you have to leave the bar, following the checking procedures for accepting payment (see page 99).

Following workplace rules

The rules in your workplace for handling cash and taking payment are there to protect everyone. The emphasis depends on the sort of transactions you have to deal with. Typical rules include:

- in some pubs – only cash may be accepted, and before giving change for a £20 or £50 note, a colleague must be asked to observe the transaction

- in some restaurants – besides cash, certain cards can be accepted, but authorisation from the card issuing company must be obtained for amounts over the floor limit, e.g. £50

- in some hotels – customers can ask for their bar bill to go on their accommodation account, when they should be asked to produce their room card and sign the bill.

From time to time there may be particular concerns, e.g. a large number of forged notes circulating in the area, or a customer using stolen credit cards to pay local restaurants, hotels and shops.

Some customers will tell you to ignore workplace rules. With others, you may feel you know them well enough to rely on their honesty. Don't be persuaded. Customers should respect – and most will – that you have to carry out company procedures. If they insist that an exception should be made, call your manager or the publican to take over.

Pre-opening procedure

Before the bar opens, or you start your shift, check that you have sufficient change to give customers paying with £5, £10, £20 notes, etc. There should be a reasonable quantity of each coin, as well as some £5 notes. Normally a reserve of change is kept in a safe, elsewhere. Top-ups from this supply are given in exchange for notes of the same value, and coins are usually pre-counted in bags of particular values, e.g. £1 of 2p coins, £5 of 5p coins.

Your manager or the publican may see to this, providing you with a *float* which you are responsible for handing back at the end of the session. You should check that the float is correct and, if requested, sign that you have done so.

As necessary, check that you have sufficient stocks of till rolls, credit card vouchers (for hand-operated machines), customer bills and pens (to loan to customers to write out cheques or sign credit card vouchers).

During operation

Keep an eye on the change available, and get more as necessary. You should not have to ask customers for the exact amount because you're rather low on change.

It is a security risk to have too much cash in the till. In busy bars, your manager will ask you to open the till, and in your view collect most of the notes, any cheques and credit card vouchers and put them in a bag with the till number or your name. The filled bags are kept in the safe (the process is repeated as necessary) and counted at the end of your shift.

Some bars have a note safe bolted to the bar counter. It can only be opened with a key (which the manager or publican will keep). A few £5, £10 and perhaps one £20 will be kept in the cash drawer, all other notes being put straight into the note safe.

When you are putting money paid by customers in the till, put the coins and notes in their proper compartments. This makes it easier to find the change you need, and reduces the risk of giving the wrong value coin or note by mistake. Notes and cheques should all be facing the same direction, and the same way up.

Closing down

After taking out the float you started with, the total value of cash, cheques, etc. in the till, plus any that have been put in the safe during your shift, should agree with the till reading for total sales. You may be asked to check and count this with your manager, who will keep a record of the total and any differences with the till reading.

What your employer does about differences will be explained to you. Differences can arise because customers were given too much or too little change, or some orders were not rung up properly on the till. Occasional discrepancies may be accepted, but repeated problems will not. If all the barstaff use the one till and one cash drawer, everyone will be under suspicion.

Once emptied at the end of a session, the cash drawer is usually left open. Should someone break into the bar after closing, it will be obvious that there is no cash in the till to steal.

Dealing with payments

No one likes mistakes over money. They arise from carelessness or a genuine misunderstanding. Unfortunately, customers, colleagues and your employer may suspect dishonesty.

Suspicions are less likely when each step of the transaction is clear and easy to follow.

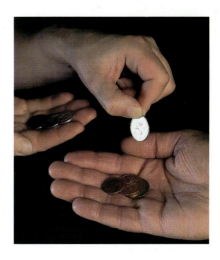

Be careful to give customers the correct change.

How much customers are being asked to pay

When the order is for a standard item, and the prices are well displayed in the bar, you can assume customers know the price. But if you are offering alternatives, something special for the customer (e.g. a double portion of chips), or selling a more expensive item, you must be careful to tell customers the price, or point to the specials board where the price is stated, or offer a menu or drinks list that gives descriptions and prices.

If you feel the customer has asked for something that will cost a lot more than he or she might expect, find some excuse to clarify what is being ordered. In doing so, you can mention the price, e.g. 'We have two very good malt whiskies, a single malt which is excellent value at £3, or a 20 year old at £5'.

How the calculation was arrived at

Bills presented to customers in the restaurant or cocktail bar are usually itemised, so that customers can check prices of individual items against what they were served, and any extras such as service charge. If customers query whether they have to pay the service charge, perhaps because they feel the service was unsatisfactory, get your manager to take over. The customer does have the right to refuse, but it is not an easy situation to deal with.

To check prices of individual items in a pub, customers would have to watch you ring up the charges on the till. Whether or not they do this, pub customers are more likely to query the amount when you ask for payment. You can put their mind at rest by stating the price of each drink and if necessary making the addition a second time, in their hearing. If the customers do not understand English well, write down the prices and total.

You may feel nervous about remembering the prices in a face-to-face situation like this. Making mistakes, or appearing uncertain, may make the customer suspicious that you have overcharged. Get a copy of the price list – that will reassure the customers and help your memory.

What change is due

Confusion often arises (or is created) because of doubt about the value of the note handed over by the customer. To help your own memory, and make it clear to the customer that you are not likely to be confused or mistaken:

- state the value of the note when the customer hands it to you, e.g. 'That's £20 you've given me, thank you', or 'Change for £20 coming up'

- stand the note above the cash drawer (in the clip if there is one) while you count the change

- count the change to the customer, working up from the cost of the order to the value of the note handed over, e.g. '£2.80 (the cost of the drinks), £3 (as you hand over a 20p), £4 and £5 (as you hand over two £1 coins), your change for £5, thank you.'

Ideally, you should not put the customer's note in the cash drawer and close the till until you have given the change to the customer. If all is well, close the till. If there is a query, the note is still in view, and the customer will find it difficult to argue that he or she gave you a higher value note.

But if you have to move away from and perhaps turn your back on the till to give the change to the customer, it is unwise to leave the note out, or cash drawer open.

Reporting errors and problems

The sooner you tell your manager of a mistake you have made, or a problem which has arisen, the greater the chance of it being sorted out. It is more difficult at the end of the day, or some days later, trying to explain why the cash in the till was short, or why a transaction went wrong. Delaying such explanations might suggest you were planning on the error going unnoticed.

If the customer complains before you have said anything to your manager, you put your manager in a more difficult situation than is necessary. Instead of being ready to explain why the problem occurred and put matters right, your manager will get the customer's viewpoint first. This may be to your disadvantage. Your manager will have to ask for time to investigate the problem, and meanwhile the customer is left dissatisfied.

Being polite and helpful to customers

Dealt with in your usual polite, helpful way, taking payment will form a natural part of your other exchanges with customers, greeting them, serving their order, etc. But because of people's attitudes to it, money has much potential for difficulty and ill-feeling.

To reduce the risk of customers taking offence:

- always say 'please' when asking for the money and 'thank you' when given it

- be ready to explain the bill if customers look puzzled or worried

- give customers who get their bill at the table, a chance to study it

- count the change into the customer's hand, on to the counter or table, or present it on a plate – whichever seems most acceptable to the customer

- give the change promptly – particularly in a restaurant or bar where customers pay at the table and you have to take the money to the till. Delays suggest you are hoping to keep the change as a tip

- when checking notes for forgery, and lists of credit cards which have been stolen/withdrawn, do so discreetly. If the customer queries what or why you are checking, give a reason that can't be challenged, e.g. 'the banks have asked us to take more care'

- write the total on credit card vouchers – leaving it open (for a tip) irritates many customers

- if authorisation on a card is refused, tell the customer discreetly, if possible out of the hearing of other people in the customer's party

- when the bill is for a couple, present it to the woman if she has booked the table, ordered for both people, etc. (indications that she is entertaining the man)

- for groups of people where you do not know who the host is, or the bill is being shared, place it at the centre of the table.

Some customers like to show off with their money. Beware it is not a front, designed to distract you from taking the standard precautions, e.g. requiring a cheque guarantee card, or getting authorisation on payments by card.

If customers query the amount charged or their change, do not take offence. Respect their right to do so. You may have made a mistake, or it may be the customer's poor numerical ability, poor understanding of English, or unfamiliarity with British currency.

Do not rush customers with sight difficulties. Offers to help can be appreciated, but the customer may worry that you are trying to take advantage of his or her disability. If your offer to help is accepted, give the customer a chance to check each coin and note (which can be done by feel and weight) before finally handing it over. When you return the change, identify the value of each coin and note so the person can put them away safely, e.g. notes folded in a particular way.

Forms of payment

In pubs and bars, customers have to pay for their drinks at the time they receive them. It is illegal to give credit. Regular customers cannot pay for their drinks at the end of the week, as they might do for milk deliveries.

If the bar is in a restaurant or hotel, the charge for the drinks can be added on to the customer's meal or accommodation bill.

Cash

The main risk is from counterfeit money. Small businesses like pubs are favourite targets, because it is assumed the staff will not check for forged notes, especially if a time is chosen when they are very busy. To reduce the risk, some publicans refuse to serve customers wanting to pay with £50 notes – as these notes are legal tender, the argument is that the customer is being refused, not the money.

Forged notes are worthless. The police will keep them as evidence and to help prosecute the people involved. But the business will not get compensation and it takes a lot of drink sales to make up the profit on a £20 or £50 note which proves to be a forgery.

Suspected forgeries

If you suspect a note is forged (see illustration), ask the customer to wait while your manager comes to check properly. It may help to say that there have been a number of problems recently and you have instructions to get the manager every time a £20 or £50 note is presented – whether or not this is true.

The situation is not easy. You want to avoid:

- embarrassing the customer unnecessarily – he or she may not know the note is forged

- making a mistake – your suspicions may be wrong

- losing money for the business – by not acting on your suspicions.

If your manager is not near, get a colleague to call him or her, or use a telephone or the emergency bell. Wait with the customer and apologise for the delay. Keep the suspect note in your hand, in view of the customer. If you leave the customer's sight with the note, you could be accused of changing it. If you give the note back, and it is a forgery, the customer and the note are likely to disappear.

note feels crisp, not limp, waxy or shiny

thread embedded in paper

serial number (horizontally or vertically)

colours clear and distinct

printing sharp, well-defined, no blurred edges

watermark visible when held up to light

Watermarks
Bank of England:
The Queen
Bank of Scotland:
Sir Walter Scott
Clydesdale Bank:
sailing ships
Royal Bank of Scotland:
Lord Islay

Partially-sighted symbols
on Bank of England notes

○ £5   ■ £20

◇ £10   ▲ £50

Travellers' cheques

Pubs and bars which are popular with tourists and business people from outside the UK will usually accept these. They are equivalent to cash, but more secure as the person using them will be refunded if they are stolen. The value will be in £ Sterling, US $ or the currency of the country that the visitor has come from. The customer is asked to sign the cheque a second time, before payment is accepted (see checklist on page 99).

Sales incentive vouchers and cards

These encourage customers to spend more – typically in the restaurant. Handing over the voucher or producing the card gives the customer certain items free, or a reduction off the whole bill. Conditions may be set down, e.g. two adults must pay full price, and then the meals for up to four accompanying children are half price.

Luncheon Vouchers are accepted as payment for food in some pubs and restaurants. Purchases over the value of the voucher(s) must be paid in cash. It is not in the customer's interest to purchase items less than the voucher's value, since you cannot give change. Check that the voucher has not expired.

Cheques

In some pubs, only the publican decides whether or not to accept a cheque. This avoids problems arising from barstaff accepting a cheque without a valid cheque guarantee card and the customer has insufficient funds, or the cheque comes from a stolen cheque book, or the cheque was wrongly filled out. In any case, as cheques have to be paid into a bank account, it takes a few days to clear payment, and there is a per-transaction charge.

In pubs which serve food, and in wine and cocktail bars where the average bill is quite high, cheques may be accepted. The customer must produce a cheque guarantee card. Provided the amount is not more than the limit printed on the card (£50, sometimes £100 or £250), and conditions for use are met, the bank will honour the cheque.

The disadvantage of cheques is that the bill for food and drinks for a party of people will come to more than a £50 cheque guarantee card limit. This means asking customers to pay the balance in cash or taking a business risk, as some shops and supermarkets do. The customer is asked to produce a driver's licence, other cards, or some identification, and to write his or her address on the reverse of the cheque.

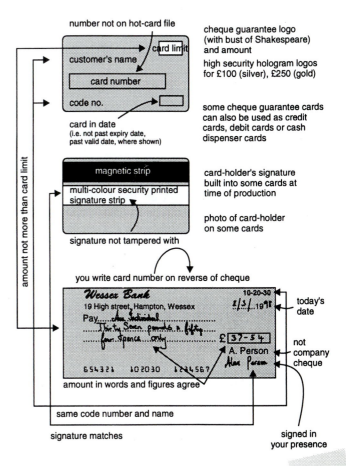

number not on hot-card file

cheque guarantee logo (with bust of Shakespeare) and amount

high security hologram logos for £100 (silver), £250 (gold)

some cheque guarantee cards can also be used as credit cards, debit cards or cash dispenser cards

customer's name

card number

code no.

card limit

card in date
(i.e. not past expiry date, past valid date, where shown)

amount not more than card limit

magnetic strip

multi-colour security printed signature strip

signature not tampered with

card-holder's signature built into some cards at time of production

photo of card-holder on some cards

you write card number on reverse of cheque

Wessex Bank
19 High street, Hampton, Wessex
10-20-30
1/3/.199?

today's date

Pay ...
Thirty Seven pounds & fifty four pence only

£ 37-54

A. Person

not company cheque

654321   102030   1234567

amount in words and figures agree

same code number and name

signature matches

signed in your presence

Cards

Many hotels and restaurants, as well as bars and pubs with restaurants and accommodation, accept various 'plastic' cards. Many customers like to pay in this way. They don't have to carry a lot of cash and get other advantages depending on the type of card:

- *credit card*, e.g. Access and Barclaycard – all the customer's payments can be settled once a month with one cheque, or the repayment to the credit card company spread over time – although interest is charged and a minimum amount must be paid each month

- *charge card*, e.g. American Express or Diner's Club – gives the convenience of settling all payments once a month but with no extended credit

- *debit card*, e.g. Connect or Switch – the amount is immediately taken out of the customer's bank account. Some customers prefer this. Unlike a cheque, the transaction is verified by the bank as it is made (usually automatically), so there is no need for a £50 or £100 limit. Provided there are sufficient funds in the customer's account, the transaction can be for any sum.

Customers may earn bonus points, Air Miles or similar incentives through using their card. Some credit cards earn money for charity each time they are used. These are called *affinity cards*, and those who benefit include Oxfam, the National Trust, as well as charitable organisations that the cardholder has a connection with, e.g. professional association, trade union, university or college they studied at.

When making the agreement to accept a particular card, and on a regular basis thereafter, the business has to pay the card company a fee. The business does not get the full amount paid by the customer (because of the card company's commission). Card companies are anxious for their cards to be widely accepted, and some offer incentives and marketing support to businesses.

Businesses which do a lot of card transactions have an electronic machine which reads the information recorded on the black band on the back of the card. Being linked to the card company's computer, an immediate check is made with the customer's account number. If credit is available, the transaction goes ahead.

With a manual machine, the card company will set a limit which can be accepted (typically in the range £50 to £100). Above this, authority for the transaction must be obtained by telephoning the card company.

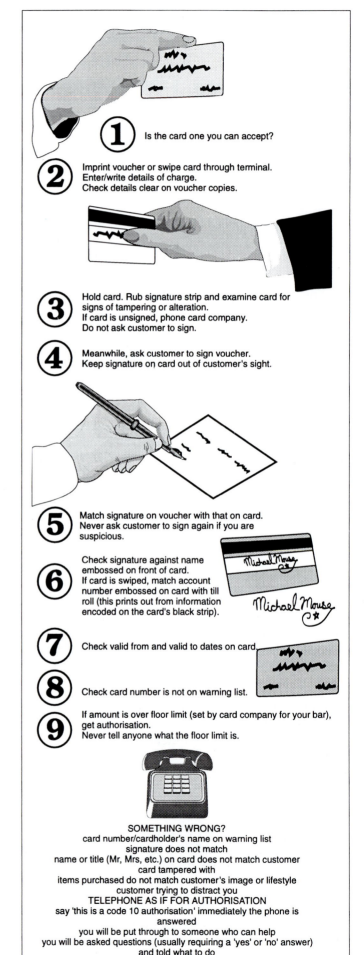

(1) Is the card one you can accept?

(2) Imprint voucher or swipe card through terminal. Enter/write details of charge. Check details clear on voucher copies.

(3) Hold card. Rub signature strip and examine card for signs of tampering or alteration. If card is unsigned, phone card company. Do not ask customer to sign.

(4) Meanwhile, ask customer to sign voucher. Keep signature on card out of customer's sight.

(5) Match signature on voucher with that on card. Never ask customer to sign again if you are suspicious.

(6) Check signature against name embossed on front of card. If card is swiped, match account number embossed on card with till roll (this prints out from information encoded on the card's black strip).

(7) Check valid from and valid to dates on card.

(8) Check card number is not on warning list.

(9) If amount is over floor limit (set by card company for your bar), get authorisation. Never tell anyone what the floor limit is.

SOMETHING WRONG?
card number/cardholder's name on warning list
signature does not match
name or title (Mr, Mrs, etc.) on card does not match customer
card tampered with
items purchased do not match customer's image or lifestyle
customer trying to distract you
TELEPHONE AS IF FOR AUTHORISATION
say 'this is a code 10 authorisation' immediately the phone is answered
you will be put through to someone who can help
you will be asked questions (usually requiring a 'yes' or 'no' answer)
and told what to do

Taking payment

Some tills only add up the items sold. Others tell you what change is due. Some have pre-set keys or codes for each drink, which automatically enter the price. Some record who handled the transaction, the time and date, the number of customers in the party, etc.

Another name for automated tills is EPOS, which stands for electronic point of sales systems. These may be linked to the bar control system, comparing the numbers of each drink sold with stock issues, and producing detailed sales information.

General procedure for taking cash payment, using a till

1 Enter the price of each item that the customer has ordered, or use the pre-set key or drink code.

2 When two or more of the same item is ordered, enter the price for one item, then use the multiplication key followed by the number ordered.

3 When all the items are entered, press the total. Tell the customer what this is.

4 Enter the value of the money given to you by the customer, and press the key to tell you what change is due, if any.

5 Count the change out into your hand.

6 Count the change to the customer, working up from the cost of the drinks to the amount you were given.

In some pubs, barstaff calculate the cost of the drinks in their head (or on paper), ask for the amount due, then enter the total on the till, get change, etc.

Taking payment for food

When customers are ordering a meal and drinks from their table, it is usual to ask them to pay at the end of the meal. A hand-written bill might be prepared. The details, or the separate totals for food and drink are entered in the till once payment has been received.

If food is ordered or collected from the bar counter or a self-service buffet, payment is usually required at the time of ordering or collection. Ring up the cost of the items ordered on the till. As required, give the customer a receipt or a numbered ticket, so that the food can be delivered to the right table when it is ready.

Dealing with errors

If you make an error, e.g. ringing up £17 instead of £1.70, it is usually best to cancel (or *void*) the transaction and start again. Check with your manager how such problems are dealt with.

There will also be rules about opening the till to give change (usually discouraged), and what to do if a customer says one of the drinks was not ordered, after you have served it and rung up the amount.

CHECK **T**list
Taking payment

✔ close cash drawer after each transaction

✔ be clear to customers what they are to pay

✔ be ready to explain how the charge was arrived at

✔ be polite, say please and thank you at each step

✔ keep the cash drawer tidy

✔ ask for more change before you run out

✔ tell your manager if you make a mistake

by cash

✔ state the value of the note the customer gives you

✔ check notes for forgeries

✔ keep note outside the cash till until you have counted the change

✔ count change back to the customer

by cheque

✔ cheque details correct and customer produces a valid cheque guarantee card (see illustration)

✔ only accept one cheque per transaction

✔ cheque does not carry words 'not to be used with a cheque guarantee card'

✔ card returned to customer, cheque put in till

by travellers' cheque

✔ date and payee details correct

✔ customer signs cheque in your presence

✔ this signature matches other signature on cheque

✔ signature checked with passport/other identification

✔ customer given change if value of cheque higher than amount due

✔ cheque put in till, passport returned

by card

✔ card is valid and details are correct (see illustration)

✔ authorisation code imprinted/written on voucher

✔ card returned to customer with customer copy of voucher

✔ carbon sheets from vouchers torn up in view of customer

1 What must you check when getting the till ready at the start of your shift?

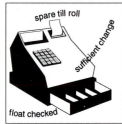

2 If you run out of change during service, what has gone wrong? What problems will be caused? What can you do to reduce these?

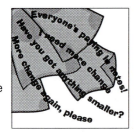

3 What mistakes might explain why the amount of money in the till at the end of service is a) too much, b) too little?

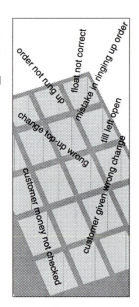

4 What steps can be taken to reduce the loss which would occur if the till was robbed a) during service, b) after closing?

5 Give the main points you should check when accepting payment a) in cash, b) by cheque, c) by card.

6 What do you do if there is a problem with what the customer has given you as payment? What special points should you consider if it is a) a forged note, b) a stolen cheque or credit card, c) you are asked to retain the card when seeking authorisation, d) the card has expired?

7 What should you do if you a) ring up the wrong amount on the till, b) write the wrong amount on the payment voucher for a card, c) find you have got the wrong amount when counting the change back to a customer?

Use this to check your progress against the performance criteria.

Element 1

Maintain the payment point

Deal with customers in a polite and helpful manner ☐ PC1

Get equipment, cash, etc. and stationery ready for use ☐ PC2

Maintain payment point during service ☐ PC3

Get cash etc. available for collection during service ☐ PC4

Inform customers politely and promptly of any delays ☐ PC5

Close down the payment point ☐ PC6

Deal with unexpected situations effectively & inform appropriate people ☐ PC7

△ Discrepancy in payment or change, suspected fraud

Prioritise and carry out your work in an organised, efficient and safe manner ☐ PC8

Element 2

Deal with payments

Deal with customers in a polite and helpful manner ☐ PC1

Enter information into payment point correctly ☐ PC2

Inform customer of the payment amount ☐ PC3

△ Cash, cheques, credit cards, cash equivalents

Acknowledge and if necessary validate receipt of payment ☐ PC4

Place payment in secure approved location ☐ PC5

Carry out transaction in optimum time and give confirmation to customer ☐ PC6

Deal with unexpected situations effectively & inform appropriate people ☐ PC7

Prioritise and carry out your work in an organised, efficient and safe manner ☐ PC8

Drink service from the bar

Preparing and serving drinks

Preparing and serving drinks to customers is when everything comes together ... your customer care skills ... your knowledge of hygiene, health, safety and security ... the law on who can and cannot be served alcohol ... knowing what your bar sells and how you can promote sales ... working effectively.

Dealing with customers helpfully

Many customers only have contact with you when you serve their drink. In a busy bar, you won't have time for long conversations. In any case, some customers don't want this, especially if they are with friends.

What all customers want is a look that says 'welcome, I'm pleased to see you' when they come to the bar, and a polite, helpful response when they ask for their drinks (see Section 1). If you are busy serving others, give those waiting a smile and if they are within speaking distance, say you won't be long.

Working safely

Show that you want customers to enjoy their drink safely. They can see much of what you do behind the bar. How you hold their glass, the care you take to keep drinks equipment clean, how you look, how you behave ... these all tell the customers what hygiene standards are like in your pub (see Section 2).

Who can be served alcohol

To be able to serve customers at all, your bar needs a licence. To avoid problems you must work within the licensing laws. There are strict rules on who can and cannot be served alcohol, on the times alcohol can be served, and on the measures sold (see Section 3).

Providing information on drinks

Customers get a good impression when you know what your bar sells. You won't be required to be an expert on every drink. But customers do expect you to know about the main types of drink, to offer suggestions on what they might like, and to suggest alternatives if their choice is not available (see Section 4). There is also certain information you should know yourself or at least know how to obtain. This includes the prices of drinks, the quantities they are available in, their main ingredients and their alcoholic strength.

Hospitality

1 Did the barstaff acknowledge waiting customers and attend to them as soon as possible?
2 Were the barstaff quick, efficient, pleasant, helpful?
3 Did the barstaff confirm the total cost of your drinks before your money was taken?
4 Were you thanked by the barstaff on completion of your order?
5 Were the barstaff helpful when you placed your order, e.g. if you ordered a pint of lager, were you offered a choice?
6 Do the staff appear to give equally good treatment to all customers at all times?
7 Did anyone acknowledge your departure by saying goodbye or thank you when you left?

Quality

1 Was all glassware polished and at correct temperature?
2 Was your order well presented with appropriate accompaniments?
3 Was the beer bright, clear, with a good head? Did it taste sound?
4 Was the temperature of the drink correct?
5 Was it served in an appropriate glass?

appearance

clean and tidy with no weeds
nd around the building edges?
arden neat, well kept and grass
ee from litter?
hanging baskets blooming and
ants in good condition/free of dust?
external signs clear and clean?
xternal lighting working?
windows clean throughout?

omfort

emperature and ambience on
he building?
r areas clean and tidy?
eet smelling, clean and tidy and
well stocked with soap and toilet paper?
4 Hand dryers working, hand towels stocked and all toilet doors lockable?
5 All light fittings and lamps clean, in use and in good working order?
6 All AWP's and cigarette machines in working order, clean and switched on?
7 Background music and/or juke audible at appropriate level?
8 All air filters and extraction fans clean and in use where applicable?

Standards of customer care and service are seen by many employers as the key to increasing sales. Mystery drinker and diner surveys are one of the methods used to monitor standards. Each 'yes' answer to this questionnaire earns 3 points in the hospitality section, 2 in the quality section, and 1 for the remaining questions.

Promoting drinks

Suggesting what drinks customers might enjoy promotes sales in your bar. You can also do this at other contact points you have with customers – telling them about special offers, new drinks, drinks for special occasions, etc. (see Section 5).

Dispensing and serving drinks

What your customers want is reflected in the drinks available in your bar, the methods for dispensing them, the glasses and other equipment for serving them.

The small pub serving the local community will be a very different operation from the bar of an exclusive hotel. In the pub there will probably be a choice of glasses for serving pints of draught, but only one type of liqueur glass or possibly no liqueurs at all. In the hotel bar you will have a wider range of glasses for spirits, wines, liqueurs, cocktails, etc., several different garnishes, but perhaps no draught beer and few pint glasses.

There will be differences too, in what you serve customers who ask for a type of drink but do not name the brand. Many pubs and bars have preferred brands which you should serve when a customer asks for a whisky for example, but does not name the type. In other bars, you would always tell such a customer what brands were available, and perhaps the characteristics of each.

Serving temperature

There is a generally accepted serving temperature for many drinks. Treat this as a starting point rather than a firm rule. Customers sometimes have their own, very different preferences which you should do your best to meet. New drinks as well as different ways of enjoying old favourites are adding other possibilities.

The general rules are (for variations and details of temperature ranges, see illustration):

- British bitters and traditional cider are enjoyed slightly cool, lager and other types of cider cold. Many customers in the north of Britain prefer their beer a few degrees cooler than those in the south

- imported beers, especially those made in hot climates, are mostly served very cold

- spirits are served at bar temperature. The temperature is adjusted by the customer's choice of accompaniments – ice, water (normally at bar temperature), lemonade, cola, etc. (chilled). Customers may warm cognac by holding the glass in their hands. A few bars use special glass warmers

- red wine is served at bar temperature, white and rosé wine chilled, sparkling wine and Champagne well chilled.

In-line chillers are used to cool draught beer and other drinks dispensed in bulk. Bottled drinks should be placed on chilled shelves and refrigerated display cabinets in good time to reach the right temperature before service (see page 85). Where necessary, a bottle of white or sparkling wine can be chilled in about 20 minutes – place in an ice bucket filled with ice and water.

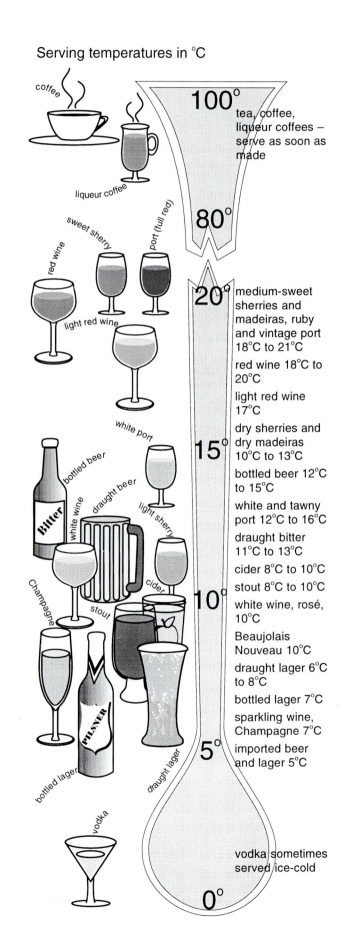

Serving temperatures in °C

100° tea, coffee, liqueur coffees – serve as soon as made

80°

20° medium-sweet sherries and madeiras, ruby and vintage port 18°C to 21°C

red wine 18°C to 20°C

light red wine 17°C

dry sherries and dry madeiras 10°C to 13°C

15° bottled beer 12°C to 15°C

white and tawny port 12°C to 16°C

draught bitter 11°C to 13°C

cider 8°C to 10°C

stout 8°C to 10°C

10° white wine, rosé, 10°C

Beaujolais Nouveau 10°C

draught lager 6°C to 8°C

bottled lager 7°C

sparkling wine, Champagne 7°C

5° imported beer and lager 5°C

vodka sometimes served ice-cold

0°

coffee, liqueur coffee, sweet sherry, port (full red), red wine, light red wine, white port, bottled beer, Bitter, white wine, draught beer, light sherry, cider, Champagne, stout, bottled lager, PILSNER, draught lager, vodka

The accompaniments should be what the customer wants. And they should make the drink look good.

A tidy, organised back bar makes your job easier and looks good from the customer's side of the counter.

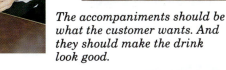

Drink accompaniments

Accompaniments serve one or more purposes:

- *ice* – to chill the drink and to give it an attractive appearance – but as the ice melts it dilutes the drink, so it is not added to drinks like beer and wine. Some customers do not like ice with mineral water, since the ice is made from tap water

- *water* – to dilute the drink without adding any particular flavour. Some whisky drinkers prefer soda water, some a natural mineral water

- *cordials* – to add flavour to the drink and sometimes colour

- *food garnishes for drinks* – to add colour, shape and flavour. Standard items include slices or half slices of lemon and orange, and maraschino cherries. Special garnishes include sliced cucumber, lime, kiwi fruit, apple and pineapple, twists of the outer peel of lemon, lime and orange, olives, leaves and sprigs of fresh mint and borage

- *decorative items* – to add novelty and interest, e.g. long plastic stirrers or spoons, paper umbrellas and sparklers. As customers often keep these as a memento of their visit, they are a form of advertising when marked with the name or logo of the bar

- *for hot drinks* – white and brown sugar, speciality coffee sugars, diet sugars, milk and cream.

Learn the accompaniments that suit particular drinks served in your bar (see Section 4). Then you know what customers expect to be offered. If customers want something different from the usual, remember it is their drink to enjoy as they wish. Never insist on putting ice and lemon in gin and tonic, for example.

Service equipment

Keep service equipment clean, ready to use and in its proper place (see page 112). This gives customers a good impression of the bar. The range will include:

- *bottle openers* – the only safe way to open bottles of beers and minerals which are closed with a crown top (those with screw tops can be opened by hand). If the opener is fixed to the bar counter, there will be a container to catch the tops. If bottle tops fall on the floor, remove them before they cause someone to slip

- *corkscrews* – to pull the cork out from a bottle of still wine or a vintage port. Besides the various hand-held types, there are bench-mounted models

- *spirit measures (Optics)* – to dispense spirits and sometimes fortified wines (Optic is the registered trade name of the makers). For whisky, gin, vodka and rum, the measure must be a government certified type, to deliver an exact 25 ml or 35 ml (see page 107). Many bars use a similar measure for brandy, and one which delivers 50 ml for popular fortified wines, e.g. vermouth. These do not have to be certified models. Clean spirit measures regularly with the cleaning agent made for this purpose

- *thimble measures* – made of stainless steel or silver plate, to hold an exact measure when filled to the brim, e.g. 35 ml. Measures used for whisky, gin, vodka and rum must be government-stamped. Clean thimble measures between use, so you do not spoil the drink's flavour with whatever was last poured into the measure

- *pourers* – inserted into the neck of the bottle, these help direct and control the flow of liquid into the glass. Some types do not seal the contents of the bottle, so are more suitable for fast-selling cordials and fruit syrups etc. Some types of pourer deliver a controlled quantity of liquid, e.g. lime cordial, but are not made to the strict specifications required for government-certified measures

- *knives and chopping boards* – for preparing drink garnishes, e.g. slicing lemons and oranges. There are boards made for bar use, which are smaller than those found in kitchens, and are fitted with containers for the sliced fruit

- *ice buckets and tongs* – to serve ice for customers' drinks, often placed on the bar counter and usually insulated so the ice will keep longer

- *trays* – to carry drinks to customers, and to help clear empty glasses, etc. from tables. Clean trays regularly so they do not become sticky

- *coasters and drip mats* – to put glasses on, on the bar counter or table. Often used to advertise particular drinks or the bar itself (i.e. if overprinted with the name or logo). Drip mats collect the moisture which forms on glasses containing very cold drinks, preventing it from collecting on the table surface and dripping over the customer. Replace coasters and drip mats which are stained or torn.

Glassware

Many drinks have to be served in a particular glass. Sometimes, you may be able to offer customers a choice, e.g. a balloon or straight glass for brandy. The decision on what glass to use for each drink is made by the publican or management, taking account of:

- practical considerations – how much the glass costs, how easy it is to clean and store, how it will stand up to bar use, etc.

- tradition – certain styles of glass have become established as appropriate for particular drinks, e.g. a stemmed glass for wine

- expectations of customers – when customers are paying high prices for their drinks, they expect a finer glass, e.g. a cut crystal glass for spirits

- how the quantity of drink sold is measured – for draught beer and cider, wine sold by the glass and sometimes sherry and liqueurs, the amount served can be measured by filling a particular glass to the top, or to the maker's capacity mark. If the glass is not used, then beer and cider must be dispensed from a metered pump, and glasses of wine by using a measure (see page 108).

Service style

When you are serving customers *at the bar*, you can ask if they would like ice as you pour the drink, or how much tonic you should pour, etc. If their order is for a bottle of beer, they see you fill the glass and know it is from the right bottle.

If you are serving drinks *at the table*, get the information you need from the customers at the time you take their order (see pages 113 to 115). If mixers are dispensed, ask how much tonic etc. they would like. If mixers are in bottles, take the bottle on the tray to the table. If this is the practice in your bar, pour some for the customer and leave the bottle. Usually bottled beers are poured at the table, to give a more personal level of service.

Glasses

A fine glass adds to the pleasure of a fine drink.

For draught beer, a handled mug is more popular with older customers. Younger customers prefer a straight glass.

Some regulars have their own tankard behind the bar of their local. The beer should be dispensed into a government-stamped glass and then transferred into the tankard at the customer's request.

For bottled beers, spirits and some minerals, use a glass that will hold its destined contents with comfort, and look good.

Finally, nothing lowers the tone of a house more than serving a drink in a chipped or cracked glass. They are both dangerous and unhygienic. Always watch out for damaged glasses and withdraw them from use at once.

Illustrations of glasses with thanks to John Artis Limited

Draught beer

This is dispensed into the glass at the bar counter. The quantity – including the froth if it is a beer served with a head – must not be less than a pint or half-pint (see box) unless it is part of a mixed drink, e.g. a shandy. How this is measured depends on the beer dispense system, and decisions the publican or manager has made about the sort of glasses to use for beer. Some bars have more than one combination, so you have to know which glasses to use for each type of beer.

1 Get a clean pint or half-pint glass. Check if the customer would prefer a straight or handled glass (if available).

2 If customers ask for their glass to be refilled, thank them and say it is no trouble to use a clean glass. Refilling a glass is likely to spread bacteria, e.g. staphylococci from the customer's lips on to the dispense nozzle.

3 Holding the glass by the base or the handle, place it under the dispense nozzle. Tilt the glass to an angle of about 45° so that the beer runs down the side. The nozzle should be close to, but not touching the glass.

4 If you are using a beer engine, pull the handle towards you in one steady movement. Stop when the handle has gone as far as it will go, or the glass is full. Otherwise, fully open the tap, or push the button or switch.

5 Straighten up the glass after it is half full. The aim is to get the right head on the beer. To get more head, pull the glass away from the nozzle so that the beer falls a greater distance and into the centre of the glass. With practice, you will find the best time to tilt the glass for each beer.

6 When the glass is full, or the beer has stopped flowing from a metered dispense, it is ready to serve.

Tell your manager if, in spite of the care you have taken, the beer is very frothy or lively, or has sediment in it. There are several possible causes for problems like this (see pages 73 and 81).

Some pubs use a long nose (or *swan neck*) on the beer dispense. Hold the glass straight, with the nose not quite touching the bottom of the glass. When the glass is nearly full, pull the glass away so that the nose is just under the surface of the beer as the glass is filled to the brim or line. Some disapprove of this method of dispense, because of the risk of spreading bacteria if a clean glass is not used every time.

If you are dispensing the first pint or half-pint of draught beer of the day, or since the beer line was cleaned, examine the appearance carefully. This is an extra precaution and there should not be a problem – checking that the beer tastes and looks good is part of the procedure for cleaning the beer line and connecting a new cask (see page 77).

Beer with soft drinks (i.e. shandy) or cordials

Mixtures of draught beer with soft drinks or cordials can no longer be described on the price list or drinks menu as a pint or half-pint (because of the change to metric quantities). As the beer is mixed, it does not have to be an exact measure, so you do not need to use a government-stamped glass. But because this is what customers are used to, it is likely that your pub will continue to serve the equivalent of pints and half-pints, describing them as 'large' and 'small'.

Some pubs offer one type of shandy – lager with lemonade. Or the customer is given a choice of lager, mild or bitter and lemonade or gingerbeer. Dispense the beer into a pint glass or half-pint glass, filling the glass to about one-third full. Top up with the lemonade or gingerbeer, pouring it down the inside of the glass carefully to prevent too much frothing.

Add cordials to the top of the beer, so they gradually mix through the liquid. Popular mixtures are lime or blackcurrant juice with lager, and blackcurrant with Guinness.

Serving draught beer

There are three legally-acceptable ways of measuring the quantity of draught beer (see Section 3):

1 From a beer engine or free flow tap into a government-stamped glass that holds at least one pint or half a pint when full to the brim – a *brim-measure glass*.
  The head on the beer is an integral part of the drink, provided that it is not excessive. A measure of draught beer should contain at least 95% liquid after the collapse of the head.
  If at the time of service the quantity of beer does not satisfy the customer (because of the head), and the customer asks for a top-up, this should be served.

2 From a beer engine or free flow tap into a government-stamped glass that holds exactly one pint or half a pint when full to the line printed on the glass – a *line measure glass*.
  Sufficient beer should be dispensed so as the ensure that if the head collapsed, the liquid in the glass would be level with the line.

3 From a *metered dispense* system – which pumps the beer from the cask or keg to the bar, delivering an exact pint or half pint – into an *oversized glass*. This has no government stamp and holds slightly more than a pint or half-pint.

Bottled beer

Your pub may use particular glasses for certain bottled beers. The glass should hold slightly more than the bottle, to allow room for the head.

1 Open the bottle slowly – to let the gas escape gently and to avoid damage to the neck of the bottle.

2 Hold the bottle in one hand, by its centre, turned so that the customer can see the label. Hold the glass in the other hand, by the base or stem. Hold bottle and glass at chest height, and face the customer.

3 For beers which may otherwise form a large head, hold the glass at an angle of about 45°. Put the neck of the bottle just inside the glass. The bottle and glass should not touch. Tilt the bottle so the beer runs down the inside of the glass, steadily and without stopping.

4 Gradually bring the glass upright as it fills. Keep the neck of the bottle out of the beer. If you want more of a head, raise the bottle above the beer and pour into the centre of the glass. If too much head forms, apologise to the customer, put the glass and bottle down for a few minutes, then continue pouring.

5 When you have filled the glass, place it on the bar counter for the customer to pick up. Put the empty bottle away – some types are returnable (see page 69).

In some bars, the opened bottle and glass are given to the customer to pour the beer. Or just the bottle – it has become fashionable among some customers to drink from the bottle. But if other customers find this unacceptable, the manager may decide that all bottled beers must be poured into glasses. You may need to tell the customer that this is a house rule and if this is not accepted, to get your manager to deal with the situation.

Draught and bottled beers mixed

Some customers like a mix of part-draught, part-bottled beer, e.g. black and tan (Guinness and mild). Pour half a pint of draught beer into a pint glass, then top up with the bottled beer. If some beer remains in the bottle after the glass is full, give the customer the bottle to empty later. Some customers prefer to pour the bottled beer themselves.

The half-pint of draught has to be an exact measure. It will be, if you are using a metered dispense, or a pint glass with a half-pint mark. Otherwise, dispense the draught into a government-stamped half-pint glass, then carefully pour it into a pint glass and add the bottled beer.

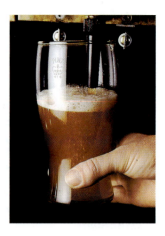

Above: *pulling a pint of cask conditioned beer into a government-stamped glass.*

Right: *keg beer from a metered dispense.*

Move the glass into an upright position as it fills. Keep the neck of the bottle away from the rim of the glass.

Bottled beer with sediment

Like cask conditioned beer (see page 80), some types of beer go through the final stages of maturing in the bottle. To avoid sediment getting into the glass:

• handle the bottle gently and keep it upright as much as possible, so that the sediment remains undisturbed at the bottom of the bottle

• hold the bottle and glass at eye level when pouring, so you can see the beer moving through the neck of the bottle

• stop pouring as soon as you see sediment enter the neck.

Done carefully, you will leave only a small amount of beer in the bottle.

Cider (draught and bottled)

Draught and bottled ciders are poured in a similar way to draught and bottled beers. Cider does not produce a head of foam.

Spirits

In most bars, bottles of the most popular spirits (whisky, gin, vodka, brandy and perhaps rum) hang upside down from brackets fixed to a bar shelf, or a free-standing bracket that holds two, three or four bottles. In the neck of each bottle is a spirit measure or Optic which dispenses the exact quantity of 25 ml or 35 ml.

1 If the customer does not say, ask what is required with the spirit (see page 47 for the most popular mixers), and whether the customer would like a single or double. If available, use a smaller glass for a spirit on its own, and a brandy balloon for cognac on its own.

2 Hold the glass at the base or by the stem, place under the spirit measure and release a single measure. Use a firm push (upwards or backwards, depending on the type of measure), and hold the glass in that position until the spirit has stopped flowing and the sight glass is empty.

3 Pull the glass away. For a double, allow the measure to refill, and push the glass against the release arm or button for a second time.

4 Add ice and any garnish (e.g. lemon slice) if required. In some bars, the ice is put in the glass before the spirit.

5 If a mixer is asked for, open the bottle. Pour a little into the glass, and give the bottle to the customer to add more as required. Some customers will say how much to pour. If the mixer is served from a dispense point at the bar or a hand-held gun, ask the customer how much is required. If the customer wants water (e.g. with whisky), ask how much to pour, or put a jug of water by the glass for the customer to use as required.

When the bottle is nearly empty, make sure the glass of the spirit measure is completely full before dispensing a drink, otherwise there is a chance of serving a short measure.

Using a thimble measure

There may not be a spirit measure on the bottle – if it is one sold infrequently, e.g. a malt whisky, or this is the style of service, e.g. for the bar of a small private function. In these cases use a thimble measure:

- unscrew the cap from the bottle
- place the glass on the bar counter
- pick up a single measure – hold by the base or the handle over the centre of the glass (for a double, use a double measure or pour two singles)
- carefully pour the spirit into the measure, right up to the brim
- tip the contents into the glass in one quick movement so that nothing spills
- let the measure drain before putting aside.

Spirit measures are inserted into the neck of the bottle, which is held upside down in a bracket. The chamber holds the exact quantity of spirit. This is released into the glass by pressing the side of the glass against a button, or pushing the glass upwards.

Measures and popular accompaniments

Wine by the glass

The range of wines available and how they are dispensed depends on the pattern of wine sales. In a bar specialising in wine, customers may have a choice of three or four red wines by the glass, a similar number of whites and perhaps one sparkling or Champagne.

These will be selected to please knowledgeable wine drinkers, and to offer them a range of quality and styles. The wine will be served from the bottle, kept on the bar counter or in a chiller, and recorked or restoppered between use. Special stoppers are required for sparkling wine. For still wines, some types of stopper extend the drinking life of the wine by replacing the air in the bottle with a vacuum or a special gas.

Because wine does not keep for long once the bottle has been opened, many bars restrict the choice to one or two wines of reasonable quality and value. For customers who want something different, e.g. a full-bodied red to go with their meal, there is usually a wider range sold by the bottle.

In bars where white wine by the glass is a good seller, it may be dispensed from a tap at the bar counter, connected to a bulk container in the cellar (red wine is not suited to this method). Wine display cabinets are another option, holding bottles of white wine at drinking temperature. Into the neck of each bottle, which fits through a hole in the bottom of the cabinet, is fitted a push bar or button dispense measure similar to those used on spirit bottles.

Whichever system is used, the quantity of wine served must be not less than 125 ml or 175 ml (see page 39). This can be measured by:

- filling a wine glass to the maker's capacity line – good-quality wines should then be poured into a larger glass so that the bouquet can be appreciated more fully
- dispensing the wine through a measure (fitted to the bottle or the supply line from the cellar).

Fortified wines

Where there is space, and a brand sells well, bottles of vermouth will be displayed alongside the whisky, gin, etc. fitted with measures that dispense 50 ml. Otherwise, pour the drink into a thimble measure, then into the customer's glass.

Pour sherry and port into the glass. Elgin glasses and schooners are usually filled to the top. One of these glasses can be used as a measure if you are serving sherry in a larger glass (e.g. a copita), or fill the glass to the correct level by eye (check with your manager).

Liqueurs

Fill a liqueur glass to the top, or a thimble measure (25 ml is the usual size) and pour into a larger glass. Some liqueurs can be served in special ways, e.g. Crème de Menthe on crushed ice or Tia Maria with double cream poured over the top.

Soft drinks, minerals and juices

Open the bottle or can and pour contents into a glass. If you are using a dispense point on the bar, fill the glass to the correct level (e.g. about 10 mm from the top). Some dispense systems deliver a measured quantity.

Bar drinks standards

DRINK	MEASURE	GARNISH	POPULAR ADDITIONS	SIZE OF GLASS
Mineral water	Fill glass	Ice & lime wedge		34 cl (12 oz)
Minerals	Bottle	Ice		34 cl (12 oz)
Juices	Fill glass	Ice	Lemonade, tonic	34 cl (12 oz)
Vermouths	50 ml	Ice & slice of lemon	Lemonade, soda, tonic	34 cl (12 oz)
Pernod	25 ml	Ice	Cordials, water	20 cl (7 oz)
Dubonnet	50 ml	Ice & slice of orange	Lemonade	34 cl (12 oz)
Campari	25 ml	Ice & slice of orange	Lemonade	20 cl (7 oz)
Sherry	50 ml			9 cl (3 oz)
Liqueurs	25 ml	with Sambucca serve an odd number of coffee beans and set alight		5 cl (1½ oz)
Baileys	50 ml	Ice		20 cl (7 oz)

Hot drinks

With coffee, offer white and brown sugar, milk and cream (if available). With tea, offer white sugar and milk. Some customers like a lemon slice, not milk.

Coffee and tea are best freshly made, using freshly drawn, freshly boiled water. The tea pot should be warmed first. If you are pouring the tea, give it a few minutes to infuse.

In bars, fresh coffee (i.e. not instant) is usually made by one of three methods:

- a single-serving, ready-to-use, disposable filter – place on the cup, fill with boiling water, cover with the lid, and serve to the customer. If the customer is not familiar with this method, explain that the water filters through the coffee into the cup. Once the top container is empty, the filter is put to one side, resting on the upturned lid (to catch any drips)

- a cafetière – place the coffee in the jug (check with the packet how much to use), pour on the boiling water, insert the plunger, leave for a few minutes to allow the coffee to infuse, then push down

- filter machine – place fresh filter paper in the holder, add the coffee (usually a pre-portioned pack), and return to its position. Fill the pot with cold water, empty into the top of the machine, then put on the warming plate under the filter. Do not remove the pot until the coffee has stopped dripping through the filter.

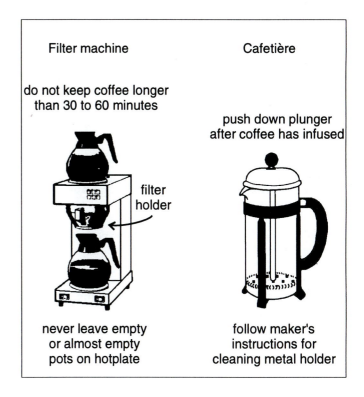

Filter machine — do not keep coffee longer than 30 to 60 minutes — filter holder — never leave empty or almost empty pots on hotplate

Cafetière — push down plunger after coffee has infused — follow maker's instructions for cleaning metal holder

Maintaining customer and service areas

Many customers like the atmosphere of a busy bar – particularly if they see the place is kept looking tidy.

Maintaining customer areas

This requires some careful judgements, so customers don't have to wait for their orders:

- use every free moment to collect glasses, empty ashtrays, etc.

- make each journey worthwhile – if you take an order to customers, return with empty glasses from nearby tables

- work as a team with your colleagues behind the bar, so that one person is not left with the less pleasant jobs to do

- let colleagues know what you are doing, so that everyone is not away from the bar clearing tables at the same time.

When you are among customers, check that all is well. Offer, if this is appropriate, to bring more drinks, or the food menu (see page 53).

Be sensitive to signs of trouble among groups of people, drug dealings, or under-age drinking (see pages 31, 32 and 33). Tell your manager about these as soon as possible.

Environmental control systems

Being busy and moving about, you may think the bar is warm enough, or too hot, perhaps. Because you like the music you may want to turn the volume up. But it is the comfort of customers that matters.

Be aware of how customers are reacting to the environment in the bar. Did you hear someone mention the loud music? Or how hot or cold it is? Or see someone trying to open a window or close the door? Check with your manager before adjusting heating or air conditioning equipment.

If your bar has mostly natural lighting during daylight, lights will have to be turned on when this fades and perhaps curtains closed. The atmosphere should be welcoming, not gloomy nor too bright.

'Eyes down for a full house' is a comment you do NOT want customers to make about your bar. What the customers are saying is that the barstaff are too scared to look up, because they know what they will see and feel they can't cope.

Notice what is going on in the bar. Do tables need clearing? Are customers ready to re-order? Are they comfortable?

When the bar is very busy, keep taking a look round the bar as you're serving. Greet each new arrival – at least with a smile or friendly nod – so the customers know that you have seen them. Make a mental note of the order in which they have arrived, so you can serve people in turn.

If you need to, ask 'Who's next, please?' If this doesn't help, work from one end of the bar to the other, serving each customer in turn. Then go back to the starting point and repeat the process. Customers will see that you are trying to handle the situation fairly, and feel reasonably confident that they will get served before too long.

Maintaining service areas

Less busy moments during service also give you the chance to:

- tidy the bar counter – emptying ashtrays, collecting glasses, wiping the surface, changing drip mats, etc.

- put away empty bottles – returnable bottles separate from other bottles in a skip or container

- dispose of rubbish – broken glass should go in the bin or a container kept specifically for that purpose

- wash and put away glasses – keeping up with the flow of dirty glasses reduces the risk of running out of a particular glass, or finding that glasses are still warm after coming out of the glasswasher (see page 91)

- restock shelves, etc. – on cold shelves and in refrigerated cabinets, put the new stock to the back, so that it has time to get chilled and stock is properly rotated (see page 85)

- replace bottles of spirits – remove from the stand, change the spirit measure to a full bottle and replace on the stand (see box)

- prepare more accompaniments – refill ice buckets and water jugs, slice extra lemons, etc.

- clean service equipment – wipe trays, wash thimble measures, empty and clean drip trays.

The label of the bottle should face the customers.

Changing a spirit measure

1 Take hold of the bottle with one hand, the spirit measure with the other. Holding them firmly, pull them towards you, away from the holder. On most stands there is a safety catch behind the spirit measure which has to be released first.

2 Turn the bottle slowly upright. Any liquid in the measure will drain back into the bottle.

3 Pull the spirit measure out of the bottle carefully. Clean thoroughly in a cleaning agent for spirit measures.

4 Open the new bottle. The seal should be intact. If it has been broken, check with your manager before proceeding.

5 Pour the remains of the old bottle (there should be very little) into the new bottle.

6 Push the spirit measure firmly, but carefully, into the new bottle.

7 Take a firm hold of the bottle with one hand, the measure with the other. Turn them slowly upside down to allow the spirit to drain into the measure.

8 Replace them in the bracket. The label of the bottle should be facing outwards. Check bottle is secure before letting go of it: screw-type safety catches must be tightened first.

9 Examine the measure to see it is not leaking.

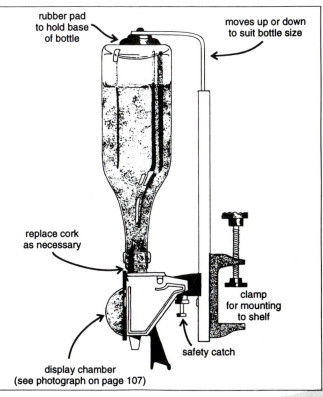

rubber pad to hold base of bottle

moves up or down to suit bottle size

replace cork as necessary

clamp for mounting to shelf

safety catch

display chamber (see photograph on page 107)

Illustration with thanks to Gaskell & Chambers Ltd

111

During the session

Unless it is a very busy session, there is time that you can use in between serving customers.

Never stand around doing nothing. There is **always** something to be done behind a bar:

- change/clean dirty ashtrays, emptying contents into a metal container
- tidy up and wipe down the counter
- tidy the back counter
- replenish the ice, lemon, etc.
- wash, dry and stock glasses
- collect glasses from customer areas
- wipe down tables
- reposition chairs
- chat to your customers
- mop up any spills
- organise product display.

Remember – serving customers takes priority over any of these tasks.

Closing the pub

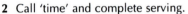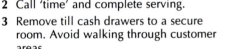

1 Call last orders.
2 Call 'time' and complete serving.
3 Remove till cash drawers to a secure room. Avoid walking through customer areas.
4 Keep customers aware of drinking-up time.
5 Check toilets and other customer areas.
6 Lock all doors, windows and gates, ensuring that fire exits are secure.

Taking customers' orders at table

In many pub restaurants, like other types of licensed restaurant, both food and drinks are brought to customers at their table. This may be your main job, or something you do as well as serving behind the bar.

Some bars provide table service of drinks for customers who do not want to go to the bar, or only offer table service, e.g. in the more expensive hotels, and some wine and cocktail bars.

The staff who serve drinks at table may collect what the customers want from barstaff. If not, you will also be involved in keeping the bar stocked and dispensing all types of drinks. In either situation, there are some tasks that:

- can only be done at the bar, e.g. dispensing draught beer
- can be done at the bar or at the table in view of the customers, e.g. pouring a bottled beer – this depends on the style of service offered
- are usually done at the table, because this is what customers expect, e.g. opening the bottle of wine ordered with a meal.

Preparing service equipment

This may include:

- *glassware* – you may have your own stock of glasses, water jugs, ashtrays, etc. Check these are clean, polished and ready for use. Throw away chipped or cracked items or put them aside if they have to be accounted for before destroying
- *trays* – to carry orders to the table, and help clear glasses, etc. which customers have finished with
- *service linen* – napkins for the presentation and opening of bottles of wine, to line the tray (in some places), and to polish glasses
- *pen/notepaper* – to write down customers' orders.

Greeting customers and taking the order

Usually customers find a table, sit down and wait for you to come and take their order. The delay should be as short as possible.

1 Welcome the customers. If this is the style, say your name and tell them you will be looking after them this afternoon/evening.

2 Offer a drinks (and food) menu if there is not one on the table. Some customers will want to order at once, perhaps because they are in a hurry, because they already know what they want, or because they are ready to make up their mind quickly when you have told them what is available. Other customers enjoy choosing what they will have. After telling them about the specials, say that you will be back as soon as they are ready to order.

3 Return when customers are ready to order. Usually you can tell this, for example, because they have put the menus back down on the table, or they are continuing with their conversation. Customers should not be kept waiting so long that you find them looking anxiously around the room, or they come over to you at another table and say they would like to order.

4 Take the order, making suggestions as appropriate and checking the details of what the customers would like, e.g. the sweet or medium house wine. So that you can give each drink to the right person when you return with the order, note on the order who is having what, e.g. 'red jumper' by the order for wine.

You may be able to greet customers as they enter the bar, help them to their seats, hand them a drinks menu and tell them about the specials.

When the bar is busy, you may find customers have sat down at a table which hasn't yet been cleared. This is not ideal, especially if there are other tables they could have gone to. But you cannot criticise customers for choosing the table they want.

Each time you move through the room fetching and serving orders, take a look at all the tables you are responsible for. Update the picture in your mind of who is sitting where. Notice what stage customers have reached. Are they ready to order? Are there empty bottles or glasses which you can clear? Might the customers want to order again? Are they about to leave? In which case you can help with the chairs, putting on coats, etc. and say goodbye and thank you.

Who can and cannot be served alcohol

As in the bar, it is against the law to serve alcohol to anyone under the age of 18 – certain drinks are exceptions if the customers are also eating a meal. But there are no legal age limits on who can be in a restaurant or areas of the bar set aside for eating food. In these areas, adults, if they wish, can buy alcoholic drinks for youngsters under the age of 18 accompanying them. (See Section 3 for more details.)

Promoting drink sales and providing information

Customers ordering their drink at the table are not able to look around the bar shelves to see what is available. The drinks list will give prices and possibly descriptions. Drink mats and tent cards on the table may promote particular drinks. There might be a display board to highlight special drinks, or describe the wines and cocktails.

What you can tell customers about drinks will often play a powerful role in what they decide to order. Listen and look for clues. Ask questions. Make suggestions. Try and match what you say to what they want (see Section 5). It irritates customers when you insist on giving what is obviously a standard sales pitch.

Drinks service at table   *Coppid Beech Hotel*

1	Approach table. Ask if ready to order.	
2	Offer alternative where appropriate.	'Would you like Booth's or Plymouth Gin, Sir/Madam?'
3	Offer appropriate accompaniment.	e.g. ice and lemon.
4	Repeat the order to guest.	To confirm that you took the order correctly.
5	Leave the table.	Don't forget to thank the guest first.
6	Print guest bill on till.	Check all items are correct before printing bill.
7	Collect drinks from dispense bar.	Use a tray.
8	Serve drinks from the right. Ladies first.	Say 'Here is your gin and tonic, Sir/Madam.'
9	Leave the table.	

10 Drink service from the bar

Serving drinks at table gives you that extra opportunity to provide personal service.

Unit 2NC9, Element 2

Serving orders at table

When you serve drinks at table you can meet all the customers in a party, not just those that come to the bar.

If you have taken the order, you should be able to give each drink to the right person. Asking 'Who is having the ...?' irritates customers who feel you should remember.

Serving drinks at table

Get as close to the table as possible before putting the drinks down. Try and do this without:

- getting between customers who are deep in conversation

- stretching over or in front of people – if someone moves suddenly and knocks you, the glass or the tray, there could be an accident.

Hold glasses by the base or the handle, your fingers well away from the rim and inside of the glass. Hold bottles by the body, not the top.

If the customers are at a table in the restaurant, place the glass on the right-hand side of each customer. If the glass has a handle, it should also be on the right so that the customer can pick up the glass more easily. If you see that a customer is left-handed, place the glasses on the left of the place setting.

Wines with food – the grape types

with fish – Sauvignon Blanc, Sauvignon/Semillon, Semillon, Chardonnay

with white meat and poultry – Semillon, Semillon/Chardonnay, Chardonnay

with red meat – Shiraz, Cabernet Sauvignon, Cabernet/Shiraz, Cabernet/Merlot, Cabernet/Malbec, Pinot Noir

with French dishes – Cabernet Sauvignon, Shiraz, Chardonnay, Sauvignon Blanc

with Italian dishes – Shiraz, Shiraz/Cabernet, Cabernet Sauvignon

with Greek dishes – Cabernet/Merlot, Sauvignon Blanc, Chardonnay, Semillon

with Indian dishes – Cabernet Sauvignon, Riesling, Dry Muscat Blanc

with Chinese dishes – Rhine Riesling, Dry Muscat Blanc

with Japanese dishes – Chardonnay, Sauvignon Blanc, Sauvignon/Semillon

with Thai dishes – Sauvignon Blanc, Sauvignon/Semillon, Riesling

with vegetarian dishes – Riesling, Dry Muscat Blanc, Semillon/Sauvignon, Pinot Noir, Cabernet Malbec, Cabernet/Merlot

with cheese – Shiraz, Cabernet Sauvignon, Cabernet/Shiraz

with desserts – late picked or botrytis styles of Riesling, Semillon, Sauvignon Blanc

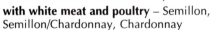

---

with thanks to the Australian Wine Bureau

Sauvignon/Semillon indicates a blend of the two varieties

Holding the tray safely

When you are able to hold the tray safely and comfortably in one hand, you can use the other hand to unload the tray. If not, put the tray down on the table, or on a nearby table if there is no space.

Unload your tray carefully, so that it does not over-balance. It may help to put bottles on the table first, and to move heavy items to the centre as you unload.

Order for serving customers

Serve women before men. Serve guests before their host and/or hostess. But if it is a woman entertaining a man, e.g. a business colleague, serve the man first. He is her guest.

In a family party or group of adults and children, serve:

- children first – otherwise they are likely to get impatient

- very elderly after children – shows respect for age

- wife before husband – even if the wife has ordered

- the person who will be paying the bill, last – even if this is a woman.

Pouring drinks at table

You give customers a more personal service if you pour their drinks into the glass at the table. This is not possible for draught beer, spirits, wine sold by the glass, minerals from bulk dispensers, cocktails, mixed drinks, etc. It is usual – except in some very busy bars – for bottles and cans of beer, minerals and soft drinks. Bottles of wine are always poured at the table.

You may be able to pour mixers and soft drinks into the glass before you remove them from the tray. For mixers with a spirit, pour some into the glass. Place glass and bottle on the table for the customer to add more mixer as required (see page 107).

To avoid getting too much head on bottled beer, you need both hands free, one to hold the glass, the other to pour the beer (see page 106). Otherwise pour just a little, then give glass and bottle to the customer.

Opening wine at the table

For most customers, to see their bottle of wine opened is part of the enjoyment of wine drinking.

1 Show the bottle to the customer to confirm that it is the type ordered.

2 Neatly cut off the top of the plastic or metal capsule which protects the cork.

3 If there is any dirt on the top of the bottle (likely with older wines), wipe it off with a moistened paper napkin.

4 Carefully remove the cork. The shaft of the cork-screw should go into the centre of the cork, deep enough to get a good grip, but not right through the cork. You want to avoid some of the cork remaining in the neck of the bottle, or bits falling into the wine.

5 Ask 'Would you like to taste the wine?' (some customers say no). If so, pour a little wine into the glass of the person who ordered it.

6 When you get approval, pour some wine for all the customers who are drinking it. Fill the glasses not more than two-thirds full, to allow the bouquet of the wine to be enjoyed.

Presenting the bottle (above), opening the bottle using a waiter's friend corkscrew (right).

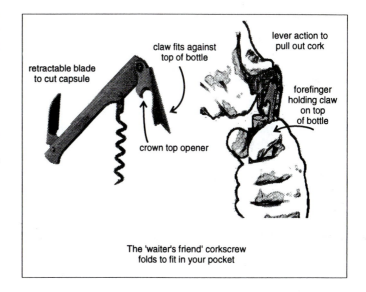

retractable blade to cut capsule

claw fits against top of bottle

lever action to pull out cork

forefinger holding claw on top of bottle

crown top opener

The 'waiter's friend' corkscrew folds to fit in your pocket

Opening sparkling wine

As the wine in the bottle is under great pressure, take care that the cork does not fly out, injuring you or someone else in the room, or damaging an object. The wine sometimes gushes out of the bottle immediately the cork is released. Have a glass nearby, and be ready to pour the frothing wine into this.

1 Hold one thumb over the top of the cork. As an extra safety precaution, place a napkin in your hand first.

2 With the other thumb and forefinger, break into the foil, take hold of the ring of the wire muzzle and twist until it breaks.

3 Keeping your thumb on the top, twist the cork gently in one direction, and the bottle in the other direction.

4 Keep a firm grip of the cork as it loosens. It should let out a gentle hiss.

The napkin is an extra safety precaution, reducing the risk of the cork shooting out of the bottle and injuring someone.

If the wine froths too much in the glass, stop pouring for a few moments until the froth subsides.

shaker Boston shaker bar blender ice crusher

pourer

chopping board

knife

Hawthorn strainer

mixing spoon

juicerator

Illustrations with thanks to Lockhart Catering Equipment

Unit 2NC10, Element 1

Preparing for cocktail service

To many customers, cocktails offer something new, exciting and fun, perhaps for a special occasion. Some have become classics, known and made to the same recipe the world over. Others are associated with the place they were created, or their creator. Some remain in-house creations, popular with the customers of that bar but not copied elsewhere.

Preparing equipment

Check the equipment you need is ready to use:

- *cocktail list / menu* – tells customers what is available, the prices and usually a description

- *squeezers* – for extracting the juice from fresh fruit, e.g. lemons, oranges and limes

- *knives and chopping board* – for slicing fruit and other garnishes

- *ice scoop* – made of plastic or metal. Do not use your fingers (unhygienic) or a glass (damages the glass and a safety hazard if the glass breaks)

- *pourers* – inserted in the neck of bottles of syrups and cordials so that the liquid pours easily

- *blenders* – electrically operated, used to mix some types of cocktail. Because of the power and speed at which they work, the result is creamier and lighter than you get using a cocktail shaker

- *shakers* – the type used for making a single cocktail or sometimes two of the same type, has an in-built strainer. Once shaken, the cocktail is poured into the glass. The *Boston shaker* is larger, the upper half or top is sometimes glass, and there is no strainer

- *mixer glasses* – for cocktails that are stirred with a spoon to mix. Generous size, plain shape, made with strong glass. *Mixer tins* are made of stainless steel, for use with an electric, hand-held mixer

- *stirring equipment* – some drinks are mixed with a long-handled spoon, sometimes known by the American name of *muddler*

- *strainers* – so that the ice used to make some cocktails, and pips etc. from freshly squeezed fruit juice do not go into the customer's glass. The metal coil around the outer edge of a *Hawthorn* strainer fits over the side of a mixing glass (see illustration on opposite page)

- *glasses and jugs* – for serving and presenting cocktails. Some barstaff pre-chill the glasses, to serve the cocktail at exactly the right temperature.

Preparing ingredients and accompaniments

Ingredients for the cocktail recipes used in your bar may include:

- *fruit* – oranges, lemons and cherries, plus a much wider range if fruit cocktails are a speciality

- *fruit juices* – lemon and lime juice are usually squeezed from the fruit as required. Juices available ready-to-use fresh include orange, grapefruit, pineapple, apple, grape and various blends

- *soft drinks* – most flavours

- *cream and milk* – for a rich dairy taste

- *pre-prepared mixes* – used in some bars to provide a wider range of flavours and to save time

- *alcohol* – spirits, liqueurs, aperitifs, wine.

Fruit should be of the best quality. You may be able to slice some in advance. If it is to be squeezed to make juice, this is usually done at the time the cocktail is made.

Keep milk, cream and fruit juices chilled but not beyond the use-by date. Follow package instructions for keeping, once opened.

Accompaniments include:

- *ice* – to chill the drink, or sometimes to add to the appearance and texture (when crushed ice is blended with the ingredients). Some cocktails are shaken or stirred with ice, and then strained, so the ice chills the drink but does not dilute it

- *food garnish* – olives, slices of cucumber, leaves and sprigs of mint and borage, pearl onions, fruit (see above)

- *salt and sugar* – to decorate (or frost) the rim of the glass – the rim of the glass is moistened (e.g. with lemon juice) then dipped into the sugar or salt. Sugar is an ingredient in some cocktails

- *decorative items* – e.g. plastic stirrers, paper umbrellas.

Cocktail-making at TGI Friday's provides a memorable show for customers.

Serving cocktails

Making and presenting cocktails gives you the chance to demonstrate your skills. For many customers it is part of the experience to see their cocktail shaken or mixed by an expert.

Types of cocktail

Customers choose a cocktail because they know it, they have been told it is good, or from the description.

When you are learning about the different cocktails, you may find them classified by what they are made from:

- *spirit based* – the principal ingredient(s) is a spirit, e.g. whisky, rum, brandy

- *non-alcoholic* – suitable for customers who do not want alcohol and those too young to buy alcohol.

Cocktails are also classified by how they are made. Depending on the kind of ingredients used and the final look to be achieved, they are:

- *shaken* in a cocktail shaker – for drinks which need thorough mixing, often because they include a cloudy or opaque liquid (e.g. cream, egg or fresh fruit juice)

- *blended* in an electric drinks mixer – where a frothy, light mixture is required, where crushed ice is mixed in with the ingredients, and where fruit is puréed as part of the recipe

- *mixed* in a mixing glass using a long-handled bar spoon – for drinks with clear ingredients which mix readily

- *built* or *poured* in the serving glass so that the ingredients do not mix but form separate layers, giving a colourful effect. The heaviest ingredient is poured first, the next heaviest second, and so on.

Making cocktails

You see the experts pour some of this and a little of that. But until you know the ingredients and can judge quantities as accurately as they do, follow recipes carefully.

Pay attention to the terms used. Many recipes use the cocktail-making terms – mix, shake, blend and build (see above) – as a form of shorthand. Typically the term 'mix' will include:

- adding ice to the mixing glass to chill the ingredients

- stirring the ingredients and ice thoroughly

- straining the mixture into the serving glass.

Promoting cocktails

In a lively bar where the emphasis is on fun, and the customers are mostly young, the whole atmosphere will encourage the sale of cocktails. They may have outrageous names. Descriptions may emphasise exotic flavours and places, or have a romantic appeal.

You can build on this when customers ask you to suggest a cocktail. Link what you say to what they are likely to find interesting (see Section 5). Is this a long or short drink? Sweet or dry? Strong, low in alcohol or no alcohol? Does the customer like particular flavours, or have a favourite liqueur or spirit? Is it before or after a meal?

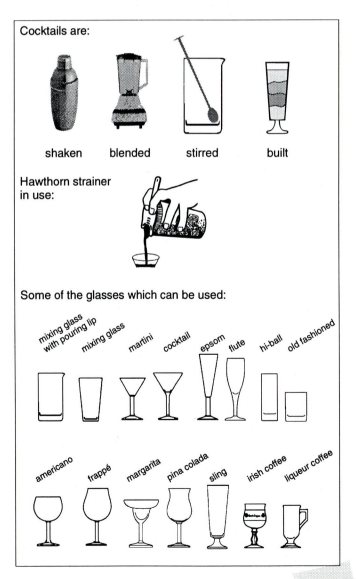

Cocktails are:

shaken   blended   stirred   built

Hawthorn strainer in use:

Some of the glasses which can be used:

mixing glass with pouring lip   mixing glass   martini   cocktail   epsom   flute   hi-ball   old fashioned

americano   frappé   margarita   pina colada   sling   irish coffee   liqueur coffee

Illustrations of glasses with thanks to John Artis Limited   **117**

10 Drink service from the bar

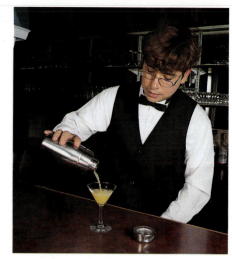

Driver
by Royal Naval Supply School

300 ml orange juice
300 ml alcohol-free wine
2 – 3 dashes angostura bitters
dash of grenadine syrup

Stir and serve over ice in a hi-ball glass.

Dim Sim
by Royal Naval Supply School

2 measures vodka
1 measure cointreau
25 ml light red wine

Shake vodka and cointreau in crushed ice and strain into a cocktail glass. Pour red wine (which must be at room temperature) on top so it floats.

Singapore Sling
by Royal Naval Supply School

1 measure gin
1 measure cherry brandy
1 measure lemon juice
1 tspn caster sugar

Shake gin, brandy, lemon juice and sugar. Serve over ice in a hi-ball glass. Top up with soda water.

Americano
by Campari

25 ml Campari
25 ml red vermouth

Half fill the serving glass (e.g. hi-ball or old fashioned) with ice. Pour over Campari and vermouth. Stir. Top up with soda water, if required. Decorate with half a slice of orange or a twist of lemon zest.

John Collins
by Beefeater

large measure Beefeater gin
2 tspn lemon juice
2 tspn gomme (sugar syrup)
dash Angostura bitters

Half fill the serving glass (usually hi-ball) with ice. Add lemon juice and gomme. Top up with soda water and stir. Decorate with ice and lemon. Serve with straws.

Daiquiri
by Rum Information Bureau

30 – 40 ml Lamb's white rum
juice of 2 fresh limes
1 tspn sugar
dash grenadine (optional)

Stir all the ingredients with lots of ice in a jug. Serve in a cocktail glass. Add a dash of grenadine for pink daiquiri.

Mai Tai
by Rum Information Bureau

1 part Lemon Hart Rum
1 part dry sherry
1 part lime cordial

Vigorously shake all the ingredients. Pour into martini glass over crushed ice. Top with a slice of lime and kiwi fruit.

Arctic Almond Coffee
by Finlandia Vodka

1 part Finlandia vodka
1 part Amaretto
1 part Kahlua or other coffee liqueur
2 parts cream

Stir together, strain and chill.

Golden Glory
by Buchanan Aitken of the International Bartenders' Association for Ballantine's

1 part Ballantine's Finest whisky
1 part amontillado sherry
1 part dry vermouth

Mix with ice in mixing glass. Strain into glass. Add zest of orange.

Acropolis
by Buchanan Aitken of the International Bartenders' Association for Ballantine's

1 part Ballantine's Finest whisky
1 part ouzo
1 part retsina
1 part lemon juice

Shake and strain into glass. Garnish with lime slice.

Bass TAVERNS

Cocktail-making checklist

- follow the recipe – changing anything alters the whole drink
- always clean measures and equipment immediately after use
- use correct glass and garnish
- never overfill the glass, causing the drink to spill

Blending
- place jug correctly on the motor
- set blender at correct speed
- never place a jug on or remove it from a turned-on blender
- never blend a solid on its own (ice, ice cream)
- never put your fingers or bar equipment inside jug while it is blending
- do not rock the blender to and fro, as this damages the motor

Shaking
- make sure lid is on tightly so that contents do not spill
- shake with vigorous, long motions not short, sharp ones
- do not over-shake as this will break up the ice and dilute the drink excessively

Mixing (using an electric hand-held mixer)
- set mixer at correct speed
- hold the tin firmly so that it does not slip
- hold the tin upright to avoid the mixer blades scraping against it

Building
- have the correct glass, filled with cubed ice if recipe requires
- pour ingredients in recipe order
- do not over-pour – there is no room for error

↗
Activities
Serving drinks
↙

NVQ SVQ
Skills check
Provide a drinks service for
licensed premises
Unit 1NC6
level 1

1 What is wrong with these glasses of draught beer, and what can you do to correct the problem?

cloudy beer

2 Which of these pint glasses is filled to the correct level? Say why.

3 Describe how to serve each of the five most popular drinks in your bar, and give the serving temperature and accompaniments.

White wine service tips
check if customer wants dry, medium, etc.
serve wine chilled 10°C
pour to line on glass
pour with bottle label facing customer
hold glass by stem
No accompaniments

4 Mark where you hold these glasses when dispensing a drink. What is the reason?

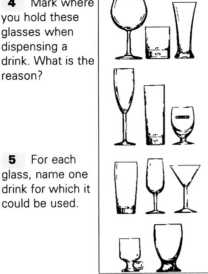

5 For each glass, name one drink for which it could be used.

6 How do you put ice in a customer's drink? What is the purpose of the ice scoop?

7 Name the drinks served in your bar with which ice should be offered.

8 How can you discourage customers from using their fingers to handle ice? Why is this a problem?

Element 1
Prepare and serve alcoholic and non-alcoholic drinks

Deal with customers promptly, politely and helpfully ☐ PC1

Serve alcoholic drinks only to permitted persons ☐ PC2

Give customers accurate information and identify requirements correctly ☐ PC3
▲ Information: price, promotions, special offers, relative strength, legal measures

Dispense and serve drinks correctly (temperature, equipment, accompaniments) ☐ PC4
▲ Drinks: draught and bottled beers/cider, spirits/wines with Optics, spirits/liqueurs free poured with measure, soft drinks, minerals/juices, hot drinks
Equipment: bottle openers, corkscrews, Optics, measures, pourers, knives, chopping boards, ice bucket, tongs, glassware, trays, coasters, drip mats
Accompaniments: ice, cordials, for hot drinks, food garnishes, decorative items

Serve drinks at the bar/table ☐ PC5

Deal with unexpected situations effectively & inform appropriate people ☐ PC6

Prioritise and carry out your work in an organised, efficient and safe manner ☐ PC7

Element 2
Maintain customer and service areas during drinks service

Deal with customers politely and helpfully ☐ PC1

Store and maintain at required levels drinks and accompaniments ☐ PC2

Keep service equipment clean, tidy and ready for use ☐ PC3

Keep customer and service areas clean, tidy, free from rubbish ☐ PC4
▲ Counters, shelves, floors, waste bins, bottle containers, tables, chairs

Empty waste bins and bottle containers as necessary ☐ PC5

Secure service areas from unauthorised access ☐ PC6

Deal with unexpected situations effectively & inform appropriate people ☐ PC7

Prioritise and carry out your work in an organised, efficient and safe manner ☐ PC8

Illustrations in questions 4 and 5 with thanks to Durobor SA

119

9 What is wrong about this, and why?

10 What do you say to the customer who asks this?

> Same again in this glass, please

11 Describe how to pour these two drinks. Why is the angle of the glass different?

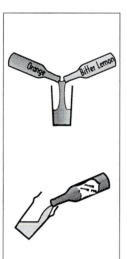

12 During service how can you help keep the bar looking tidy, and running efficiently?

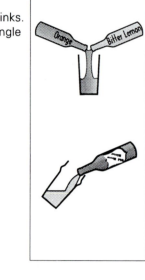

13 What should you do if a drink is spilled over a) the bar counter, b) a table covered with a cloth?

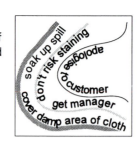

soak up spill — don't risk staining — apologise to customer — get manager — cover damp area of cloth

14 Comment on the way this tray is loaded.

15 Show how you would arrange these items on a tray.

16 Describe how to open a bottle of wine using each of these corkscrews.

17 Why is it wrong for this to happen in a bar or restaurant?

Element 1
Prepare and serve alcoholic and non-alcoholic drinks

Deal with customers politely, helpfully and identify their requirements ☐ PC1

⚠ Those who: comply with licensing legislation; act in drunken manner; violent or disorderly; under-age; under exclusion order; requesting service outside hours

Serve alcoholic drinks only to permitted persons ☐ PC2

Give customers accurate information ☐ PC3

⚠ Price, promotions, special offers, ingredients, alternatives, relative strength, legal measures

Promote drinks at all appropriate times ☐ PC4

Dispense and serve drinks correctly ☐ PC5

⚠ Draught & bottled beers/lagers/cider, spirits/wines with Optics, spirits/liqueurs free poured with measure, soft drinks, minerals/juices, hot drinks
Bottle openers, corkscrews, Optics, measures, pourers, knives, chopping boards, ice bucket, tongs, glassware, trays, coasters, drip mats
Accompaniments: ice, water, cordials, food garnishes, decorative items

Serve drinks at the bar/table ☐ PC6

Clean service equipment and keep free from damage ☐ PC7

Deal with unexpected situations effectively & inform appropriate people ☐ PC8

Prioritise and carry out your work in an organised, efficient and safe manner ☐ PC9

Element 2
Maintain customer and service areas during drinks service

Deal with customers politely and helpfully ☐ PC1

Maintain stocks of drinks, sundries & accompaniments at required levels ☐ PC2

Store, arrange and rotate stocks and accompaniments ☐ PC3

Keep service equipment, customer & service areas clean, tidy, ready for use ☐ PC4

Maintain environmental control systems at required levels ☐ PC5

Deal with unexpected situations effectively & inform appropriate people ☐ PC6

Prioritise and carry out your work in an organised, efficient and safe manner ☐ PC7

18 How can you help customers with a) sight difficulties, b) very shaky hand, when choosing the glass, and serving the drink?

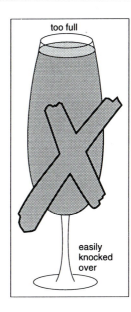

too full

easily knocked over

19 What questions do you ask customers ordering these drinks at table?

1 x G & T
1 gl red wine
1 x coffee
1 pt bitter
1 lg shandy
1 x mineral water

20 Number these customers in the order in which you would serve them.

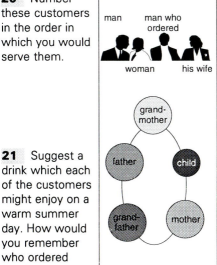

man   man who ordered

woman   his wife

grand-mother

father   child

grand-father   mother

21 Suggest a drink which each of the customers might enjoy on a warm summer day. How would you remember who ordered what?

22 This family ask if they can sit in the bar. What do you say to them? What drinks would you recommend for the children?

23 If the family ask what food is available, what would you suggest?

24 A mixed-age group in the bar are all drinking pints of beer or spirits. Some of the group are, you think, under age. What do you do, and why?

25 One of the adult customers from the group comes to the bar to order more beers and spirits. What do you do, and why?

> **CAUTION**
> **YOUNG PERSONS**
> **under 18 years of age**
>
> **IT IS AN OFFENCE**
> for any person under the age of 18 to buy or attempt to buy intoxicating liquor for his (or her) consumption in the bar.
>
> **IT IS ALSO AN OFFENCE**
> for anyone to buy or attempt to buy intoxicating liquor for consumption by a person under the age of 18 in this bar.

26 Bottles of soft drink at the front of the chiller cabinet are warm, those at the back are cold. Why is this wrong and what should have been done?

27 How can you tell that the heating, ventilation or music needs to be adjusted?

Element 1

Take customer orders

Check service equipment and get ready for service ☐ PC1

△ Glassware, trays, service linen, pen, note paper

Greet and deal with customers politely and helpfully ☐ PC2

△ Those who: comply with licensing legislation; act in drunken manner; violent or disorderly; under-age; under exclusion order; requesting service outside hours

Identify, record and deal with customers' requirements ☐ PC3

Promote drinks to customers at all appropriate times ☐ PC4

Give customers accurate information ☐ PC5

△ Price, special offers, ingredients, alternatives, relative strength

Deal with unexpected situations effectively & inform appropriate people ☐ PC6

Prioritise and carry out your work in an organised, efficient and safe manner ☐ PC7

Element 2

Serve orders to table

Deal with customers politely and helpfully ☐ PC1

Keep service equipment clean and free from damage ☐ PC2

Serve drinks to meet customer requirements ☐ PC3

△ Draught & bottled beers/cider, wine, spirits, soft drinks, minerals/juices, hot drinks

Serve alcoholic drinks only to permitted customers ☐ PC4

Give customers accurate information on drinks ☐ PC5

Deal with unexpected situations effectively & inform appropriate people ☐ PC6

Prioritise and carry out your work in an organised, efficient and safe manner ☐ PC7

NVQ
SVQ

Skills check
Prepare and serve
cocktails
Unit 2NC10

level
2

1 In which of these recipes must the minimum measure of spirit be 25 ml or 35 ml? Why?

American dry martini:

5 parts gin, 1 part dry vermouth

Side car

2 parts brandy, 1 part cointreau, 1 part lemon juice

White lady

2 parts gin, 1 part cointreau, 1 part lemon juice

---

4 For each of these cocktails, identify the method of making and the equipment required.

2 Name the glass to use for each of these cocktails.

Kir Royal

½ measure crème de cassis, top up glass with Champagne

Bloody Mary

1 measure vodka, 2 measures tomato juice, 2 dashes Worcester sauce, 1 dash lemon juice, Tabasco sauce, cayenne pepper and black pepper to taste

Cointreau frappé

fill glass with crushed ice, pour over cointreau

Pimms

ice, Pimms No. 1, lemonade or ginger ale. Decorate with cucumber peel, borage or mint, slice of lemon or orange

---

5 Now use your own words to describe each cocktail as you would to a customer.

6 For each of the following customer requests, name and briefly describe a cocktail from the range offered at your bar, or from those given on this page and page 118:
a) with no alcohol,
b) with vodka,
c) long and refreshing,
d) before a meal,
e) after a rich meal,
f) for a child.

3 Why should a pasteurised product be used in cocktails which require egg white, egg yolk or the whole egg?

RISKS FROM SALMONELLA POISONING

Bartenders advised not to use raw egg in cocktails. Pasteurised egg products are safe because the process kills the harmful bacteria.

FRUIT DRINKS

Turquoise Blue
A combination of rum, triple sec, blue curaçao. Sweet & sour. The colour of the sea off an Hawaiian isle.

Scarlett O'Hara
Like a southern belle, this blend of cranberry and lime juices with Southern Comfort bewitches and beguiles.

FROZEN DRINKS

Mexican Runner
Fresh strawberries, tequila, dark rum. Sweet & sour. Banana and blackberry accents.

Peach Margarita
Gold tequila, peaches, peach schnapps and lime blended and served with a sugar rim.

SPARKLING DRINKS

Wine Spritzer
Crisp white wine served over ice with a hint of soda. Served with a lemon twist.

Poinsettia
Cranberry juice, Champagne and triple sec make this refresher blushingly bubbly and fruity.

ICE CREAM & SHERBET

Chocolate Mint
A refreshing blend of chocolate, white crème de menthe, white crème de caçao and vanilla ice-cream. Our version of the after-dinner mint.

Friday's Freeze
Vodka, orange juice and orange sherbet, topped with whipped cream and a cherry.

FLINGS & SMOOTHIES

Grapefruit Blast
Grapefruit juice, orange juice, sweetened and topped with soda.

Blueberry Triathlon
Yogurt, blueberries and grape juice combined with coconut, honey and pecans.

With thanks to TGI Friday's

Element 1

Prepare areas and equipment for serving cocktails

Keep work areas clean, tidy and ready for use — PC1

Ensure cocktail making equipment is clean and free from damage — PC2

⚠ Equipment: pourers, blenders, shakers, mixer tins, stirring equipment, squeezers, strainers, knives, chopping boards, glasses, jugs, ice scoop, cocktail list/menu

Prepare and store cocktail ingredients ready for use — PC3

⚠ Ingredients: fruit, fruit juices, soft drinks, cream, milk, pre-prepared mix, alcohol

Store cocktail accompaniments ready for use — PC4

⚠ Accompaniments: ice, food garnish, salt, sugar, decorative items

Deal with unexpected situations effectively & inform appropriate people — PC5

Prioritise and carry out your work in an organised, efficient and safe manner — PC6

Element 2

Serve cocktails

Deal with customers politely and helpfully — PC1

Identify customers' requirements correctly — PC2

Give customers accurate information on cocktails — PC3

⚠ Price, ingredients, relative strength, measures

Promote cocktails at all appropriate times — PC4

Assemble cocktails using correct equipment and accompaniments — PC5

Finish and serve cocktails using correct equipment and accompaniments — PC6

Serve alcoholic cocktails only to permitted persons — PC7

Deal with unexpected situations effectively & inform appropriate people — PC8

Prioritise and carry out your work in an organised, efficient and safe manner — PC9

Index

Index